PEACE IN THE RED ROCK VALLEY

Darlene

Getting to know
you Has been a
bright spot in my life.
I hope that you enjoy my
book.

Gary
Gilna
7/22/2005

PEACE IN THE RED ROCK VALLEY

....AS LONG AS THEM GUNS HANG THERE

James E. Gilmer

Writers Club Press
San Jose New York Lincoln Shanghai

Peace in the Red Rock Valley
....as long as them guns hang there

Writers Club Press
an imprint of iUniverse.com, Inc.

For information address:
iUniverse.com, Inc.
5220 S 16th, Ste. 200
Lincoln, NE 68512
www.iuniverse.com

ISBN: 0-595-18071-X

Printed in the United States of America

To Nancy, without whose patience and help and indomitable love, this book would never have been completed.

To my children, Tanya, Jim and Alan for their encouragement and understanding, and for loving me again.

To Bobby Lee, my late Alcoholics Anonymous sponsor, without whom I might not have lived to tell this story.

INTRODUCTION

My intent in beginning this writing was simply to record my memories of some of the extraordinary times of my life that I feared would go with me to a grave someday, untold. I wanted to share the funny stories and pleasant memories because some things are just too precious to not be shared, but I needed to share my feelings about those things that weren't so funny or pleasant because some things are just too haunting to not be reconciled.

I especially wanted to share my experiences, be they glad, sad, funny, or serious, with my children in hopes of removing some of the shroud of wretchedness that has obscured the alcoholic's true perplexities since time immemorial, and of giving them a better perspective of their dad. I soon realized that I also wanted to share those same things with everyone whose lives have been altered in some way, even inadvertently, by an addiction.

As I began to piece my story together, I began to be able to see, from that distant hill of time, the workings of an alcoholic mind, and how events, going back even to my childhood, established my values, and produced my behavior.

Even though some of those memories are indeed hilarious, I began to see how the accumulation of my experiences was grooming me for an inadvertent entry into the hell of alcoholic addiction well before some of those who were to be affected by it were even born.

It became like stepping back to look at a jigsaw puzzle in its entirety instead of only seeing, up close, the one defective piece of it at a time, as I had struggled to make it fit, somehow, someplace.

I found myself being able to see, from that distance, the entire scenario of my addiction, realities that I couldn't see while I was close to, indeed embroiled in it. I could see how truly merciless my addiction became, my fear of being unable to overcome it, and of my being so ingrained in the hopelessness of it that I accepted it as my way of life, until I was finally forced to do anything to escape it.

That anything was, as a last desperate measure, to turn to the mysterious spiritual, and having been forced to do that how I was then introduced to a simple yet genuine belief in, and a reliance upon a power greater than me that enabled me to stop drinking alcohol. My story is not one of faith; it is more a story of fear.

More importantly though, it is a story of proof of the existence of such a power for anyone, but especially for those who might be searching for a way out of a seemingly hopeless dilemma.

If you don't have a problem with alcohol or drugs, and you read this book anyway, I hope that you might get a few laughs and perhaps experience an invasion of the heart. Maybe you might also gain some insight into us addicted people, and hopefully have a better understanding of an addicted friend, spouse, child, parent or someone close to you. You might also learn that we drunks, and addicts aren't just sorry as hell, but that we are simply good people who are mentally retarded where alcohol and drugs are concerned, and that we didn't plan on becoming what we became or doing the things that we did, be they funny or tragic.

Finally I have written of the joy of life in recovery, and of the peace that has come in a conscious companionship with that spiritual entity.

PRELUDE

As an aficionado of old western movies, I reckon that I've seen most all of 'em. The one that stands out in my memory is a Red Ryder movie in which Red Ryder, played by Wild Bill Elliot, known as the "peaceable man," and Little Beaver, Red's young Indian sidekick, had out-smarted, and whupped or jailed or killed all of the bad guys in the Red Rock Valley. The bullets had finally stopped flyin'.

The bank vault was secure, and the central waterin' hole was now open for the sodbusters and the sheepherders as well as the cattlemen. Horses were again tied to the hitchin' posts, along the dusty street, peacefully swishing their tails at an occasional horse fly, and snortin' now and again while waiting for their riders to return. Law, and order reigned supreme.

As the final scene of the movie phased in, Red Ryder, Little Beaver, the Duchess (Red Ryder's aunt), and the town's leading citizens were gathered in the home of the Duchess, nestled there in the valley, to celebrate the restoration of order. They were overjoyed with it, and were heaping loads of praise, and accolades upon Red Ryder, and Little Beaver.

The high noise level of the mixed conversations began to fade away as all eyes turned, curiously, to follow Red as he, in his peaceable way, had begun to walk across the room. The soft clump, clump of his boots and the jinglin' of his spurs were the only sounds to be heard by now.

Red stopped at the fireplace, took off his gun belt, with his two trusty six shooters in their holsters, and hung them all on a wooden peg over the mantelpiece. He then turned to face the folks gathered there and said, in his authoritative yet very peaceable sounding voice————-; "As long as them guns hang there, there'll be peace in the Red Rock Valley."

Chapter I

MY NAME IS JAMES——, I'M AN ALCOHOLIC

As is customary, I stopped in for a cup of coffee one morning at my sister's restaurant, in our little hometown of Buford, Georgia. The restaurant also doubles as the town's news center, as most small town restaurants do.

Amidst the clamor of conversing customers and waitresses scurrying about pouring coffee and shouting out orders to the cooks, a friend beckoned me to his table. Now Glad, short for Gladston, was in the egg business at the time. He was also known as the area's finest "dirt road philosopher."

Of course, I used the standard greeting in such a setting, usually, "Hey boy, you workin' hard?" He replied that he was indeed and that he had already been aaaall the way to Cumming and back (all of twenty miles round trip) and that he had already delivered twenty cases of eggs that morning.

Quite an accomplishment I thought, for this early in the day and then I, having a college education and an engineering background and the waitress having just brought me my coffee and having had my first sip of it, began to analyze the situation.

I said, "Glad, ain't there thirty dozen eggs to a case?" He replied, "Yep, 'at's right." Then I said, "Well, that makes three hundred and sixty eggs to a case don't it?" He replied, "Yep, 'at's right." After a quick mental calculation, I said, "So you've already delivered twenty cases which makes, oh, seven thousand and two hundred eggs this morning, right?" He replied, "Yep, 'at's right." Then I said, "Ain't it a miracle that we live in a world where only yesterday seven thousand and two hundred of your chickens each laid an egg, the most incredible food item that God provided for His people, for you to deliver today for happy consumers to enjoy eating and to be nourished by?" Of course he replied, "Yep," and after a short, studious pause, obviously considering the inconvenience that a chicken must go through in the act of laying of an egg, added, "And there wadn't nary one of 'em that **WANTED** to do it!"

I reckon that it's human nature to want to share good things with others. If, for no other reason, than to let them know that we got there first or maybe that we've got something that they ain't got. Don't we love to tell someone else about the good restaurant that we've been to or a good movie that we've seen, or especially a good doctor or surgeon that fixed us up, a good vacation spot or probably the most shared experience, how we quit smoking. That one always pisses the smoker off and gives us non-smokers a feeling of superiority! Then, there is the sharing of our favorite fishing hole, a good book and all sorts of things!

What I want to share with you through this book is the way that I found out of an addiction dilemma that I one day discovered that I was deeply submerged in, that I couldn't come out of and had come to believe would end with my death or long term incarceration. I had been warned all of my life that once hooked on alcohol or drugs, it was next to impossible to get unhooked. I came to know that I was hooked and as much as I wanted to, I couldn't stop what I was doing.

Yes, I am very much aware that when we share our good things with others, not everybody rushes out to try them, but once in a while, someone might come back and say, "You were right! Thanks for telling me about that place, or person, or thing," or whatever it was that we were braggin' about.

So, as you travel through this narrative, please remember that your writer is somewhat educated, but he ain't too smart. In fact, I was driving through a local parking lot recently looking for a place to park close to the store entrance of course and wondering why I couldn't seem to ever get there ahead of all them other cars that are parked in all of the close-up spaces and of course, cussin' because not ONE of the handicapped spaces was taken and thinking of all the hell I was gonna raise if I ever caught a handicapped person parked in one of OUR spaces!

Suddenly I spotted an empty space about four or five down in the next row over, so I went "hell bent for leather" to get around to it. Well, just as I rounded the turn and headed for that coveted space, I realized that I was zooming past an empty space that I had overlooked and it was the very first space and it was not a handicapped space and a car had turned in behind me and was very comfortably pulling into that space. So, in my zeal for something good, I missed something much better.

And so it was, when I began to realize that there could be a life again without alcohol in it. I thought, "I'm going after it all," and I started reading every book on recovery that I could get my hands on. The more psychological the title looked, or the more educated the author was, the more I thought I needed to read it. Inner child, parent, Ego, Super Ego, I'm Ok, You're OK, anything that could outline ways to come back from what I had become, to some semblance of normality. Man, I wanted them books to be complicated so that I could feel like I was workin' hard for it, but as I struggled through them I discovered that I couldn't understand nothin' that they were sayin'! I even tried to impress a friend once with some of my newfound book learnin' from one of them books by asking him if he had been in touch with his "inner child" that day, to which Mike bluntly replied, "Yeah and he's a real son-of-a-bitch!" So much for that!

So, I analyzed the situation and came down to the fact that I, without alcohol, am an average person. On the ol' bell shaped curve, I fall smack dab on the middle line.

I believe in my country, America, yet I don't crusade to stop the evil forces confronting her, even though I know that I should. I eat normal foods, no snake, alligator, possum, roasted bugs, escargot and such. I have a mortgage payment to make. I change the oil and filters in my cars and I'll try to fix anything several times before I'll pay to have it fixed—-, plus pay for gittin' what I tore up fixed while I was trying to fix it!

I've learned of the fallacies and pitfalls of using credit cards. I vote for the man, not the party. I won't eat the yellow or green or black jelly beans until all of the other colors are gone. I gripe about what the world of professional sports has come to, yet I still watch 'em and I always root for the underdog. I, in this their very worst season, am the only Atlanta Falcons fan left and that's including the team members themselves. (*GO FALCONS!*)

I love old Laurel and Hardy films and I'd much rather see Indiana Jones outrun a train on his hands and knees and then de-rail it with his pocket knife, than to see a true-to-life movie. I rarely know the answers to any of them questions on "Jeopardy," and I don't believe that them contestants can be THAT smart either!

The only real difference in me and the average denizens of the world is that I, without knowing that it was happening, became addicted to alcohol. It seems logical then, that if there were a separate bell shaped curve for us alcoholics, I would fall smack dab on that middle line, too. I'm an average alcoholic.

So it occurred to me, when I began to figger out that being a drunk carried far too many unpleasantries with it to make it really worthwhile and that being one is like baptizing a Cannibal, "It's a whole lots of trouble fer nuthin," that I began to recognize my need for a way out of my alcoholic dilemma and that there hadn't been very much that I, being average, had understood, or even gave a shit about in those many books, threats, treatment centers, doctor lectures, D.U.I. schools, ministerial counseling's and warnings from judges, loved ones and policemen of things to come. It had all been too psychological, complicated and demanding, cold and clinical and of course that ol' wrecking ball couldn't git me, ol' "Dead Eye" James! HAH! I got more smarts than that! I'd see it comin' in plenty of time and just flit right on out of harm's way like a gnat.

So I figger if I'm an average alcoholic and couldn't find something to hold my attention and help me, something that I could understand and feel, then there must be many, many more average alcoholics out there now looking for something understandable that they can identify with too. Or maybe those average friends and relatives of us average alcoholics might want some understandable insight into our unbelievable ways.

So, my intent in this endeavor is to share the true story of my unintentional and unknowing entry into and the miracle of my way out of an alcoholic addiction that I had come to believe was hopeless. I want to share the humor and the tragedy of my journey through it and finally, the peace that has come in having escaped from it and the joy of being totally free from it's unbelievably merciless domination. I hope to make my story understandable for average folks like myself and just maybe convince someone that the only really difficult part of recovery is discovering how truly simple that it is. If this is true for average me, then it must be true for many others.

Please don't let these words discourage you complicated folks; you fit in too. Because whichever way any of us do it, if we're trying to beat it, we're doing it right! I personally don't believe that anyone can be moving in any direction that takes us away from a mind-altering addiction and be going the wrong way.

I hope that if these words ever reach someone who wants an escape from his or her alcohol or drug dilemma that they will be simple and meaningful and you might be glad that I told you about the way that I have found.

So, enjoy my story, laugh a little and perhaps cry a little, but please believe that we addicted people who have been fortunate enough to have stumbled onto a path leading out of our dilemma, look back on the hell that we were put through by our addiction and know now that we were like my friend Glad's chickens—-; Didn't nary one of us **WANT** to do it!

Chapter II

HOW COULD YOU HAVE BEEN——THAT IGNERT?

I had begun to put my "blazin'" story into some readable form and had asked my wife, Nancy, my children and my siblings to read what I had put together up to where I had gotten to so far.

Their comments had been highly complimentary so I was feeling pretty good about it and was beginning to think of the "Pulitzer" or maybe even a "Nobel" prize once in a while.

We had a family gathering later which included a couple of uncles that we hardly ever see. When we do see 'em it's usually at a funeral home to launch a loved one to that Promised Land——, we hope! In fact, we hadn't seen one of 'em since Dad's funeral about five years earlier.

My book became the topic of conversation at the party and my sister, Sue Ellen, produced her copy of what I had given her to read and insisted that I read some of the episodes for those who hadn't heard them. I, like ol' Goober of the Andy Griffith show, weakly said, "Aw, shucks—- naw—-," but I was, like him, very easily persuaded to do it.

When I had finished reading and the laughter had died and the tears had dried, my Uncle James, Colonel, U.S. Army, retired, the one that we hadn't seen for such a long time, my hero from my childhood (I was proud to be named after him), a West Point graduate; in my mind, the single handed winner of World War II, ol' Dwight Eisenhower's right hand man, Hitler's main nemesis, appeared to have enjoyed the reading and he sensed that all of our eyes had quietly focused on him, waiting for his learned critique.

He had a very scholarly yet quizzical look on his face as he gazed over his glasses at me for what seemed like hours, while he organized his thoughts. We were all anxious as he was obviously about to speak. I was especially anxious and all set to receive his words of wisdom and hopefully favorable comments when finally he, obviously choosing his words very carefully, broke the silence by inquisitively saying, to my chagrin—-; "How could you have been—- that ignorant?"

Of course the group went hysterical with laughter. I didn't repeat them, but I couldn't help but think of the words of that old song. I reckoned that I had "laid around and played around this ol' town too long."

Uncle James really had enjoyed the reading and he did me the honor later of reading my manuscript and he did pay me some very high compliments on my work, but his question that night had again made me aware of just how truly bizarre some of my escapades must have seemed to someone who has never been controlled by an addiction.

I thought about a time in my youth when Dad, who would give anyone the shirt off of his back, invited a mentally retarded man to our house to spend a Sunday afternoon. It was a church thing, but thinking back, it was probably also an attempt by dad to raise the intelligence level of his own kids by exposure to a higher level. After all, our doin's often drove dad, in a fit of frustration, to call us "a bunch of nuts," and to add that we were all about half-cracked!

Anyhow, there weren't many ways that I could entertain that person so I soon lost interest in trying. I resorted to my usual Sunday afternoon boyish activities and ended up in one of our apple trees. I was very comfortable lying on a limb up there eating an apple, when I heard a noise beneath me.

I looked down to see the retarded gentleman walking around and around the tree in a small circle, happily mumbling to himself. He had wandered away from the house, probably to find some relief from dad's philosophical directions on how to get his life onto the right track.

Not having a mature appreciation for his condition, I saw this as a comical thing and chuckled silently to myself at the poor guy. I remembered feeling a sense of superiority over him and wondering how he could be that ignorant.

I know now that if that man could have been around when I had relinquished my own mind to my addiction, he could have watched me as I went 'round and 'round in aimless circles, often mumbling to myself! He may well have laughed silently to himself at me. He would have felt superior to me as he watched some of my actions and he would have wondered, how can he be that ignorant?

For example, Interstate eighty-five goes through my hometown to Atlanta and just before entering the city, it merges with interstate seventy-five. They become as one through the city and then, on the other side of town, they split off again. Interstate seventy-five then goes on past Moultrie to Valdosta, Georgia and then into Florida. Interstate eighty-five goes on to Newnan, Georgia and then into Alabama.

I had traveled both of these roads many times, especially Interstate seventy-five because I had lived in Thomasville, Georgia, just down that road.

At this time in my alcoholic life, I was changing jobs again and was to start a new job in Moultrie, Georgia, the first thing on a Monday morning. I had planned to drive down on the Sunday night before so that I could be fresh and ready early, come Monday morning.

Of course I did some heavy farewell imbibing with some friends that Sunday and I continued with my own private farewell party as I left for my destination in my little Volkswagen Rabbit that night.

I was singin' and hollerin' as my little Rabbit and me whizzed through Atlanta and southward, on our way to another new life of fame and fortune in Moultrie. Night was already upon us as we reached the southern outskirts of Atlanta.

My side of the road had narrowed from six to four to two lanes and traffic was light, it being a Sunday night. The little rabbit was at its peak and its little engine was singing my song, "Big wheels keep on turnin'!"

The ol' kidneys were working fine and I had made a couple of pit stops along the way already and had cautioned myself against any more libations. I had begun to feel that I wasn't at full capacity by this time, but onward we sped——, into the night.

I soon began to realize that I was getting pretty sleepy and was becoming pretty limber. I finally pulled over onto the shoulder of the road to get out and walk a little of it off and I found myself having to hold onto the car to stand up.

When I got back into my trusty little Rabbit, lo and behold she wouldn't start. She wouldn't even make a noise when I turned the key to the start position.

After several attempts to fire her up and lots and lots of cussin', I got out and began my staggering quest for the nearest exit, which turned out to be a mile or two on down the road. By the time I got to one I was really wobbling and felt fortunate that no police had come along. I was desperate to find a place to rest up for a few minutes and I happened upon a grassy area by a motel pool and laid down there to pull myself together.

After a short while, I got up and made my way to a gas station nearby. I must have left the motel just before the police got there because when I told the guys at the station of my predicament, they told me that I had already been reported and that the police were looking for me as of that moment. They had heard it all on their police scanner.

Of course they wanted a towing fee more than they wanted to turn me in so one of them graciously took me to my car to either fix it or tow it in. (I'm glad that there wasn't a reward on my head!) Then, when he tried to crank the car, the little bitch started right up!

He had done something that I had neglected to do. He put the gearshift in neutral. After getting the car started up and before resuming my journey, I asked him about how much further it was to Moultrie. He replied, "About two hundred miles man—-! You're in Montgomery, Alabama!"

"WHAT HAPPENED? HOW HAVE I COME TO THIS PLACE?", I wondered. "THIS AIN'T WHERE I'M SUPPOSED TO BE! THIS AIN'T THE WAY I HAD IT FIGGERED OUT *A'TALL!*" This kind fellow then followed me to a motel where I spent the night.

I wouldn't fully realize until the next morning that I had, the night before, been somnambulistically hurtling down the wrong leg of a geographic right-angled triangle toward Montgomery, Alabama while gleefully, idiotically singin' and hollerin'. The other leg of that triangle led to Moultrie, Georgia and the hypotenuse of that triangle was the two hundred-mile road from Montgomery to Moultrie that I now had to travel.

I'm sure that that retarded man that dad had brought home from church all those years earlier, would have found this scene very amusing and probably would have chuckled silently to himself and wondered about my ignorance. I reported late for my new job that Monday. Yes, I finally got there, but what a tense way to do it!

I also think a lot about the last time that I was processed into a jail, possibly to stay for a long while. I was among five or six other men who were also being greeted into the facility. All of us stood stark naked for our orientation which included a good de-lousing. My turn came for that special treat and I was directed to stand on a certain spot over a drain in the already wet and sticky concrete floor.

When I was informed of the purpose for this I quickly assured the friendly officers that I was an educated man and that I certainly did not have any lice or any other form of creepy crawlers on me and that I was innocent of the charges anyhow and would probably be leaving there in a few minutes and that this procedure would certainly not be necessary for me and would be a waste of our taxpayers money.

I was informed that I was in an equal opportunity facility and that I would certainly not be deprived of my de-lousing privilege and even if I didn't have any bugs on me right then, at least I wouldn't get any during my stay there, however long it might be.

I was then instructed to raise my arms and turn to face an officer who was standing about fifteen feet from me, gleefully brandishing a "heavy duty" squirting apparatus filled with the miracle delousing fluid. He was also wearing rubber gloves, a rubber apron and rubber boots.

I was about to discover that this wouldn't be the first time that he had done this job. My next hysterical thought was, "Why is he so well protected from that stuff and I'm standing here stark naked——? Could this possibly be a secret facility where habitual offenders are exterminated?" I wondered!

He hit my head hair first and then each underarm got a squirt, then my chest and then, of course, the ol' pubic area. Then came those words that still ring in my ears——; "Turn around, bend over and spread them cheeks!" I promptly obeyed and then discovered just how deadly he was with that squirt bottle! He scored a dead center bulls-eye and *OOOOOOOOHHHH*——, that stuff was cold!

As I stood there in that chimpanzee-like position, dripping delousing fluid, I recalled many years before, when in a management seminar, we participants had been instructed to make a list of the things that we would have wanted to accomplish twenty years from that day.

My list included being at least a vice president of some large company, a Sunday School superintendent, president of Civitan or Rotary or some other worthwhile civic club, to own a country estate complete with horses, swimming pool, fishing pond and so forth, member of the school board, all of the good stuff. I was confident at that time that I could do it all!

So while I was crouched in that chimpanzee pose, in that jailhouse, many years later, dripping that awful insecticide, I mentally screamed, "WAIT—A -MINUTE—-! WHAT WENT WRONG—-? THIS, FOR DAMN SURE, WADN'T ON MY LIST—-! THIS IS DEFINITELY NOT SOMETHING THAT ANYONE IN HIS OR HER RIGHT MIND WOULD EVER WANT, LET ALONE PLAN ON OR ASPIRE TO ACHIEVE—-! THIS IS PLAIN SORRINESS!"

I'm sure that that retarded man that I had sniggered at while he walked around in circles under that apple tree, wouldn't have just been chucklin' to himself at this revoltin' scenario, he would have been laughin' his ass off at me!

Then I wondered, "How have I come to this?" This was one more of the many humiliating experiences that I had gone through and was to go through before it would all be over.

In that setting, hopelessly incarcerated, totally subject to their authority, I tried to ease my pain by dreaming of what might have been had I not, except for my very bizarre combination of ignorance and insanity, become a drunk. Why, I wondered, did events such as these not cause me to stop what was obviously causing them? Uncle James' question was a legitimate one. How could I have been that ignorant? I also wondered, "Where did ignorance leave off and insanity begin?"

When I try to figger out the difference in those two mental conditions, my mind goes back to when I was a rising young executive, newly graduated from college and finding that my first position in Civil Service was much too "blah" for me. I dreamed of revamping the industrial world with my new education and vigor and I couldn't do that from behind my civil servant's desk filling out "invitations for bid" forms for airplane parts, nuts, bolts, tires and such things as that, never knowing if they got purchased or not.

The actual buying was done by someone at some other desk in some other building located God only knew where, filling out some other forms. After all, I was a college graduate and was wasting away on a menial job like that! So I quit that job and went into the industrial arena. Shit Far,* I wish I had it back!

*I've used the phrase "Shit Far" in this writing already, so an explanation of the phrase seems to be in order here for it to be meaningful, both now and further on in my story.

The phrase, "shit far," has nothing to do with distance. It is rather a derivative of "Shit Fire," probably Latin, which is an expression used for emphasis only. I reckon I could use "Jumpin' Jehosophat," or something similar, but that is much too troublesome to say, let alone to write. "Shit far" is a very comfortable phrase to say, write and think and it covers the entire spectrum of human emotion.

Some people prefer to use a different phrase for each of their feelings, such as "Heavens to Betsy," or "Awesome," or "Far out," "groovy," "Out of sight," "Gross," "Cooool," "Jumpin' Jehosophat," and so on, but I find that "Shit Far," covers them all; happiness, sorrow, disbelief, surprise, fear, anger, remorse, regret and so on.

So, as this phrase appears in this narrative, please bear in mind that it is your writer's humble effort to drive the point home, yet to keep it simple. Anyway, if I had kept that civil service job, I'd be retired now. I see now that quitting it was my first major ignorant act, but I learned from it.

Number two on my ignorance list was my move to El Paso, Texas. There were two of us "up and coming" engineers in the company working our ways to fame and fortune. Richard T. Lucey hereafter referred to as Richard and I had become close friends working together on various projects. I had just finished a major, very successful project in our distribution center in Bridgeport, Connecticut, our home office area and was enjoying the prestige that comes with such a huge success. Richard was making his waves in our Southern plants.

We had both already been dazzled by all of the travel, adventure, challenges and accomplishments that we had experienced so far with this company. So we were "ripe" for it when we were picked to be the key players in a big cost reduction project that was to be undertaken in our largest production plant in Juarez, Mexico. The Mexican project would require at least a year, maybe more, to do and would mean relocating our families to El Paso, Texas.

We were approached by our leaders with a sales pitch that, of course, pointed out all of the advantages in moving there; a pay raise, future advancement with the company, an opportunity to see the old West and old Mexico, the prestige of it all, the good schools, living in a thriving, bustling city such as El Paso, learning a new language and much more.

Then of course there were the good things that Richard and I assumed would come along; cheap booze, fiestas with the Mexican hat dancers and the mariaches serenading us with songs like "Blue Spanish Eyes," and "Granada", or maybe "Adios, Mi Corazone". Our wearing cowboy boots and cowboy hats with lots of feathers on 'em and fittin' right in with them folks (where you're judged by what you're wearin' on your head and feet) instead of standin' out like a couple of clowns at an opera, like we would've looked back home and riding on them dune buggies in the painted desert at sunset.

It was a dream come true. We didn't just consent to it, we would have kissed their asses and then crawled to El Paso on our hands and knees to get to go. We were ready to be cowboys "Driftin' along with the tumblin' tumbleweed." It was "John Wayne—-, git outta my way!"

Several weeks after our transition my bosom buddy and I were once again sitting in that *loooooong* line of traffic, waiting to go through customs, at the border, twelve to fifteen hundred miles from where we really longed to be, our respective homelands. We were waiting to cross back into El Paso, which by now we were calling "the gravel pit of Texas." The sun was beating down upon us unmercifully as we inched along.

We had already purchased and were each devouring a popsicle from one of the many Mexicans who strolled among the many weary travelers selling them out of their little igloo coolers.

We had already had the windshield washed twice by the Mexicans armed with their squirt bottles filled with a soapy solution and with a rag. They slip up on you from the driver's side from behind and before you know it they reach around and squirt the soapy stuff onto the windshield. Then you had better let them wipe it off. And you'd better give them a dime or more or you'll get another good squirt or two that won't get wiped off.

We had spent our mandatory nine and a-half hours at the plant, which didn't include the one to three hours that it took to get to and from there. We had discovered by now that the Mexican plant didn't close for the American holidays, another "itty bitty" detail that we had overlooked.

So instead of celebrating the Fourth of July, Labor Day, President's Day, Thanksgiving Day and others with our families, we celebrated Cinco De Mayo, Guadalupe Day, Mexican Independence Day and other Mexican holidays at home, in El Paso, alone while our kids were in school and our wives were doing whatever Americans did during Mexican holidays.

The crushing blow came when we were informed that we didn't even get our usual Christmas turkey out there. We put our foot down on that one and demanded our damned turkey. To our surprise we got one and the other Americans assigned there got one too. *Ooohhh* thank you, Mr. Scrooge. We called it the Mexican-American turkey revolution.

It was unbelievably miserable for us and especially for our wives and we had at least a year of it to do. We couldn't quit, we were to far from home for that. We were hooked!

It must have been that damned popsicle that caused Richard to make a statement that we would both use frequently after that day. He turned to me and choosing his words carefully, broke the gloomy silence by very emphatically saying—-; "Dead Eye—-, we've been whanged!"

"*Yeaaaaaahhhh boy,*" I replied—-, "ignert wad'nt no name."

I'm sure that the people in the car behind us were amazed at the unusual gyrations of the two big cowboy hats, **with lots of feathers on 'em,** in the car in front of them, as our heads rolled in desperate, hysterical laughter. I also learned from that experience.

Now, we recovering alcoholics and drug addicts have a good excuse for our ignorance and insanity, which is; "That nothing happens in God's world by mistake." I ain't too sure about that now. I don't figger that He's gonna strike us dead for figgerin' that He made a few mistakes in his creation. After all, didn't God put too many seeds in the watermelon and He made flies and gnats and mosquitoes and far too much pollen and P.M.S.—-, **I CAN'T BELIEVE THAT HE PUT THAT ONE IN HIS PLAN ON PURPOSE!**

He gave us wisdom in our old age when we needed it in our youth (a BAD mistake,) and He released me into the world before my brain was completely developed. The underdeveloped part must have been the part that would have enabled me to discern between ignorance and insanity.

I have to admit that there was a serious malfunction in my head when I realize that although Nancy makes the best rice pudding known to mankind and I love it, I have never eaten enough of it to make me throw up and if I did eat that much of it, I wouldn't go back for more of it, not right then anyhow and if I knew that eating it would get me thrown in jail, I wouldn't touch it! NO WAY! I ain't that ignorant.

Yet I didn't have that much smarts when alcohol was involved. I would drink enough of it to throw up and to be thrown into jail and worse things would happen, but I would hurriedly, eagerly go right back to it with no hesitation whatsoever, just as if the things that had happened to me hadn't even registered on my mind. I didn't seem to be able to learn from those happenings; therefore I must conclude that contin-

uing to do them had to be pure insanity. There just ain't no other explanation!

Now, please remember that I'm just ignorant, I ain't no dummy
because there were things that made such a lasting impression on me
that I have never done them again.

I remember once, as a small child of five or six, scrounging around in
mom and dad's bedroom and discovering the laxative, Ex-Lax. It sure
looked and smelled like chocolate candy and it tasted like chocolate
candy, so I thought that it must be chocolate candy and it had been left
there for me to find.

There were about six squares of it and I ate them all. Lordy! Lordy!
Lordy! The results made such a lasting impression on me that I haven't
eaten that much of it ever again and don't plan to. I quit eating Ex-Lax.

I grabbed hold of an electric fence once in my youth, never suspecting that a harmless looking piece of wire out in the open spaces could
hurt me. **WRONG!** I must have been well grounded, I was probably
even barefooted when I took hold of it because the jolt made such a
lasting impression on me that I have never done it again and don't plan
to! I quit grabbing hold of electric fences.

Another lasting impression came after I had gone into the industrial
arena and was with the second company that I was to work for during
my career. I had been selected to attend a management seminar in a city
about a hundred miles from where I was living at the time.

I was simply overcome with joy and pride when I was informed that
I was to spend two weeks there at the company's expense. My first business trip! Big stuff, especially for a person who had grown up in a small
town of about twenty-five hundred people. We didn't even have a
school bus!

There were thirty-five students in my high school graduating class,
but that turned out to be an advantage in life because I have always been
able to truthfully say that my scholastic average placed me in the top
thirty-four of my class.

I might point out that I was one of three in that class to graduate from a four-year college. I was right proud of that. I have to say though that one of my ol' high school chums who, I later discovered, had been inwardly smoldering ever since our teacher and classmates had over-whelmingly proclaimed me as the smartest student in our geometry class, brought me down to earth about my college education.

He and I had laughed and joked about our high school rivalry for that limelight, so I was rudely awakened to his true resentment about it some years later when some of us classmates had gotten together and were talking about our successes so far.

I'll have to admit that I got carried away and overdid it some when I reported on my accomplishments since leaving high school. Fortunately, one of the other members of the group kindly validated my braggin' with, "Yep, all you gotta do to make it to the top is have a col-lege education and love Jesus."

My ol' geometry buddy however wasn't so kind. He smirkingly said to me "Where's that college that you went to located at?" I jokingly, but mistakenly replied, trying to rub a little of my "higher" learnin' off on him, "First let me correct your grammar; 'At' is a preposition and you never, ever end a sentence with a preposition!" "Well then," he promptly replied. "Where's that college you went to located at, —- *ASSHOLE?*"

He went on to become very successful, but alas, the mills of the Gods had condemned him to dwell in the shadowlands of my having been the unlikely, however undisputed star of Mrs. Mclain's geometry class.

Anyhow, for a young man with a rather simple background, this upcoming trip was certainly a thing of grandeur that I had been blessed with! Thank You, Jesus!

It was an exciting two weeks and on the last day of the session, the host company invited the group, about twenty of us from around the state, to a luncheon at the businessmen's club in that town, which we all graciously accepted. Now, it was obvious that this was not just an ordinary restaurant like I was accustomed to. It was a high-class place, an old southern mansion that had been restored.

They had linen tablecloths, crystal, china and waiters in tuxedos each with a white linen towel draped over his arm. I felt as if I had discovered the meaning of the word "elegance," and if this was to be my world, I was ready to take my place in it.

I was seated close to one of our hosts and heard him saying that this place was world renowned for it's hot horseradish and that we must try some of it for a true dining experience. Little did he know that he was leading me into one of the most significant experiences of my life, dining or otherwise. I tried to appear suave and worldly-wise, as I remarked, "Sure, why not? I love good ol' hot horseradish!"

What a lie! I'd never even heard of it. We were poor when I was coming up. Lots of folks will say that they were poor back then, but that they didn't know it, well we knew it! We couldn't afford fancy foodstuffs such as Bagels, Toastems, Cap'n Crunch and the like. We had to get by on country ham and sausage from our hogs, milk from our cow that I milked morning and night, homemade biscuits and corn bread, fresh green beans and fried chicken that we raised and such stuff as that.

We did have a "store bought" item once in a while that we considered a luxury. It was a canned, meat by-product called Breakfast Sausage and we went for that stuff like Russians go for Caviar, when mom could afford to get some and fix it for us.

I saw some of that same brand of breakfast sausage in a store not too long ago and I simply had to have some, for old time's sake. It tasted repulsive to my now refined taste. Ain't it strange how things change over a period of about thirty years?

I read the ingredients on the label of the can for the first time ever and I am now convinced that the meat processors make it by grinding up whatever is left over after they've finished making the potted meat and we all know what parts of the animals go into the potted meat, so this stuff had to be bad! I reckon that all things are relative, but damn, that sausage was good back then!

So we didn't have Bleu Cheese, Ranch, Thousand Island, or Italian dressings and such and we sho' 'nuff didn't have any horseradish, much less HOT horseradish, so I had never even seen any, let alone ever eaten any of it. We did have things like ketchup, mustard, hot pepper sauce and mayonnaise and the closest comparison that I could make with the horseradish when I first saw it was to mayonnaise.

Now everyone knows that mayonnaise is not eaten in ittsy-bittsy smidgens, but more like in blobs, a blob being about as much as one would dip from a jar with a knife to be spread on a piece of bread to make a banana or a tomato sandwich, or to be piled onto a cracker to be eaten in one big bite with a Vienna sausage or some potted meat, or with a hunk of cheese, or a sardine, or some other delicacy on it.

Now, if you've never had freshly ground hot horseradish, maybe you have had hot mustard in a Chinese restaurant, or maybe you've taken a deep breath from a newly opened bottle of ammonia. If so, then you know that the fumes from either of these causes a sensation in one's head that really cannot be described.

It's not a pepper hot taste in the mouth type of thing, but a fume thing from a small taste or sniff of either of these that can take a person's head clean off. I didn't know these things at that time, nor did I know, till now, that the fumes that come from just grinding horseradish roots will blind a person! Well, multiply either of these feelings by ten thousand and you have the reaction brought about by swallowing too much freshly ground hot horseradish in one blob.

So I didn't know what hot horseradish was, but if it was served in this swanky place, it had to be heavenly. I know now that awesome ain't no name for it, but by then I had conjured up in my mind a taste which surely must be known worldwide, among the affluent, that was going to be the envy of everyone back home when I casually and nonchalantly told them about the divine hot horseradish that I'd had at the businessmen's club in Greenville and I would, sarcastically, recommend that they also try some of it the next time that they just happened to be up that way.

The die was cast, there was to be no turning back now for I had gone beyond the point of no return. The wheels were in motion for this new adventure. I very calmly and cooly ordered a shrimp cocktail, definitely with hot horseradish for my appetizer. Then I waited——, like an innocent lamb for the slaughter.

I didn't want to appear "un-refined", so I sat calmly, with a knowing, disdainful countenance, as the waiter placed before me the silver vessel with those succulent shrimp hung around it's rim and the delicious looking horseradish heaped inside of the cup. It was just waiting there for me to dig into it, in what I assumed should be mayonnaise fashion, "blob" eating.

I was calm, but in reality I couldn't bear waiting any longer for the others to be served so that I could taste that stuff, so I very discreetly picked up one of the knives by my plate, dipped me up a knifeful of that harmless looking, yet subtly, highly volatile horseradish, the equivalent of at least a heaping tablespoonful and hungrily, eagerly, yet very suavely plopped it into my mouth and swallowed it——————.

*SSSSSSSSSHHHHHHiiiiiiiiiiiiiiiiiiiiiiiiiiiiiiiiiiiiiiiiiiiiiiiiiiiiiiiiiiiiiTTTTTTT
FFFFAAAAAAAAAAAAAAAAAAAAAAAAAAAAAAAAAAAAAARRRRRRR!*

I might just as well have swallowed a hand grenade! The impact was sudden! The effect of the fumes from that freshly ground horseradish was at its peak instantly. They were like an air bag in a car, they filled my head **SUDDENLY!**

My head felt like it was a hot, un-opened can of "sody pop" that had been vigorously shook or dropped and the gasses couldn't escape and on top of that, as if someone had stuck a high voltage wire in each of my ears. My head felt like it was the size of a basketball with my hair standing straight out. My eyes and ears seemed about to pop out under the pressure and tears were streaming down my cheeks.

My first hysterical thought was that I was having a massive brain hemorrhage because I had heard before that internal bleeding causes a tingling sensation and my sensation wasn't tingling—-, it was *SIZ-ZLING!*

In that instant, I resigned myself to the fact that I was about to be *GRAVEYARD DEAD,* that I was thinking my very last thoughts on this earth. I thought that I was about to shake hands with God, Jesus, The Holy Spirit, Peter, Paul and Mary and I was definitely not ready, nor did I want to meet *ANY OF THEM RIGHT NOW!*

A million thoughts raced through my head. It is truly amazing how fast we can think when we believe that we are dying—-; "Will they get my body home? What will Sue do now? My kids are orphans! Will I go to hell? Will my insurance pay off? How will I look in my casket? Why did it have to happen here? I wish I had been a Christian! *I WONDER IF IT'S TOO LATE TO GET SAVED REAL QUICK?* I wish I had never started drinkin'!

"*DAAAAMMMMM* **THIS WHOLE**—-! Whoa Nellie! *CAN'T BE CUSSIN' RIGHT NOW!* I've always loved y'all, God and Jesus! *PLEASE* don't send me to hell!"

Then I realized that while I was panicking, the feeling in my head was abating and that I was still in this world. **THANK YOU JESUS! THANK YOU O LORD OF HOSTS! BLESS YOU O MIGHTY JEHOVA!**

Then, I thought that I had had a stroke and was only going to be paralyzed for life, but boy howdy, I wouldn't be dead! I was definitely thrilled with that alternative! "Thank You, Heavenly Father! Thank You! *THANK YOU, THAAAAANK YOU O BLESSED REDEEMER!*"

I must have been carrying on like the coyote in that "road runner" cartoon after he had been clobbered real good, because the group seemed to be frozen for an instant in the act of doing whatever it was that they had been doing when my dilemma captured their attention and they all looked at me with that "What the hell's wrong with him?" look.

Needless to say, the very least of my worries at that juncture in the eons of time, was whatever them folks might be thinking about my table manners or my suavity, for I've never known of anything changing more quickly than my going from the extreme of sheer ecstasy in elegant living, to sheer terror in believing that I was fixin' to die from some kind of physical seizure and it had come, I thought, by some strange coincidence, the very instant that I had swallowed that horseradish.

I know now that the fumes from just a little smidgen of hot horseradish causes a hell of a sensation in a persons head and I had swallowed **WHAT HAD TO BE THE EQUIVALENT OF A HEAPIN' TABLESPOONFUL** of what I expected to be the nectar of the Gods.

I then began to check out my hands, arms, legs and other parts and discovered that they weren't paralyzed. In fact, to my surprise, I felt normal all over, yet there was no doubt that something had happened, but what? I had no idea. I certainly had not imagined all of that agony. So I figgered that I had just had my first fit of some kind, maybe epilepsy had started in me (now I know why epileptics have gotta have something to bite down on) and that I would go to a doctor when I got home and get myself checked out. In the meantime I said; "*Oooooohhh* Dear

Lord JESUS! Please don't let that happen again, not here anyhow!" I thought surely that God wouldn't let one of His creatures——, even a sinner like me——, ever go through that kind of agony twice in one lifetime.

It was hard to appear calm after a sudden horrendous surprise like that, but having settled back down, I was ready to resume my journey into ecstasy land. I recalled what I had been doing when that awful thing happened to me and was aware that because of that damned whatever it was (back to cussin' already), I had been unable to concentrate on the taste of the horseradish. So, I confidently dipped me up another knifeful and swallowed it.

Yep, it was much worse the second time——, like getting smacked again in the exact same place that's just quit hurtin'!

"*OOOOOOHHH, GOD!*" I moaned, this time sho' 'nuff drawing the attention of the crowd. I wrapped my arms around my head and held on because I knew by now that this thing was like gittin' raped by a gorilla—— it wouldn't be over 'til the gorilla was done. It also became very clear to me just what was going on. The whole picture came into full focus.

I've already mentioned several times that I am indeed an educated, college trained, but still somewhat ignorant man and finally my education paid off. I called upon all of my learning and training and figgered out that the horseradish was doing it. I also realized that it wasn't a hemorrhage or stroke that I might die from this time, yet I was terrified that the human body might not be able to survive that much pain in that short of a time span. I vowed that if I survived this second blast that I would never, ever put another smidgen of horseradish of any kind into my mouth. And I haven't. I quit eating horseradish!

The significance of this true story for me is that I put a substance into my body that literally disrupted my normal functions and that my body violently objected to it in such a way that I thought it was going to kill me. Yet I wasn't capable of connecting the upheaval within me the first time to the real cause of it in any way and I blindly, unknowingly, put more in. Now that is ignorance at it's finest, yet I learned from it. I overcame it. I quit doing that too!

I look back on the horseradish experience now and see it as one of life's little hilarious lessons, but rest assured, it wasn't a bit funny at the time and it made a *LASTING* impression on me.

So, you might say that I have become a good social Ex-Lax eater and I totally abstain from touching electric fences or eating hot horseradish because of the impressions that they made on me. I remember those things. I learned from those experiences. I was capable of overcoming that ignorance. So my Intelligence Quota must have been high enough all along.

The results of my drinking alcohol were more terrible toward the end than the effects of the Ex-Lax, electric fence and the horseradish all combined, but time after time after time, following the violent reaction from it; jail, delousing, divorce, being fired from job after job and all the others, I still couldn't make the connection and I would again pour alcohol down my goozle and wait for the next violent reaction. Why? I hadn't the slightest idea then why I had to do it, but for thirty years, I did it. I couldn't quit doing that!

Looking back, I can see that even with my first drink of alcohol, I had a bad reaction, the horrible taste of it, but true to my alcoholic nature, that malfunction in my head, I took another drink. The reactions over the years went from the bad taste to hangovers, to all of the reactions that drunks and addicts have that grow progressively worse. It's as if we're saying, "I think I'll drink again and just see what happens next!" Something negative always did. Now that's got to be insanity!

It was thirty years after my first serious drinking when I finally felt like the cat that was in love with the skunk and realized that he had enjoyed all of this that he could stand. It was the morning of January thirty-first, nineteen hundred and eighty-six, that I woke up once more feeling like I had been eaten by a buffalo and shit over a cliff. I was in our old home place where my aging dad still lived back in Buford.

I had slept in this room as a boy and as a young man until I had gone off to college. It was now twenty-eight years later and I was back home again and had been there since July. I had returned to the home place six months earlier after having been fired from yet another job as a result of my alcoholism, my fifth good industrial engineering position since my alcoholic avalanche had begun. On this day, the violent reactions to my alcoholic drinking included being unemployed, financially broke and having to live with dear ol' Dad again. I was divorced, apart from my children; the youngest was Alan, my thirteen-year-old son.

My transportation was a ragged Volkswagen Rabbit, but that was all that I needed to transport my meager material possessions. When my wife then, Sue, had kicked me out seven or eight years earlier, I needed my pickup truck to haul my stuff, but by now the back seat of this little compact car was sufficient.

My last place of residence had been a very comfortable mobile home, permanently set up on about two acres in the North Carolina country-side. I had finally lucked up on a job situation there because the last company that I had been working for had gone bankrupt. The bank-ruptcy gave me a good reason for leaving that job. (That was one job that I didn't get fired from.) Those circumstances had enabled me to land a good job finally.

I loved the new area, the job, the people and the town and had entered into a loving relationship with a very lovely and highly respected lady there. I had started to dream of living there for the rest of my life with her. I had been very warmly accepted in the community and was on my way back up, but in spite of my good intentions, plans and desires, my alcoholic mind took me once again to the people and to the places and to the things that would guide me onto a course leading away from my dreams once more, another bad reaction that I couldn't yet connect to my mysterious craving for alcohol.

I lived in that place for a couple of months after being fired, feeling sorry for myself and easing my pain with alcohol until my money ran out. I owed rent for those two months and of course, couldn't pay. Once again, running time had come and just as I had done four job firings before this one, I loaded up my now meager possessions and under cover of darkness, I drove away from my new dream. As usual, I couldn't think of anyone who might be terribly crushed because I hadn't said goodbye.

Other reactions brought about by my alcohol consumption included blood pressure so high that I wouldn't have it checked because I didn't want to know just how high it was. I didn't have to admit to myself that it was dangerously high if I didn't know the numbers. I would attempt to give blood now and then, hoping that the Red Cross people wouldn't give me a little slip of paper advising me to see my doctor. There were lesions on my hands that had split open. My wrists and ankles were blue from the bursting capillaries because of the blood pressure.

I had hoped to be dead from a quick heart attack before this day arrived because I was to face a judge today for the eighth of nine arrests for driving under the influence of alcohol (the eighth and ninth both in the same week!) Alas, the fateful day had arrived. It was in my face.

I was seriously behind on child support and the ninth drunk driving charge was yet to be atoned for. I knew that I was about to do some serious jail time. I was to face the judge at five o'clock in the afternoon that day and I was reasonably sure that when I left home to go to the courthouse that I would not return for a long, long time. Habitual offenders in Georgia can be sentenced to up to five years in prison and I was certain that the judge would have records of the first seven offenses. He would probably condemn me to life in the electric chair! My mind was searching desperately for some solution to my dilemma. I had about eight hours before court time and I thought that surely I could figure out some way around this. I didn't know yet that my "figgerin'" days were over.

So I went to my chest of drawers (that's where most of us advanced drunks end up keeping our liquor) before I even got dressed and took out my quart bottle, about three-fourths full of cheap vodka (that's what most of us end up drinking once we get over that "I drink for the taste of it" illusion) from the top drawer. Like that first knifeful of hot horseradish, I didn't yet know what was causing these horrible reactions. I wasn't in denial because one has to be aware of something before one can deny it. I didn't know yet that I am an alcoholic.

So, in spite of all these reactions to alcohol, what seemed more logical and what I wanted more than anything else right then, was another drink of it. I was mentally sick enough by now to believe that alcohol was all that I could rely upon to keep me sane.

I walked over to an armchair in that room and sat down with my bottle and without anything to drink with it or mix with it, I sucked two or three good, long, soothing, searing gulps from it, convinced by my alcoholic mind that I was simply having a cocktail and then I began to apply my college trained mind to try and come up with answers to the questions that I had by now asked myself many times over; "What happened—-? What went wrong with my plan—-? Where did I turn in the wrong direction—-? Where are those who once loved me—-? The things that I once possessed—-? The sparkling career—-? The joy of living—-? Where—-? When—-? Did they all slip away?"

Then, with my bottle, the source of all of my problems, *IN MY HAND*, I asked myself once more—-, "What has brought me to this?" We drunks call it "drinkin 'n' thinkin."

I wasn't aware, at that moment, that this day, January thirty-first, nineteen hundred and eighty-six, would be the day that I would take my very last drink of alcohol.

Chapter III

YOU AIN'T A-GITTIN' A-HOLT ON ME!

A little over ten years has passed since that last drink went down and on this particular morning, a friend and I were to attend a business meeting in a neighboring town. Since this was a weekly meeting, we usually met somewhere and rode to the meeting together.

One of our favorite meeting places is on top of the earthen dam that holds back lake Lanier in Georgia. The road across the top of the dam is part of the route that we usually take, but there are parking spaces on top of the dam so that folks can stop and enjoy the view.

On one side, of course, is the lake where the water level reaches up quite high on the dam. On the other side you can see all the way to the bottom of the dam where the Chattahoochee River resumes it's natural flow.

The view from that side is absolutely magnificent, especially early in the morning when there is very little commotion to distract one's attention from "Old Man River." I was enjoying this pristine display of nature when Stan arrived to pick me up, then off we went. To my surprise, as we rode along, Stan picked up a little clear plastic cup from his console, one like you'd find in one of them economy motels these days. Taking a small sip from it, he said that he'd had a little stomach problem that morning and he figgered that a little whiskey just might help it.

I have known this man for years and I knew that he did not have a drinking problem, so I wasn't alarmed that he took a little sip of alcohol for any reason, even at that time of the day. What I was very much alarmed about was my feelings about the fact that he could take only a little sip and put what was left in the cup back down as if it weren't even there.

I had that feeling that I have when someone performs a magic trick or something like that. I wondered, "How in the world did he do that?" Not only had he just taken a little sip, he didn't even touch it again until after our meeting some two hours later, when on our way back to my car, he finished off what little was left in that cup. It only held another small sip.

As I've already said, I hadn't had a drink in over ten years at that time. I haven't even wanted a drink since that January thirty-first night. I do not even wish that I could drink alcohol. I do not fear it. I am free from it. Yet when Stan took those little sips, my alcoholic mind began to rattle it's cage and screamed out; **"Where is the rest of it? Ain't he going to finish that?** He must have a half-gallon of booze in the trunk of the car!" I instinctively thought, "He must have enough stashed away somewhere to finish the job that this first drink has started!"

This occasion once again laid bare to me the fact that this man and I are as different as night and day where alcohol is concerned. We are in the same type business, we have mutual friends, mutual interests, we can converse about common things, we enjoy the same events, places and such, but he can take a sip of alcohol for his stomach and stop with that. My mind automatically asks, "Where is the rest of it? Surely he must have more!" Right about the time that he had taken that second sip, we arrived back at my car.

Instead of going home right then, I found a secluded place to sit for a while on the grassy side of the dam to admire the view. As I sat there looking down upon that ol' river peacefully flowing along, my mind began to drift with it into that twilight zone of deep thought.

I realized that once again my alcoholic mind had reared its ugly head, even after all those years, to let me know that it, even though caged, was still very much alive. I felt a wave of anger at how, for so many years, that mind had controlled me, how it had taken me to the brink of death and how it had flourished and grown stronger within me with each drink that I took, while telling me; "You need me. I'm all that you can depend upon." That mind had me convinced that alcohol was all that was keeping me alive and sane. I also began to wonder why it is that some people, like my friend Stan, can drink alcoholic beverages with indifference, but I must have more after that first sip.

My mind drifted back to those words that I had, many years before, been exposed to; "The phenomenon of craving" that only exists in the mind of the alcoholic and how long it had taken me to learn that even though I don't understand it, I've got it.

As my thoughts continued to drift on that ol' river's current they took me back to events in my life that caused me to come to know that I possess that "cussed thang."

They drifted back to when I was seven or eight and we, the family, lived in what would now be considered a country setting, but what in reality back then was considered sort of "tobacco roadish," no running water or inside conveniences. In fact, there wadn't much of anything. We actually marveled at rich folks back then, when we learned that they, instead of going outside, actually went *INSIDE OF THEIR HOUSES* to use the toilet! You see, we lived in the country when livin' in the country wad'nt cool!

There were seven of us, Mom and Dad, three sisters, Betty Ann, Donna Jean and Sue Ellen. Then there was my brother David and me, yours truly, "DEADEYE" James. Betty, the oldest, was in high school at the time.

Our home had five rooms. The room that I slept in with David and Mom and Dad (them in one bed and me and David in another, of course) separated the kitchen and sitting room from the other bedrooms, which were used by the girls.

Betty had spend the night company one night and after the corn poppin' and other activities that we entertained ourselves with back then had ground to a halt, we had all gone to bed, but for some reason or other Carol, Betty's guest, had to go to the kitchen for something or other and of course she had to come through the middle room where David and I had already bedded down, but hadn't yet gone to sleep. Carol was pretty, I thought.

Now Carol was in her nightgown when she came through and being so scantily clad, she came through rather briskly. The hurried movement was her way of acknowledging that she shouldn't be in the presence of two impressionable young boys in her gown, but it was also a statement that it wasn't that big of a deal. The briskness was a token of penance, more or less.

Anyhow, because of that briskness of her movement she stirred up enough wind to cause her gown top to blow wide open and I beheld for the very first time in my young life, a full view of a female's fully developed breasts—-, **BOTH OF THEM**—-, *ALL* of both of them! My eyes must have been as big as saucers! It was NOT an optical illusion! I was looking at the real things and fully developed ones at that and they were on a real live high school girl! I had heard about 'em, but boy howdy, this was *REAL*! I was really seein' some and it was very obvious that when God made Carol, He sho' 'nuff meant for everybody to know that she was a girl!

I didn't know nothin' about sex then. I had only heard a little talk about it, but I was very much aware that I had been affected by that glimpse of her in a *"MIGHTY PECULIAR WAY," and* I liked the feeling.

That was probably the first time I ever said or at least thought the words, "SHIT FAR!"

I couldn't analyze this situation in my street mind (I'll explain later) based on my limited knowledge of such things, but something within me had been awakened and I wasn't satisfied with just the glimpse—- I had a desire for more. I didn't know what I was feeling, but I sho' 'nuff knew that I wanted to feel like that again! New avenues were certainly being illuminated for me that night for future exploration!

That experience also scared me half to death because my momma had told me that if I ever thought wicked things about girls that I would turn to stone! I sho' 'nuff thought it was settin' in right then! "Lord Jesus," I prayed, "Please forgive me, a sorry sinner, for whatever's a-goin' on here 'cause I know that it's got to be a sin and the devil's fixin' to git me!"

It would be awhile before I would go to sleep that night, for unknown to me at that moment, I had been introduced to what I now know to be my mind's mind, that part of my mind where mysterious feelings and acts are generated and where, I was to learn in time, my chief adversary, that cussed "phenomenon of craving," lurked.

So, henceforth when I refer to my mind, I will be talking about my conscious one, my "street mind," the one that I use to decide whether or not to beat the yellow traffic light, the one that I am using when I say "I" or "me."

Of course, this is my daily operating mind that I can make decisions with such as, "If I ever get out of this jailhouse, I'll never take another drink as long as I live!" In fact, I wondered for a long time why Sue had kicked me out because I had promised her time after time that I was going to stop drinking and in my daily operating street mind I was thoroughly convinced that I was going to stop! I really meant it!

As of this moment, I can look at myself and know that I am over-weight and vow to lose some of it and really mean it, but I haven't yet done anything about it and I've known of my weight situation for ten years now. So it was with alcohol; I decided to stop drinking many times and I truly meant it every time. I really did!

I have many times decided to be a good Christian and have been gloriously saved from my sins (especially in jail!) and in my daily operating street mind, I really felt it and meant it!

Why did these things never stick? It's because, as the old song goes, "My Mind Has A Mind Of its Own," and I can't control it. It controls me and it functions off of data that it has accumulated since that day that I was spanked by the doctor who delivered me into this world and it produces my behavior. It is my subconscious, my computer.

I've got to get somewhat psychological here in order to make some of this writing meaningful, so stick with me. Don't give up now. It is a fact that even the world's most sophisticated computer can only print out whatever has been programmed into it. So, if the words "ice cream" have been put in, then the computer will print out "ice cream," but if the word "shit" has been put in, then the computer will print out "shit." End of psychological part.

And so it is with my mind's mind. It took me a long time to figger out that except for intuitive senses, the human computer starts out blank. We are then products of what gets programmed as we go along and based on this data, good or bad, that has been put into it, my mind's mind can overrule my street mind at any time and I won't even know that it has done it until my actions are either well under way or are already past history. Unfortunately, lots of shit went into my computer/mind.

For example, I'm sure that there have been times in most of our lives when we have been trying to stay out of an argument between other persons, town meeting type stuff, P.T.A, especially Band Booster discussions and in our street mind we have vowed to keep quiet. Then, to our surprise, our mouths pop open and the wrong words come pourin' out and then we have found ourselves involved in it.

On several occasions, Nancy has been in a discussion with one of the children and I could tell that it wasn't a pleasant one. My street mind would say, "Stay out of it," and then my mind's mind would have me blurt out, "What's going on here?" Then I'm in it with them! My mind's mind has always been a pesky devil!

Just as surely, my mind's mind can cause me NOT to do things. I remember when some of us boys discovered an old rock quarry that had been dug out very deep and had filled about halfway with water. The cliffs around that pond were fifty to a hundred feet high in some places.

I more than once stood on one of those lofty summits and, in my street mind, wanted to dive. "Man," I thought, "What an experience that would be and the water so soft looking and all!" I had seen others dive from fairly high up on those cliffs and in my street mind, I wanted to do it too, but my mind's mind said, "NO!" It had been programmed with knowledge of the danger involved and it over-ruled my street mind. Thank You! Thank You, Heavenly Father!

Now, based on my experiences and those that I have heard other admitted alcoholics share, I'm convinced that my mind's mind has two parts. One part is the normal part and as long as it is functioning, I act normally, I'm the real me. But when I introduce alcohol into my system, the normal part shuts down and the alcoholic part takes over.

I see it sort of like the plug that screws into the engine of the cars with electric fans. As the engine heats up, the plug heats up as well and expands, causing the gap inside the plug to close, bringing two points together so that the electric current can pass through and activate the fan. The fan will then run at full speed until the heat goes down enough to allow the points to separate and break the circuit. The fan then stops and stays stopped till activated again by the heat from the engine.

I know now that at any given time in my life, either my mind's normal mind or its alcoholic mind is connected. I know that I functioned normally, made good rational decisions and choices, had many major accomplishments, lived happily then and now, as long as the normal connection existed; but when I decided to take a drink and this choice was always made in my daily operating street mind, the alcohol closed the gap between my mind and it's alcoholic mind. My normal system would be short-circuited and would shut down and then the "alcoholic shit" in my head would "hit the fan."

Then, until I left off alcohol long enough, either by passing out, getting locked up, or for some other involuntary reason, for the gap to open and normalcy to return, I would do some strange things and afterward wonder why, what happened, because I really didn't know.

Then sooner or later, usually sooner, I would intelligently, rationally, in my street mind, decide to have that next first drink, because I was ignorant of how alcohol affects one's mind and the next thing I knew, "the shit would have hit the fan" again. I couldn't know not to do it. My mind's mind didn't yet contain the necessary data.

Just like that first blob of hot horseradish, I couldn't know that it had caused that indescribable reaction. When I took it into my body and it produced that violent and at the time I thought, deadly reaction, I never considered the horseradish as being the cause of it. I didn't have the necessary data in my minds to come to such a conclusion. I couldn't have known.

The knowledge that a foodstuff could cause that kind of feeling had never been programmed into my computer so I blamed it on the things that had been programmed that could cause such a feeling; a brain hemorrhage, a stroke or a fit. So when the crisis was over and I learned that it wasn't any of those things, I blindly put more of the same stuff in. I was ignorant about hot horseradish. I couldn't know not to do it.

When Carol came through my room that night, my street mind, based on what I had learned in church, said, *"DON'T LOOK! SINFUL! AVERT YOUR EYES! YOU'LL GO TO HELL and BE CAST INTO AN ETERNAL LAKE OF FIRE!",* but my mind's mind had already recorded some other little tidbits of data about sexual matters. That data, coupled with instinct, was enough to produce feelings that my street mind couldn't even begin to comprehend, but my mind's mind didn't have any trouble with it a'taaallll! It glued my eyes to her. Even though my street mind thought that the penalty might be hell fire, my mind's mind took over. I looked! I couldn't not look!

Just as surely, I couldn't know that a drink of alcohol activated that phenomenon of craving in my alcoholic mind. It hadn't been programmed yet. I was, at this time, ignorant of this fact.

So here I was, a normal person in all respects and appearances, wandering around with a loaded, loose cannon in my head that would do much damage before I would learn something about it. Why couldn't I have seen that?

I know now that it goes back to when my momma, in her best attempt, had told me as a young lad, that if I ever started drinking it, I would develop a craving for "likker" that I would not be able to resist. I believed her, but her understanding of "craving" was that it was like a hunger or thirst or something like that (even the dictionary uses hunger and thirst in it's definition for craving), that had to be satisfied; a demand that the body made that had to be satisfied before it would go away, a physical craving that one could become enslaved to. In fact, I heard that term in church, "becoming enslaved to alcohol." So my computer had been programmed with that definition of craving at a very young age. All of my life I lived in mortal fear of that kind of physical craving "a-gittin' a-holt on me."

Yet, while I guarded the front door against that dreaded thing happening, the real alcoholic type mental craving, the one that only we alcoholics possess, came in through the back door and slipped it's arms around me.

Mom and Grandmother, with all their best intentions and love for me, used my Granddaddy as an example of a person who had come to crave "likker" and who had become a "*soooooorrrry*" individual because of it.

Well, they made a BIG mistake using him as an example because I loved and admired that old man. He called me "Hoss" and he had a scent about him that I loved to smell. I know now that it was a combination of the Prince Albert cigarettes that he rolled and smoked and the moonshine whiskey that he drank.

I followed him around often as a boy and one day, when he didn't know that I was anywhere around, I followed him into the barn, where I saw him dig down into a feed barrel and take out a bottle of that wicked "moonshine" whiskey and take him a long drink of it. Damn, he made it look good!

I knew that I'd better be still and quiet till he got gone. It would have been a "revoltin' development" for both of us if he had seen me, so I laid low and later made my way back to the house.

I couldn't get that feed barrel out of my mind (sort of like Carol), so later on I made my way back to the barn and to that barrel and very nervously dug the bottle out. I took me a little drink of it to see just what this irresistibly wonderful stuff was all about.

It was mighty quiet in that barn. All I could hear was that ol' horse snorting while I waited tensely for whatever it was that was supposed to grab me and change my life around.

To my surprise, there was no mysterious power that compelled me to have another drink of it. In fact, it tasted bad and burned going down, so in that moment, another drink of it was the furthest thing from my mind. I waited patiently, but the "craving seizure" didn't come. I was mighty glad; I would hate to think that I would be a slave to something that awful!

I figgered then that what they were telling me about craving was all a bunch of baloney and an effort to steer me away from the good life and into the bosom of the church. After all, there had already been talk of my becoming a preacher when I grew up so I figgered that they must have wanted me to remain pure. The grown-ups wanted to keep the so-called good stuff for themselves!

I realize now that something else happened to me in the barn that day. In addition to the fact that I could drink and not crave alcohol becoming programmed in cement into my computer, I had had a feeling. Not a high, giddy, tipsy feeling; I hadn't swallowed that much. It was more a feeling of having won——, an exhilarating feeling of accomplishment in having challenged the adults by having explored this "craving likker" thing and having proved them wrong. I didn't feel cocky, but I felt confident and sort of special.

I had unknowingly taken on another personality that day. I felt ten feet tall. That little drink had affected me in a *"mighty peculiar way."* It was like holding two aces in the hole in the game of life. I knew a secret: people can drink "likker" and not crave it. I knew something no other kid knew, I thought.

I wouldn't decide to "drink like a man" for many years to come, but the connection had been made. My alcoholic mind had recorded data that there was a way to feel different. Be it rich, brilliant, spiritual, famous, sexy, suave, athletic, safe, debt-free, handsome or whatever. There was a way to feel complete. It had also stored, in my computer memory bank, that I could drink alcohol and not physically have to have it. I could have my booze and drink it too, so to speak. I could, as we drunks say, "handle it."

So at that time in Granddaddy's barn, my mind's mind/computer recorded data that my feelings changed with alcohol and that I could drink it and not crave it. After that, it was utterly impossible for me to connect my desire for alcohol and my reactions to it, to a desire somewhere deep within me, for a change in my feelings.

Lordy! Lordy! Lordy! If I could have, I sho' 'nuff would have! Like ol' Glad's chickens, I didn't want to do it (them things that the physical reactions to alcohol brought on.) I can hear the words to that old song even now; "You Made Me Love You, I Didn't Want To Do It!"

As I see it now, the difference in me and my friend Stan and in other normal drinkers, is that they are satisfied with the way that they are and they have no reason to want to change their feelings about themselves, but I needed the changes. I wasn't content with just being me. I didn't like myself enough. I wanted to be more than what I was. I didn't feel good about me.

The most fitting description that I have heard for my condition is—- that I *have "severe personality maladjustments."* Thus, for me, the craving that I couldn't and wouldn't see for many years to come, was produced by a desire for a change in me, a feeling of wholeness. This desire had to be satisfied. My mind's mind discovered that alcohol would do it—-, thus began an inner desire for the drink.

It was more like a sixth sense. Whenever whatever caused me to need the change, any kind of change, short term or long term, good or bad, happy or sad, my alcoholic mind would print out; "Alcohol will do it!" Then the blind blunder of that first drink would come. It was like a thermostat—-, when I wanted change, my alcoholic mind printed out; "DRINK!"

I knew that I shouldn't do it, in my street mind. I never chose to drink alcohol without knowing that I shouldn't do it, but my alcoholic mind overruled my street mind and I couldn't not do it. Then there had to be one more. Then another and another. There was no logic to it, it just started. If I started out wanting to feel like a prince, I drank more to feel like a king, but in time I would become a slave. After that it would start again.

Call it a disease, a personality maladjustment, a strange malady, sorriness, insanity, an inferiority complex or whatever, because by any other name, it happened in me. For lack of a better name, someone somewhere labeled it a "phenomenon of craving." I sho' do wish that momma had known more about alcoholic type craving!

My craving wore many disguises. Whenever the change was desired there was always an excuse for the drink; thirst, sorrow, stress—- and the excuse was always convincing in any of its disguises. One of the common ones was, "Shore is hot! A cold beer would be mighty good right now!" Then after a cold one, I would drink six or eight more, believing that I was still thirsty.

Now I look back and realize that I never, even on the hottest day, ever drank six or eight glasses of ice water in a short time or four or five "sody pops" to quench my thirst, but many times I consumed that many beers in one sitting, convinced that I was doing it because I was thirsty.

I also look back and know now why I many, many times would leave my place of work, get into my car, start toward a bar where I was going to have a cold beer or drink of some kind, but would reach under the seat or into the glove box, take out a bottle, usually of vodka which was often very hot from having been in the car all day and drink from it on the way to the bar. Now, that ain't social drinking, nor is it thirst quenching!

One of my favorite "thirst quenchers" around the house was gin and tonic and there have been many times when I ran out of tonic and would drink only gin, but there was never a time when I ran out of gin and drank only tonic to "quench my thirst."

One memory that prints out vividly the power of my craving is the time in my early marriage to my first wife, Sue, when she and our only child Tanya and I were driving through the north Georgia mountains during a mini-vacation there. I had snuck and had me a couple of snorts before we had left the motel because Sue hated drinking, so I didn't do it in front of her since it created a very bad feeling between us. In other words, she raised hell about it, so I snuck around her. So here I was having had a couple of drinks already, thereby pulling the craving pin on my alcoholic grenade and I put the bottle under the driver's seat because my alcoholic mind knew that I would want more before we got back.

Sure enough, as we rode and toured, my thoughts began to close in on that bottle under the seat and I started hoping that Sue would go to sleep or that something would enable me to get to that bottle.

Alas, the roads were curvy and not conducive to sleeping and the scenery was breathtaking. So she was very much alert and awake and I suffered more with every coming and going curve in the road. Man -o - Man, did I want that drink! I was quickly losing the "feeling."

It was during this time that I began to dream up a scheme in my mind to somehow rig up the windshield washer tank with a plastic tube that I would run into the car so that I could put booze in the tank and could drink through the tube, unnoticed by her. I never did do that, but what an idea during that time of desperation!

Now let me point out that I have never heard of this idea from a non-problem drinker, but having told it to many of my recovered alcoholic friends, I have found that some of them had thought of it too. If that ain't craving, Howdy Doody ain't got wooden eyeballs!

By now, I was grasping for straws to get to that bottle when the ultimate of miracles happened. We rounded a curve and behold, a big sign appeared with the words, "HELICOPTER RIDES —- TEN DOLLARS" inscribed on it. My heart soared like the hawk, especially since one of the whirly birds was waitin' and ready to go. Sue wasn't aware of it yet, but she and our little girl, Tanya, were about to embark on their first helicopter ride!

Now I'm sure that there has never before, or since, been a madder woman on a helicopter, but once I shamed her for even thinking about hurting me by turning down this once in a lifetime opportunity (that I was giving up myself so that she and Tanya could ride) they stepped aboard and as they soared over a mountain top and out of sight, I went back to the car and turned up my precious bottle and had a long, soothing, craving-satisfying drink, never once considering the hell that the poor helicopter pilot must be catching. That was definitely not social drinking.

It is rather common among us addicted people that we are somewhat off center in some of our basic human emotions. In fact, it was in an old medical dictionary that I read that we alcoholics are people with those "severe personality maladjustments." I believe that mine were the result of a lot of the bad data going into my computer while I was coming up.

Now don't think that I am making excuses for what I became; that's not the issue here. It's the fact that I'm out of it today that counts. Anyhow, it makes sense to me that the data in my computer is all that I had to produce my behavior, so my printouts were the best that I could manage to do.

I know that my attitude toward the church, God (as He was presented to me) and spirituality were warped by my early church experiences. I was raised in a Pentecostal church and believe me, the rules were strict! You see, I was Pentecostal when Pentecostal wasn't cool. In fact, normal folks frowned on it. We might as well have been snake handlers, but then at least what they do makes a little sense!

My early memories are of the old time Pentecostal Church Of God where the fear of God became automatic early in my life. I heard many horror stories told by the various preachers and so called evangelists. Stories of those poor souls who didn't respond to the conviction that came upon them to turn their lives over to God and then had left that particular church service to be run down and killed by a BIG truck or by a bolt of lightning or some other ghastly way and then, because it was too late, they were destined to spend eternity in the "ol' lake of fire," seven times hotter than any heat known to man. I had, by that time in my short life, seen a welding torch in action and if there was anything seven times hotter than *THAT*, I sure didn't want any part of it!

I remember asking momma once how anybody could go to hell, be cast into a lake of fire seven times hotter than a welding torch flame and not be burnt plum up (I must have been a heathen even at that early age!).

Of course, she couldn't explain it so she told me that I wasn't supposed to question such things. I quickly "figgered out" that I was mighty close to gittin' struck dead so I let that question drop.

I guess that she was about as flabbergasted at that question as she was one day when I was at the front door watching the rain pouring down in torrents and I turned to her and asked, "Momma, does God make it rain?"

"Yes, yes," she smiled and replied, "He certainly does, son!" She must have been proud that I was learning to appreciate God's work 'til I turned back around and saw the water washing the red mud across the yard in little rivers and innocently remarked, "Well he shore is a-makin' a mess today!" "*Looooooord* have mercy!!", she said. It was another setback for momma!

So I would, again and again, make my way to the altar, the Church of God way and go through the motions of "gittin' saved" and really feeling it, only to find that in a day or two I was right back in the clutches of the devil, doing and thinking those awful things that growing boys do and think and then I would assume that God didn't want me. At least He hadn't shown me that He did.

We had an evangelist to come to our church one summer to conduct a revival. We were told ahead of time that he was a murderer that had been convicted, imprisoned and pardoned for his crime. (I guess that's where I got my idea for a great prison ministry myself later in my story.) Now what could be more exciting than to be in a church with a man that low down that God had forgiven and received into His bosom? Boy howdy, if it happened for him, it could happen for me.

So I was happy when summer revival came around and the family would again load up in the old pickup truck and off we would go at meetin' times. I was hoping that this would be the revival meetin' that I would make the God connection in. I really did want to go to heaven when I died, but more than that, I sho' 'nuff didn't want to go to hell!

The highlight of this revival was the night that we went to the church and upon entering, saw a full sized replica of an electric chair on the platform up front. I had seen a picture of one before so I was very much aware of what it was and I again was sho' 'nuff affected in a *"mighty peculiar way"* by the presence of this instrument of death. Little did I know, at that very young age, that those so-called "Men of God" survived on the sensationalism that they created.

The church was packed when the service started and the singing and the normal praising of the Lord set the mood very well for the sermon and sure enough, it was on **"THE WAGES OF SIN IS DEATH."**

It was a hot night and there was no air conditioning in that ol' church and that preacher, a mighty big man with a booming voice, had really gotten carried away with his preachin'. He was hollerin' and pantin' and his shirt was drenched with sweat when he reached the point in his sermon where he signaled for a pre-arranged volunteer to come on up and get into that horrible structure.

When that fellow, one of the town's barbers, came up, under the power of the spirit, of course, he was seated in that electric chair and some other volunteers strapped him in and then the "electrocution procedure" was acted out. The preacher narrated very effectively as they went through it step by step.

"And they'll-huhhh, set you down-huhhh, in a chair like this-huhhh and then they'll strap-huhhh, these little 'lectrodes-huhhh, to yo're head and yo're legs-huhhh and yo're arms-huhhh and then they'll ask you-huhhh, if you've got any last words to say-huhhh and then they'll throw a switch-huhhh and shoot more 'lectric'ty through yo're body-huhhh, than it would take-huhhh to light up this whole town-huhhh and then you'll sizzle 'til you're dead-huhhh and then——, it'll be to late——-! 'Cause then you'll be standin'-huhhh before the throne of Goddddd-huhhh, probably still smokin-huhhh, fer yo're judgement----------!!

He paused for a looooong spell while slowly wiping the sweat from his brow, allowing plenty of time for all that he had hollered to soak into the hearts and minds of an awe-stricken and graveyard silent congregation.

Then, as the pianist began to play, very softly, that old hymn, "There's a Great Day Comin'!" he went for our jugulars.

"*OOOOOOOOOHH* sinner-huhhh! What will yo're judgment be? Is yo're name in the lamb's book of life-huhhh? Will He say; 'Enter thy good and faithful servant,' Or will he say 'Depart from me-huhhh, for I never knew you,' leaving you to spend eternity-huhhh, in that lake of fire—-? Are you ready to meet Him—-? **ARE YOU READY FOR THAT JUDGMENT DAY?** "

Oooohhhh shit far," I muttered, he's a-talking to me! "*Ohhhhhhh hell*—-, I've said shit and in the house of the lord on top of that! *Ohhhhhh damn*—-, now I've said hell too! *Ohhhhh lordy lordy*—-, now I've said shit, hell and damn and all at a time like this!" I then became convinced that a big bolt of lightning was on its way to git me.

"*Ohhhhh* dear lord Jesus, please don't strike your ignert servant dead! Please deliver me from this sinful enslavement cause I swear to God, I'm doing the best that I can do!

"*Ohhhhhh shit*, now I've swore and like a fool, right at God too! I reckon there just ain't no way out of this for me! If I had'a known that it was gonna be like this, I sho' 'nuff wouldn't of come to church tonight! *Ohhhhh me*, another blasphemous thought!"

I was frozen in horror by then that my chances of being delivered from this devil's sinful mire were mighty slim and that I was gonna be cast into that eternal lake of hell fire seven times hotter than anything known to mankind, before the sun would rise again!

Now that was a mighty big swing, especially for a lad my age, to be diverted so suddenly from trying to decide, just before coming to church, if he was gonna swap his genuine World War II army helmet and liner to a buddy for two good wagon wheels to finish buildin' a ho'made wagon, to being faced with fixin' to be hurled out into eternity without ever having been genuinely "washed in the blood of the lamb." *WELL AT LEAST I WOULDN'T HAVE TO BE WORRYIN' ABOUT THEM WHEELS NO MORE!*

Now us urchins of the church were usually allowed to sit in a group during the services, as long as we behaved ourselves and kept quiet.

Well, believe me the grown-ups weren't bothered by our pranks and shenanigans that night because that preacher had us riveted! Needless to say, by the time the simulated switch had been thrown and the volunteer was simulated dead, all slumped over in that chair, they had our undivided attention!

There was a whole lots of shufflin' and groanin' goin' on throughout the congregation. Evidently, all of the other sinners were having the same terrifying thoughts that I was havin', as the preacher very emphatically explained to us, while pointing to the simulated dead man, that this could be our doom unless we turned our hearts and lives and souls over to God— and right then— because we might not get another chance. A big truck, or lightnin' or somethin' else horrible might snuff us out us before we git another opportunity!

We were obviously convinced because when Hazel, Montique and Montine, the church trio, had just begun to sing the invitational hymn, "Softly and Tenderly Jesus is Calling," we were like a dam bustin' gittin' to that altar! Everybody was goin' down at the same time, pushin' and shovin'! I thought I even heard a grown up voice say, "God damn a church with narrow aisles!"

Now, in the old Pentecostal church, one had to WORK HARD for religion. We couldn't become a full-fledged Christian with a mere stroll to the front of the church, a hand shake with the preacher and a few words to him professing our faith, like them "heathen" Baptists and Methodists did, and the way them Methodists baptized, Ha! Just dabbin' a little water on somebody's head wadn't gonna git 'em to heaven. Us Pentecostal's called that "sprinklin'" or "dry cleanin'" and that sho' 'nuff couldn't work! Even I believed that them were kind of "chicken shit" ways to get saved.

In our church it wasn't that easy. One had to walk down the aisle, kneel at the altar (which was just some wooden benches without backs) in front of the pulpit and then one had to "pray through." In other words, God had to be listening to you or you were wasting your time and sometimes praying through wasn't very easy. The saints of the church had to be satisfied that you had prayed through or you weren't saved and had to do it all over again later.

Then after this session, if you had prayed through, you had to testify and tell of your glorious experience to the satisfaction of the saints and then you were saved and now qualified for "Phase II."

In "Phase II," the candidate, in a future service of either choice or conviction, returned to the altar for "sanctification," or as we called it, "gittin' sanctified." This phase took a little more praying, so most of us lost it between "gittin' saved" and "gittin' sanctified." It was just too much to expect for some of us, but a few did make it and were then qualified to go for "Phase III" which was "gittin' filled with the Holy Ghost." Man, that was BIG——! We sinners watched those sanctified folks closely, wondering when the call from God to go back down to the altar would come, because when a Holy Ghost candidate made his or her way to the altar again (another service of course), it was the main event and sometimes it took several trips to the altar for them to get it, but when one of them finally prayed through, sometimes in the wee hours of the morning, you've never seen such a commotion!

Now, if one ran the entire gauntlet and got saved, sanctified, and filled with the Holy Ghost, he or she was then held in the utmost of high esteem in the church because it was one hell of a job to get there! On a very rare occasion, someone would get saved, sanctified and filled with the Holy Ghost all in one big crack! This would make a landing on the moon pale by comparison! The only thing that could exceed this would be a personal appearance by Jesus Christ, Himself!

Back to the flooding of the altar. There was a time of rejoicing that night. Never before had there been that many sinners at the altar at one time in the entire history of the church, because nobody had ever scared the "living shit" out of us quite like that before. Shit far, I believe that if that preacher had a-been with ol' Moses, "Way down there in Egypt's land," that ol' Pharaoh would have let them Hebrew Children leave for their promised land a hell of a lot quicker and with a whole lots less trouble than he did. He probably would have given them a police chariot escort.

Anyhow, you know the old saying; "A picture is worth a thousand words." Believe me, we got the picture that night! Some of us even had to get down at the front sitting benches, it was so crowded. The saints (that's what we called the older members of the church who had already been saved, sanctified and filled with the Holy Ghost) were now trying to help us sinners pray through and they had plenty of us to pray for and they roamed around and got to us all.

Everybody was prayin' and sweatin' and shoutin'. A pack of cigarettes went flyin' across the church prompting an ear-splittin' "*DOOOOOOOOOOOOOOOO JEEEESUS!!*" from whichever saint was praying with whichever sinner that had "prayed through" and threw it, figgerin' that everything that was sinful had to go. I would have lit out after them cigarettes any other time, but right then *I was trying to "git saved" myself!*

The organ and the piano were really blasting out the music. The singers were beltin' out the message with songs like; "I'll Fly Away," "Gimme That Ol' Time Religion," "I'm Ridin' The Range For Jesus," "Ninety-nine and a half won't do,"(another name that we called the old song about the shepherd that left his flock of ninety-and nine sheep to go in search of the one that was lost) and other soul-stirring songs.

Periodically some person that I knew was a blacker-hearted sinner than I was would leap up with his hands held skyward praising the Lord for saving his soul. I was part of this mass of humanity, but for some reason I couldn't "pray through," and I really wanted to be saved.

When the frenzy died down, the preacher asked us to tell of our new-found freedom. There were some genuine testimonies of having had a spiritual experience and some of the people that I knew in those days are fine Christian people today, but it just wouldn't happen for me. So I kept on trying and faking it a lot. In fact, later in life someone asked me if I had ever been saved and before I thought about it, I replied, "About a hundred times, I guess!"

So I assumed again and again that I wasn't good enough for God. He just wouldn't take me, at least I couldn't feel it. I did, however, stay saved for about two weeks after the electric chair episode. That was probably a record for me.

As life went on, I began to try less and less to make the spiritual connection and then one night I heard another "hot shot" evangelist say that after God had tried to get you so many times with no success, that he would stop trying.

I had a lots of respect for and confidence in preachers at that age, so I "figgered" that I didn't stand a chance! These Christian people believe that everything you do is a sin anyway, playing football and baseball, watching television and especially smoking and drinkin' likker. (I hadn't got started on the likker yet.)

And carnal thoughts of the flesh would **REALLY** get you struck dead right on the spot! I had already figgered out that those were wicked thoughts about girls, or playin' "Pee Wee" under the house or out at the barn. That's the ol' "I'll show you mine if you'll show me yours" game that boys and girls in the neighborhood used to play. It was part of that exploration process that Carol had got me interested in.

I cussed myself for having those kind of thoughts, especially when I was having 'em about the preacher's wife 'cause she was mighty young and she was the first pretty preacher's wife that I had ever seen and lookin' at her sho' 'nuff did affect me in a *"mighty peculiar way!"*

Damn, I thought, a human can't git no lower down than that—-, havin' carnal thoughts about the preacher's wife and even wishin' that he could play "Pee Wee" with *her*! Them had to be unforgivable sins! *OOOhhhhhhhh* dear lord Jesus, please spare your ignert, unworthy servant of the flesh from that eternal hell fire.

There wadn't a whole lot that a person could do and still make it to the pearly gates back then. I even got to where I was afraid to scratch some places on my own body because I thought that I surely must be committing a carnal sin!

On top of all this mental anguish, I saw my friends, who went to other churches, playing ball, going to movies (I had been whipped severely for that more than once), watching television, going to parties and such with no fear at all of hell fire and damnation. So, since God didn't want me anyhow (at least He wouldn't show me that He did) I would go to church for as long as I had to (parent pressure), but I would do those fun things that I wanted to do. And I did.

I played football and baseball in high school, but my parents never saw me play. I was in the senior play, but they never saw me act. I began to do those things that seemed normal in spite of the penalties that I now believed were looming out there in "eternity" for me.

My parents didn't stay away from my activities because they wanted to shame me for doing them, it was simply because they were also victims of this religious ignorance. I never felt that my parents were being critical of me or that they didn't love me, they simply let me make my own choices with their disclaimer that "when I ended up in hell—-, I DONE IT!"

I developed a tough skin where God and church stuff were concerned. I finally reached a point where even the most heart-rending story from the pulpit didn't bother me. I had come to believe that being a Christian wasn't for me and for many years I maintained that attitude.

I know now that I have always had an inner desire for a contact with God. I was an adult before I ever heard or read the psalm in the bible, "As the hart panteth after the water brooks, so panteth my soul after thee, O God." That psalm really grabbed me when I read it for the first time, but the thought passed quickly. Still, it had affected me in a *"mighty peculiar way."*

I had become insensitive by then to spiritual things. I attended church off and on, but always for social or family reasons. Later in life I even taught Sunday school and wore the persona of a Christian and there were times when the ol' "give your heart and life to Jesus" feeling would come over me, but I would brush it off. **HOWEVER,** I have always kept my eyes peeled for big trucks and I still get inside real quick when lightning starts flashing!

The time came, in spite of how I felt about it, when I had to "git saved" the "chicken shit" way. I was Baptist by now, by marriage, but what a day of rejoicing it started out to be.

I was changing jobs, about to become a member of the management team with the cotton mill in Canton, Georgia, where church affiliation was an absolute must! I had sensed this during my interview with them and had lied when they asked about my church affiliation saying that I was a member of the First Baptist Church in Buford. I could see that this was good and that they looked with favor upon this impersonator of a fine Christian man. They hired me.

NOW WHAT? I couldn't move to my new town and then join the church by profession of faith because all of those company executives would be there and would know that I lied and that I certainly was no Christian and not fit to be a member of their team. They were to realize these things anyhow in due time.

I had two weeks before reporting to work so I decided to join the church back home, then I could just transfer my letter and all would be wonderful!

Only I knew of my scheme when the big Sunday came and much to the surprise of the hometown folks, I marched down the aisle to profess my faith. Even Sue gasped when I stepped out into the aisle to begin this eventful journey! I felt a little like Tom Sawyer. This was much easier than the Pentecostal way, let me tell you!

I happened to be the only lamb to go down that morning and the handshakes and words of welcome were all heaped upon me as folks filed by to receive me. Some were crying as they hugged me and told me of how happy they were that I had chosen to turn from my life of sin and go the straight and narrow.

The problem was that there were several of them that expressed real joy that I had given up my wicked past—-, they must have known more than I thought they did! I actually started thinking, "Man o man, I'm glad I have done this! They love me! God has truly orchestrated everything that has led me to this event today!"

As I continued to marvel over my transformation while the Christians continued to welcome me, tears began to fill my eyes and stream down my cheeks and I once again resolved myself to be a born-again Christian and once again, I MEANT IT! In my street mind, I meant it. I was overcome with love and peace. In this "*peculiar* **way**," I had, at last, found myself.

After it had all sort of died down, we went home to start our new life—-, a family dedicated to living for Jesus. I would have gleefully volunteered for the foreign mission fields that day if someone had only asked me to do it.

My, my! Sue was proud of me, the preacher was proud of me, and I was right proud of myself! It was a wonderful new beginning!

After our Sunday roast beef dinner (southern noon meal), Sue, pregnant with our second child, decided to take a Sunday afternoon nap with our little girl, Tanya, and left me alone watching the baseball game on television.

For some time, my next-door neighbor, Joe and I had been partners in a beer making operation, producing only for our own consumption, of course. We made nine gallons each time and had it down pretty scientifically. We ordered malt and hops and yeast from Nova Scotia, which gave us a little prestige and we made good stuff and **STRONG** stuff!

Now on this particular Sunday, I had six bottles left of my share of the last batch. These were the last hold that the ol' devil had on me.

Now imagine this: a lazy summer afternoon, all alone, watching baseball on TV, (truly a contented, peaceable man's game), newly born-again, at peace with God and man, full and content from a scrumptious meal. An airplane even droned lazily in the sky overhead, putting the finishing touch to the enchantment of that blessed afternoon. Then the thought of them cold brews in the refrigerator struck me. I said to myself; "I'll just pour them suckers out!", and I went to the kitchen to do just that!

When I opened the fridge, I saw the last of my sinful life before me and out of respect for it, I reckon, I decided to drink just one of those brews and pour out the other five and for some reason I decided that I would pour after I had drunk. Well, I drank that one and pouring time came again, but I decided this time to drink just one more and pour out four.

Now this was not because I was craving, but because I was again, in my street mind, making a rational, intelligent choice to do this. So it was OK since this would definitely be the last that I would ever drink or make. Of course, before it was all over, I had rationally, intelligently decided to drink all six of them and just not ever make anymore. By then, I was smashed because, as I said, we made it strong!

Now, I had settled down with this strong buzz going not realizing how tipsy I really was, resolving never to drink again and thinking that I could cover this whole thing up from Sue and from God, when I heard a car coming into the driveway.

Now I couldn't be seen "wallerin' in sin" by just anyone at this crucial time, having just gotten saved again so, to my own surprise, I wobbled, happily and bubbly, doing a little "soft shoe" routine, to the kitchen door that faced the driveway and peered through the little gap between the curtains to see who it was.

"*OOOOOHHH SHIT FAR!*" I gasped, as my newly-found spirituality sailed right out of the window. "It's the @#%&—&%$#@#@* preacher!!!" And he was already happily making his way around to the front entrance of the house!! He had come to welcome the newest "washed in the blood" member of his flock, but was soon to discover that his newest lamb had been washed in the beer!!!

I sho' 'nuff didn't want him to ring that bell and wake up Sue to catch me drunk and get her heart broke again! *GOD-A-MIGHTY!* What a revoltin' development this was turning into, her and the preacher "ketchin" me drunk at the same time and after all the emotions of my just gittin' saved again and only a few hours ago at that! I'd sooner have been drug to town and back by a team of mules by my tongue than for that to happen! Shit far, just a few hours ago I was ready for the mission fields and now here I was "wallerin' in sin" ag'in.!!

I frantically blazed a crooked trail back to the living room, broke the speed record for lighting a pipe and was desperately puffing on it as I opened the door just a split second before he put his finger to the door-bell. His big, toothy, ministerial grin faded away as I weaved and splut-tered, "*Shhhue ish assshhllleep.*"

Even I was surprised at how slurred my own words were! I did the ol' Laurel and Hardy double take at myself! It was like trying to spit after a dentist has loaded you up with Novocaine. The words just seemed to run down my chin. I stood there feeling lower than whale shit, stupidly grinnin' and weaving, holding onto the door knob, looking like the vil-lage idiot, as he, being the gentleman that he was, quietly turned and walked away.

Once again, I had been gloriously saved and had back-slid (sinned again) all in the same day, quicker than ever before.

That afternoon was an early exposure for me to the fact that one of the prerequisites for being a good drunk is to learn to adjust quickly to lots and lots of sudden, and most of them, horrendous changes in our plans and situations.

Joe, my neighbor and beer makin' partner, was a member of the same church and was at the service the day of my "profession of faith." I later learned, when I hinted that another batch of the formula might be in order, that he hadn't been all that surprised at my "sinnin' agin", and he was more than ready! So we brewed up another nine gallons.

The weather had turned warmer and bottling time was comin' fast, so I decided the next Saturday that I needed to wash up the bottles for brewin' time. I was right in the middle of that job with about a hundred beer bottles all around me in the carport just a-washin' and a-singin'.

I was "wallerin' in sin" ag'in and yep, wouldn't you know it, the preacher drove right up. He sat in his car for a moment, that seemed to me to be more like a week, trying to analyze the situation and finally just backed out of the driveway and drove away. I could have kissed him for not getting out of that car.

The "whale manure" syndrome crept over me again as I sat there frozen in humiliation and bewilderment, wondering why he had showed up at that particular time. Still motionless, with a beer bottle in one hand and a soapy brush in the other and soap bubbles all over me, my innermost, heart-felt, pre-dominant thought was—; "*SHIT FAR!* I wish that preacher would call, before he comes!"

I found out later that he had come to talk about baptizing me and had found me baptizing myself. He did baptize me the next Sunday, but I could tell that he wasn't putting his whole heart into it. I guess that he too figgered that this was like baptizing a Cannibal; "It was probably a whole lots of trouble fer nuthin!" In fact I sensed that he plunged me under the water a little more vigorously than he did other folks and that he held me under a lot longer than he did them. I guess that he was trying to get at them deep-seated stains of sin in me.

I'll bet that he busted out singing "Praise God From Whom All Blessings Flow," adding, "*They've* got that booger now!," when he later opened the letter from the First Baptist Church in Canton, asking for the letter to transfer my membership.

We moved shortly after my baptism and that preacher was close to retirement when I saw him again and as luck would have it, I was noticeably drunk and I noticed that he noticed it! I guess that it just wasn't meant to click for him and me.

This was another religious experience that didn't make me stronger in my spiritual beliefs at the time, but I see now that that preacher is indeed woven into the fabric of my beliefs today

So having been armed with my "phenomenon of craving," and my belief that I had never craved, and my severe personality maladjustments, and all of those religious misconceptions crammed into my computer/mind, I had set out on the long and rocky road of alcoholism long before I knew that I had.

I was constantly on guard for that feared craving as I traveled this road and swore that if I ever felt a need for alcohol, like a hunger or thirst, that I would stop drinking it-PRONTO! Alas, while I guarded against those kinds of cravings, the real mental alcoholic craving already had me in its merciless clutches!

I recall once seeing a television documentary on balloon flight, in its earlier days. In one segment a grounds crew was moving a huge balloon into it's launching place. There were several crewmembers each holding onto a separate rope that was attached to the balloon to hold it down. There were enough of them of course to keep the balloon from floating away under normal conditions, but a strong gust of wind gave the balloon a sudden unexpected lift and all but one of the ground crew let go of their ropes.

The one that held on to his rope for a second or two too long, hopelessly trying to save the balloon, had been suddenly lifted upward and, by then, too high to let go of it. By that time he was high enough so that the fall might have injured, or maybe even killed him. He couldn't let go, yet he must have known that he couldn't hold on for long. As he was being lifted higher and higher, he had to know that in time he would have to fall. He had found himself, much to his surprise, suddenly and unintentionally thrust into a fatal situation. The cameras recorded his plunge to his death when he finally lost his grip.

So, armed with a craving that I didn't even know about, and an alcoholic mind that kept me in the dark about it, and as far as I knew then, a total rejection of the spiritual, I set out to try and achieve the good things in life not even suspecting that I didn't stand a chance.

I was like the man holding on to the balloon flying blindly- slowly at first, then faster and faster and higher and higher——-, to some point in time when I would ultimately lose my grip and crash, destroying myself and much of whatever and whoever might be close to me. I can remember that from time to time I would know, but would brush aside the thought, that someday I would have to fall.

I was arrested about twenty years after the church-joining episode, for the ninth time for driving under the influence of alcohol. I had a blood alcohol reading of .370, close to death. The legal limit then was .100 I had steered my vehicle onto the wrong side of a four-lane highway into the path of oncoming traffic. I didn't want to do that. I didn't intend to do that. I knew what side of the median that I wanted to be on and should be on and I meant to go to that side. I tried to go to that side, but as much as I wanted to and as hard as I tried, I couldn't make the vehicle go where I knew that it should go and to where I wanted it to go. Alcohol had taken away my ability to perform that simple driving task.

Just as surely, alcohol took away my ability to guide my life. I knew where I wanted it to go. I knew where it should go and what I wanted it to do. I chose to go to college to try and better myself. I fell in love with and chose to marry Sue, a good and lovely woman. I wanted to love her and the children that we were to have, for the rest of our lives, and we did love each other for many years. I wanted to be a good, loving husband and father, to succeed for my family, to provide the good life for them, to grow old with her, with our family around us, to enjoy our grandchildren in our golden years. I wanted us to live the good life.

My eyes were on that destination, but my alcoholic mind made it impossible for me to make my plan work the way I wanted it to work, and knew that it should work. I wouldn't be able to control my destiny anymore than I could steer that vehicle to the right side of the road. Alcohol would take away my ability to guide my life and I would be hopelessly committed before I realized that I had turned the wrong way. Unfortunately, many other lives that were bound to mine would be forced to travel into alcohol's mad world with me and they would be severely affected by it.

I would, in time, come to believe that I was just a sorry person and didn't want to be any better. Then I would come to believe that I was just plain insane and couldn't do any better, but in time, I was to learn (and it would be from the most unlikely teachers), that I was nothing more than an alcoholic; mentally retarded where alcohol is concerned and that my condition, that I thought was the worst of the worst, could be fixed.

I must admit that I was a little insulted when they added, "And it really won't be all that big of a job!"

Chapter IV

COMIN' HELL! IT'S DONE HERE!

The very first alcoholic beverage that I ever purchased was after I had joined the Navy Reserves while I was in high school.

I had heard another guy telling about having gone on the two-week summer cruise with his Navy reserve unit. He told of how, during off duty time, they would all drink beer and raise hell at the Post Exchange.

He told of how they would form a human circle placing an empty fifty-five gallon trash barrel in the middle of their circle, and when one of them had drunk his beer can empty, he would try to throw it into the barrel. If that person missed, he then had to walk, stagger, or some-times, later in the evening, crawl over, pick the beer can up and put it into the barrel. Of course, when this happened, the rest of the guys in the circle would chug-a-lug what beer was left in their can and then would all throw at the barrel at the same time bombarding the hapless guy who had missed.

I figgered that if God had thought up anything that could be more fun than that for His people to do, He must have kept it for Himself!

The thought of being part of something like that rocketed me into the United States of America's Naval Reserves. Yet I haven't done that beer can throwing game to this very day.

I was on my first weekend tour of military service and had been issued a Navy uniform and had gotten acquainted with some other new recruits. That night we decided to go to town and show the world some real Navy "hell raisers!" Our first stop was the beer store. Navy men drink! We were now Navy men! We would drink!

I remember how totally surprised I was when I opened my very first can of beer and took my very first swallow of it. I had never tasted anything that tasted that rotten! I had formed my expectations of beer's taste from the old Miller beer commercial on TV. The actors would pour the beer into the tall tapered glass in a manner that would cause a big thick creamy lookin' head on the beer and of course, that head would turn clear and sparkly and look utterly delicious. Then came the jingle, with the low male bass voice singing, "Mill-eeerrrr—-," and the high female voice singing, "High Liiiffe," then both of them joining their voices in unison with; "The champagne of bottled beeeer!" Good lord, who wouldn't be turned on by that?

My first beer, however, didn't live up to my expectations-------, far from it! It tasted worse than anything I had ever tasted! So why did I ever drink the second one? Because the feeling that I had had in Granddaddy's barn so many years ago had been reawakened. I suddenly became Admiral Farragut in my Navy uniform! It was; **"Damn the torpedoes! Full speed ahead!"**

There were four of us teenagers in our Navy outfits that night and we were on one hell of an adventure! That nineteen fifty-three Chevy became a battleship in our minds. We were only about thirty miles from home, but we felt like we were on some South Sea island and that the women were searching for us!

I got drunk that night and experienced my first hangover the next morning. There would be no turning back now, because I am an alcoholic and the first drink commanded the second drink and the next drink, right up to the last drink that I would take thirty years later.

In the beginning, my craving was easy to satisfy. The bad affects were hardly noticeable. The first bad affect was the bad taste, but as I drank more, the bad taste was easily overcome by the satisfaction of being Admiral Farragut. Another bad affect was the hangover, but that was manly—- ,Navy, I reasoned.

I had again changed as a result of the drink. It was probably the perfect high that I was to pursue from then on. I didn't pay big penalties for that spree that night. In fact, I had a good time in spite of the bad affects, but alcohol would take some massive tolls in my quest for that illusive feeling, in years to come.

I was also very surprised the next time, shortly after that, when I drank again, at how much better it tasted. It was the same kind of beer. I had to have known that the formula hadn't changed, yet it tasted better. Now I know that the reason for the improved taste was because I knew how it was going to affect me and the bad taste wasn't a surprise.

So my alcoholic mind conned me to believe that it tasted better and that the taste wouldn't stand between me and the feeling that I wanted. I had already begun to develop the mental ability to block anything that could stand between me and that change of my feelings that I craved, and that would, in time, cause me to believe that the world of alcohol was the only one to live in. I couldn't know any better.

I didn't begin to drink heavily or daily right away, but I do remember that I was proud of my ability to do it and, I thought, not crave it. For years it wasn't evident, even to me, that I was getting deeper and deeper into it. I heard a lady once describe it as like being pregnant. At first it is not noticeable, then it becomes a happy, comfortable thing like; "Oh, I'm going to have a baby," type of thing. Then it becomes pure misery, like "get this thing out of me now and don't ever mention me having another one!"

Now, I am addicted to other things, such as coffee. I drink plenty of it and I don't waste my time with the decaffeinated stuff and I don't plan to quit drinking it, but I have on occasion, just forgotten to have my morning coffee. So, the addiction to caffeine is not all that powerful. It doesn't change me. Maybe it is only skin deep, but my addiction to alcohol went clear to the bone early. I possessed, even then, what I was to come to know as that mental craving.

So as I went along, I began to be aware that I drank differently from my peers. I was one of very few that went to jail in high school because of alcohol. The others just weren't doing it. I already had to do it and didn't yet know it.

I went to military college where drinking alcohol was punishable by dismissal, yet I did it anyway with a few others. I was addicted already and consequences meant nothing in my alcoholic mind. In fact I can now see that since that first drinking session, I have always been drawn to the people in my life that drank rather than those who didn't, "like a moth to a flame."

I remember wondering why it was that I would accumulate various brands and kinds of alcoholic beverages to have to offer just in case friends or guests would drop in. I wondered why I was so proud to possess it. I wondered why it would vanish so rapidly down my own gullet.

I know now that in my alcoholic mind, I felt secure in knowing that I had it. I know now that my alcoholic mind commanded me to drink it under the guise that it was simply my choice to do so. Solitary social drinking, I reckon.

I have, in my mind, compared my becoming addicted with the fish caught in a fish basket. I remember as a young lad going with my Uncle Early to what we called "run the baskets" in the ol' Chattahoochee River where the catfish got big and we always caught plenty of 'em. I always wondered what kind of fool a fish would have to be to get himself into such a fatal fix. Now I know.

The baskets were a cylinder of chicken wire about two feet in diameter and four to six feet long and in each end the wire was formed like a cone tapering into the basket. There was a hole instead of a point at the apex of the cone. This hole was big enough to allow a good size fish to just wander through it into the basket, as if swimming through a funnel. For bait, there were tasty morsels of chicken guts, chicken heads or rotten meat of some sort that had lured the fish into the basket.

The fish would swim through that funnel, starting at the big end of it, without ever knowing that it was entering a trap, and then once inside, would feast away, but then it couldn't find the small end of the funnel to come back out. It was caught. It was doomed. Man-O-Man, they were good eatin'!

I just as easily wandered through the funnel into my addiction to alcohol and feasted on the canker within it, and then discovered that when I wanted to come out, I couldn't find the small opening either. I was just as hopelessly trapped as that catfish.

I also sometimes compare my journey into addiction to the ol' pinball machine, me being the pinball. Once I was shot out onto the board (and I was with my first drink), I began my descent toward the hole at the bottom that I now see as either utter destruction or recovery.

Sure, I bounced around and sometimes even bounced back up the board for a ways and bounced around up there for a *long* time. Sometimes, I even scored big points while I bounced around, but my destination was always certain—, that hole at the bottom.

There has never been a pinball shot yet that hasn't fallen through that hole or an alcoholic that hasn't reached the moment of decision, if he lives long enough. Sometimes when the ball has almost reached the hole, there are flippers that flip it back up even sometimes all the way back up to the top of the board, but that doesn't change its ultimate destiny, it only prolongs the drop through that hole that is, for the alcoholic, either death or recovery.

Another very realistic comparison for me of my acceleration into addiction is in thinking of a time when I was about five years old and we were living in the mill village of New Holland, Georgia, where the merchants came around and delivered groceries, ice, coal and things like that to the houses in the village.

In the summertime, when the ice man would come, the kids in the neighborhood would clamor onto his truck for the chips of ice that resulted from his breaking the hundred pound blocks into the fifty, twenty five and ten pound smaller blocks depending on what was needed for the customer's ice box. Man, them small chips of ice were good on a hot summer day, especially since we got them for nothing!

On this particular day, I was the only kid in sight when the iceman came. When he stopped at our house I made a beeline for his truck. After he had ascertained how much ice momma wanted, he came back to the truck, cut it and took it into the house to put it into the icebox.

Now it was acceptable practice for us kids to climb into the back of the truck, so I clamored up to find me a sizable piece of ice to suck on. Within only a few moments, I suddenly heard his door slam shut and felt the truck start rolling.

Well, I knew that he would be stopping again soon so I decided to enjoy the ride and get off at the next stop. Alas, our house was the last stop and I soon began to realize that I was on a ride I couldn't get off of, and I didn't have any idea where it would end! It was about ten miles to his final destination—-, the ice plant—-, but that had to be the most terror filled ten miles that any human ever traveled!

It seemed as if that truck would never stop and I was being taken further and further from the safety and the familiarity of my home and my momma with every rotation of the wheels on that truck. I could tell that the truck was moving faster and faster by the wind sounds around me and the higher pitched whining of the tires rolling on pavement and the scream from the exhaust pipe. I couldn't jump off. I was trapped!

I was terrified! I was crying uncontrollably by the time the truck finally stopped and I was discovered by that big ol' friendly black man who was about as scared as I was when he discovered his cargo.

He took care of me, bought me a "Coca-cola" and took me back home. I felt safe with him, but my feelings during that ride are as close as I can come to describing the feelings of becoming addicted. I came to know somewhere along the way that I was on a ride that I couldn't stop.

I shared this experience with a friend who is also an ex-drunk and he told me of a time when he was seven or eight and he and a cousin, about the same age, were playing around a railroad siding, where a train was sitting idle. They saw that one of the boxcar's doors were open and they assumed that the engine, that was hooked to it and the other cars, wasn't ready to roll, so they decided that they would play hobo for awhile. They ran home to gather up some drinks and Vienna sausages and crackers and such to tie up in a bandana that they then tied to a stick, like hoboes in the comic strips. Then they ran back and climbed into that boxcar.

Now they were engrossed in their hobo game and didn't hear the train crew arrive, nor the engine startin' up, and to their surprise, the train began to roll! They figgered that it wouldn't go far and that they would just be real hoboes for awhile and ride till the first stop and then hop off and walk back. Alas, their ride which had innocently begun in their north Georgia hometown, ended up in Jackson, Mississippi!!! They hadn't figgered on their hobo game becoming this realistic!!

When they arrived, scared to death, they asked some of the trainmen where they were—-? They thought that they were somewhere in Atlanta! Of course they were turned over to the police who called Jeff's dad to tell him about the situation and Jeff's dad had to drive all the way down that night to get the wayward lads.

Jeff said that he could tell that his daddy was mad when he got there because he didn't say a word when he picked them up and didn't say much on the way home, but Jeff added, "I've been tempted many times to contact the Guinness record book people and see if there has ever been another eight year old kid in the world who has had his ass whupped in three different states in the same day!"

Jeff said that his momma's reaction was a little different. When she first saw him she grabbed him and set in to hugging him and hollerin', "*SWEEEEEEEET JESUS! SWEEEEEEET JESUS!*" Her baby was home! I reckon that it takes a lot to make a momma mad.

So as I soared into my addiction, my alcoholic mind put me into some awkward situations. It became more and more difficult to explain my behavior during those times when it had been activated.

When I think of how that mind worked, I think of when I started with the company that I worked for in Connecticut. There was a guy who had been working with me and who was hired by this company at the same time that I was and he and I were sent to the home office in Bridgeport for two weeks of training and company orientation before being sent to the plants that we each had been assigned to. There was a weekend between those two weeks and since it was much too far to travel home, we decided to spend that weekend in New York City.

Now get this picture; two genuine Georgia "rednecks" in "New York City" for their first time, with no restrictions whatsoever, except for the limitations of their "tobacco road" minds and tense from the stories that they had heard about the "Big Apple." Of course we had had a few "stiff" drinks by the time we got there and they were more than sufficient to erase any feelings of inferiority that we might have started out with. We boarded the train in Bridgeport and headed for New York City.

Now, being inside that train as it sped along, we couldn't appreciate the vastness of the city as we approached and when we got off the train we were inside of Grand Central Station, so we felt pretty smug having made it this far with no problems. We made our way through the station to the street level and finally thrust ourselves onto "New York City!" The impact was staggering! Awesome wadn't no name! I had truly never seen anything this big and noisy and the aroma all around us was heavenly to me! I fell in love with New York at first sight and smell!

We had one doozy of a good time that weekend mostly just walking around and looking. We started out making fools of ourselves by going into a liquor store to replenish our supply of booze. Being the high rollers that we had become (we were New Yorkers by now!), we asked the clerks behind the counter in that store, right there on Broadway in New York City, the swingin'est city in the whole world where we might find us some action in this town.

They looked at each other, instantly recognizing how ignorant we were and one of them good-naturedly replied, "I don't know, boys, but I'm going to Mass as soon as I leave here tonight and I'm gonna pray that you find some!" I thought, "Now ain't that hospitable, and him a Yankee!"

At one point, we were going up an escalator and we had stepped on right behind a very shapely young lady. She was a step up in front of me, sort of leaning on the side of the escalator with one of her feet a step up in front of the other causing her rear end to be provocatively accentuated and her shape was indeed remarkable.

Now, my partner was a step behind me and for some un-godly, heathenly reason his alcohol soaked brain caused him to reach past me, grab a handful of her rear end and withdraw his hand all in a sweeping split second leaving me to catch the wrath of her stare. I thought that surely my eyes must be a-deceivin' me

I was still in shock from having seen it happen, when she whirled around and looked me straight in the eye and called me some names that had reference to my intelligence level and to my mother! I had, in a flash, found myself in the middle of the most humiliating predicament that I could ever have possibly anticipated! I was in a state of total helplessness in the situation and quickly began spluttering and stammering, trying to defend my honor and integrity. This was also quite a cultural shock because this was a woman and being from the south, I didn't think that women knew how to talk that way. I must have looked like Will Stockdale in "No Time for Sergeants" when he saw his first female officer!

When we reached the top of the escalator, her parting shot, having picked up on my southern accent was, "You ignorant southern creep!" as she made a hasty departure from what she must have believed to be a genuine lunatic.

I was ready to fight to the death! My first words to him were, "You godless heathen, have you absolutely no brains whatsoever, what fiendish, paganistic, satanic forces possessed you to pull such an idiotical, maniatical, nonsensical trick?" *(See later on in the story.) That was a question that I would ask myself many, many times in the coming years. It was much like some of them tricks that my mind's alcoholic mind pulled on me.

If you happen to be reading this book ma'am and remember that occasion, please accept my humble apology and forgive me and my equally "ignert" partner!

I started finding myself suddenly in situations that I had to explain to others and to myself, situations that I hadn't even anticipated. I began to wonder often about some of the strange things that were happening to me whether I wanted them or not because they were becoming harder to justify.

A conflict was developing within me because I knew that those things were alcohol induced. I knew, for instance, that my companion would have never grabbed that lady's rear end if he hadn't been under the influence of alcohol, so I applied the same logic to my situation. I knew that drinking alcohol was costly, stupid, sometimes embarrassing, unhealthy and even humiliating, and enough good data had gone into my mind's normal mind for me to know beyond any doubt that drinking alcohol was morally wrong for me, so for those reasons, I had begun to want to stop doing it.

So the inner conflict was, "If I know these things, then why do I continue doing it?" Even when it became devastating for me, I still wondered why. I asked myself, "Is it because I crave alcohol?" "Naw," I answered. "I can quit any time I want to." "Well, then why don't you?" I would ask myself. "Because I don't want to right now!" and on and on—-.

My first inkling of an answer to my questions was in the words contained in that statement that I had heard or read somewhere: "A phenomenon of craving that only exists in the mind of the alcoholic." I remember wanting to know more about this, but my alcoholic mind wouldn't let me reach for that knowledge yet. It wanted to remain ignorant.

It must have been along about this time that my alcoholic mind began to invoke a phrase that I had heard from a little ol' lady in Canton, Georgia, the same town, in fact, that we had moved to after the church-joining episode. I had, of course, by this time, gotten hooked up with some of Canton's "un-refined, good ol' boys," and I, along with three of them, two co-workers and the town's fire chief, had recognized a need for a social center for the "un-refined" of the town.

We had rented an old country home place out in the woods, owned by the afore-mentioned little ol' lady, for that purpose. We called our place "The Camp," and we gathered there frequently to imbibe and "shoot the bull." We had fish fries, made turtle stews, cooked deer meat and other stuff. Our camp became quite a social center for the "un-refined" of the town.

On a few occasions, Bee, the little ol' lady, would walk down to the camp from her house, which was close by, to socialize with us. Of course we would talk about world events, national events, city and county events, neighborhood events or anything else that might come up.

Now Bee was a very sweet little ol' lady—-, until she took a drink or two or three with us and then she became rather opinionated and a little venomous with some of her remarks. In fact I've never heard anyone call someone a bastard as effectively as she could do it. She didn't just say the word bastard like most folks do. When she said it she put the accent heavily on the letter "a" and made it tremble sort of like in a sheep's *"baaaaaa"* but she stretched the word way out giving it a scathing, cutting edge. When she referred to someone as a *"baaaaaaaaaaaaasturd,"* (and she was prone to doin' that after having had a couple of strong belts), she made it sound as if a bed sheet was being ripped apart, or a jet plane was flyin' over sorta slow. We all tried to stay on Bee's good side. You can tell that she made quite an impression on me.

Now if the topic of conversation was not one that Bee liked or just wished not to be bothered with, she would cut it off by very emphatically announcing to us;*"I ain't studyin' no sech idiotical, maniatical, nonsensical shit es 'at!"** Latin for; "I refuse to talk or even think about those sorts of things.

So as the years wore on, when the "phenomenon of craving" thought would come into my head, my alcoholic mind would print out; "That only pertains to the alcoholic so we ain't studyin' *no sech shit as 'at!"*

Ignorance was becoming insanity. Maybe I could blame Bee for my becoming a drunk, but then, I'll have to admit, that that "phenomenon of craving" business had already rung a bell in my head and had affected me in *a "mighty peculiar way,"* long before I met Bee. So my cover up attempts started, just in case I had such a thing.

A fellow told me a story once about how he was in a bar having a couple of drinks (that's a requirement for being a good drunk, we must never be able to count higher than two! You know, things like; "I just had a couple", or "How about a couple of beers, or a couple of drinks."). Anyhow, he had caught the eye of a very attractive lady in the bar. They got chummy and as the evening progressed, they ended up in a motel, in the bed together. As the big moment approached, she started crying and confessed to him that this was her first experience at such as this, that she had gone to that bar because she was mad at her husband and was trying to get back at him for something that he had done. She told him that she had a beautiful family, kids, dog, cat, bird and that she never expected it to come to this. "Lordy, Lordy, the tears were just a-flowin'!", he said.

Well, as she talked and cried, he also got to thinking about his wife and kids and dog and bird and cat and such and danged if he didn't break down into an alcohol induced crying jag, too, "And," he said, "For the rest of that night, we would cry awhile and sin awhile, cry awhile and sin awhile!" The crying relieved the guilt of the transgression, somewhat.

Likewise, I found some relief in my mind if I could at least slow my alcoholic acceleration down from time to time and cry awhile thus providing myself with some justification for it, because I knew early on in my addiction, that not only did I know that something wasn't right, but that others were beginning to notice it, too.

I was on a business trip once with two co-workers, Richard and a guy named Bill. Having finished our day and returned to the motel I, of course, began to suggest going out on the town. Richard wanted to go, but Bill decided to stay in. I stepped into the bathroom, but didn't close the door all the way and I overheard Bill saying to Richard, "I don't know what it might be, but if you go out with Dead-Eye, y'all are gonna do something crazier than hell!" Damn, I was proud of that!

My heavy drinking was becoming obvious. I was doing things beyond the ordinary, strange things. My craving was becoming more demanding and I didn't know yet that I even had a craving.

I can see myself now like my dad saw me one Christmas when I had received a pair of cowboy boots from ol' Santa Claus. I loved them boots. I had waited a long time for them, but I knew that they were coming. I had already found them hidden away. I also knew that they had come from the Sears and Roebuck mail order catalog. I had seen a picture of them in there, but now I had 'em! They were mine! I was a genuine cowboy! Sears and Roebuck or North Pole—-, it didn't matter!

Now, there was a gentleman in our community named Bill Kinsey and Bill had some kind of foot trouble so that when he walked he limped on both feet as if he had a rock in each shoe and didn't want to put his weight down on either foot. He looked weightless. It looked right comical when you'd see ol' Bill walking to town.

It just so happened that my cowboy boots were a tad too small and after wearing them for awhile, my feet would begin to hurt like all git-out, but I knew where they had come from and I couldn't bear to think about mailing them back and waiting for a bigger pair to be sent to me. That would have been too long to be without my cowboy boots, so I kept quiet about it while I endured the pain.

Alas, unknown to me, my dad was watching me walk in my new boots one day and just outright asked me; "Boy, are them boots too little?" I, in fear of losing them even for a short time, replied, "Naw daddy, they're just right!" To which Dad replied,"Then why are you walking around here lookin' like Bill Kinsey?"

So in my acceleration into addiction, I began to sense that not only was I wondering about myself, others were also beginning to wonder if I was a problem drinker. Of course, I would try to make them believe, "Naw, I'm O.K." Then they and I would wonder why I was acting like one.

I began to need reasons for my behavior, an event such as a birth, a death, a happy occasion, a failure, a success, anything to avoid admitting that I didn't know why I acted like I did when I drank, or even why I drank at all. More and more I was asking myself why. I knew that there was nothing good about it. I would cry awhile and then sin awhile.

I often think back on the time in Connecticut when I wanted so badly to buy a pop-up camper for the family so that we could travel and take in all of the attractions in New England while we lived there. It seemed as if something always came up to prevent the purchase of the camper and I would use it as an excuse to drink and salve my wounds for "letting them down."

Then came the happy day when I finally could and did buy the camper. I pulled that baby home, but guess what? I was so happy over the occasion that I wanted to set it up in the driveway before Sue and the kids got home, to surprise them. Then, of course I had to celebrate with a drink in the new camper. Of course the gap closed, my alcoholic mind connected and I ended up spending the night in the new camper, passed out drunk from celebrating.

"What's wrong with this picture?" I wondered, as I came to in the dim light of dawn beginning to break. There is nothing lonelier than that time of day for a drunk—-, facing a new day too soon, not even knowing how he finished the old one and knowing that he has lost a little more of his family's respect, trust and affection, and knowing that there was absolutely no reason to offer for it this time. I drank because I couldn't buy a camper, then I drank because I could. It's pretty hard to explain that to oneself. Nope, didn't nary one of us WANT to do it!

So, as the mysterious drive to consume alcohol became stronger, I began to need reasons to *get* drunk, instead of for already having gotten drunk. I got drunk when John F. Kennedy was assassinated, when my momma died, when my son developed leukemia, Great Aunt Daisy died, Winston Churchill died, the dog died, the space program, laser surgery developed, and on, and on, and on.

Once, a janitor who worked for the company that I was working for in Connecticut, died. He was a drunk, but a good ol' boy. I went to his funeral as a representative of the company and our head maintenance man, a drinking buddy, went with me. We really weren't all that tore up over ol' Zack being dead till we stopped at our favorite bar on the way back to work after the funeral. We told ourselves that we would have one for ol' Zack because that's what he would have wanted us to do.

We never made it back to work that day. The real magnitude of Zack's demise hit us after the second drink hit us. We found it necessary to mourn him well into the night. We got tore up after all! Zack would have been proud.

Then I began to discover that there wasn't always a good occasion or a bad occasion to use right away as an excuse for making a fool of myself either before or after the fact. I needed some aces in the hole and discovered that I could always pull up an old resentment as justification for my drinking. I not only used fresh ones, but began to store up new animosities, that I didn't need right away, for future use.

I found that my wife, Sue, provided some of the best ones. I could turn her most well meant action into a personal attack on me. Just asking me why I was late getting home was, to me, a sheer lack of confidence in me and a mighty good reason for me to drink. Sick child, bills overdue, no lovin', car broke down and so forth, all good reasons and if a reason popped up that I didn't need right then, I stored it for later use. I had a warehouse full of them because I needed to justify my consumption of alcohol and getting drunk as something other than a thing, that for some mysterious reason, I could not control. My addiction was growing, yet I wasn't anywhere close to being aware of it.

I cut my fingernails this morning and the thought occurred to me, "Ain't it strange that we don't notice the growth of our fingernails each day as it is happening, but only when they get too long?" At what point do they grow long enough to cause us to know that they are too long? I've never looked at my fingernails and said, "Gonna need cuttin' in about three more days!" Nor did I gauge my acceleration into addiction and project the time when I would be hopelessly addicted.

It was like the two old gentlemen riding along in an "A" model truck who came upon a railroad crossing as a freight train was going by very slowly. The brakes on the old "A" model failed, which wasn't all that unusual back then, and it rolled into the side of the train.

Both of the gentlemen were knocked around a little, but there were no injuries. Having settled back down, the gentleman on the passenger side said, to ease the tension, "It's a good thing that train was comin' slow, ain't it?" To which the driver replied, "Comin' hell! That son-of-a-bitch **IS DONE HERE!**"

So, like my addiction to alcohol, one day it was "done here!" The first arrest for driving under the influence of alcohol; "It's done here!" Getting kicked out of my family, getting fired from a job, fired again, waking up in jail——, "It's done here! **It's done here!** *It's done HERE!*"

All of those prizes that I won were surprises! I didn't want them nor did I plan them. One day they each, in turn, were just "done here!" How did this thing slip up on me? Why couldn't I have seen this wrecking ball swinging toward me?

I've tried to figger out with my college trained mind why it was that I was able to stop eating hot horseradish, Ex-Lax and stop grabbing electric fences immediately after the experiences. Well, it did take a little time with the horseradish and the Ex-Lax, but I did quit the same day. I have come to the conclusion that the impact of the pain and discomfort from the horseradish, Ex-Lax and electric fence were sudden and at their maximum strength quickly! The source of the agony was unquestionable. There was absolutely no doubt as to the origin of the pain and my mind's mind recorded it in seconds or at least within hours and prevented me from taking the same action again, then or forever——, at least until now.

Well now, if I have already said that the pain and turmoil that came from drinking alcohol was more terrible than the above three combined, why didn't I just stop drinking it after those first bad experiences——, the bad taste, the hangovers? It's because the bad reactions from drinking alcohol were hardly noticeable at first. They were nothing worse than the bad taste, or the hangover.

The time it took to come to the realization that "alcohol is my problem and I can't stand it anymore and that me or it has got to go," took thirty years. Why so long? Because my momma, as best she could, described craving to me, but in my Granddaddy's barn, I proved her wrong and my mind's alcoholic mind locked in to the fact that I did not crave, thus could not have a problem with it. I was convinced of that until the day when there was no other explanation for it, that the source of my pain and misery in life was unquestionably alcohol. It was then and only then that alcohol took its place with the horseradish, the Ex-Lax and the electric fence, and the hurt caused by alcohol would far outweigh the feeling that it gave me and my mind's normal mind would finally say; "**NO MORE!** I can't stand another drink of it!"

No, it wasn't all bad as I traveled along that rocky road, there were some very good times in spite of it. I have some good and happy memories, but I can see now that my alcoholic mind would use the good to camouflage the bad and cause me to believe, with each good event, that I was A-OK. Ol' King Alcohol will let us win a round every now and then to keep us going. I had a great career going, I was married to a lovely lady, I had three children. They were clothed and fed and in school every day. They had never been without food or milk. How could I possibly have a problem with alcohol? There ain't no way, I convinced myself.

My attempts to succeed took us to some very interesting places and provided some experiences and chances to see places and things that some people, even today, can only dream of.

We lived in middle Georgia, South Georgia, Connecticut, Mobile, Alabama and El Paso, Texas. I was an industrial engineer in the textile and sewing industry and was good at what I did. I headed up some major projects with the various companies that I worked for that were very successful and my work is still considered brilliant by those who were involved in it with me. They still say, "You were the best until——!"

I remember being in a meeting once with the management team for some hard decision making. When we got down to the moment of truth, the go or no go choice on a project, it was made very clear to me and the group by our boss, the vice-president of a multi-plant company, that they would rely on my judgment, on my recommendations and allowed me to make the decision. I chose to proceed. The project was a smashing success and earned me a promotion and a move to headquarters in Bridgeport, Connecticut to head up an even bigger project. It, too, was amazingly successful. I was hot.

I think that the happiest our family had ever been was those four years that we lived in Huntington, Connecticut. I loved my work, the family loved the area, the ice skating on frozen ponds, snow in winter.

We went to lots of historical places in New York, Boston, Maine, Massachusetts and more. We have been on board the genuine U.S.S. Constitution and in the church where the "one if by land, two if by sea" signal was given and Paul Revere began his famous ride. We've been in the house where ol' Paul lived. We've been to the blessing of the fleet in Stonington, Connecticut, in the house of the seven gables, in Nathan Hale's home place, in a church where George Washington once worshipped, to the Macys' Thanksgiving Day parades in New York and so much more. It was such a wonderful period in our lives, just being there.

The only problem was that alcohol was in abundance for me. It was already driving a wedge between me and my family that wasn't very noticeable yet. Martinis for lunch were common and getting a little tipsy wasn't frowned on, especially if the boss was along and each success called for a celebration. We were breaking production records and cutting costs unbelievably. It was kind of like the ol' fingernail syndrome—-, I couldn't see it growing. It hadn't become noticeable, yet there was too much good for the bad to show through. I was winning lots of rounds at that time in my life.

There was also lots of air travel involved and of course, alcohol was everywhere, on the planes, at the plants, after work at the motels, management meetings in places like the Playboy Club in Great Gorge, New Jersey, The Doral in Miami, Ponte Vedra in Jacksonville, Florida, Campa de Casa, Dominican Republic.

Everything in that world revolved around alcohol and I was in love with the lifestyle. I was becoming more and more entrenched in an environment where drinking alcohol was not only accepted, but also encouraged. Our motto was; "Drink all you want but be on the job come morning!"

What I couldn't see was that I was one of a few of us that drank too much and did things that the rest of the guys would be talking about the next morning that I usually didn't remember. I was still a valuable employee at that time, so some of my actions were noticed but written off by my bosses as escaping the pressure, or something like that, but I know now that my addiction was closing in on me.

I recall now the night that this company hired me. I met with the personnel manager and then vice-president of operations at a hotel near the Atlanta airport in the lounge. They were having a drink and of course offered me one, which I accepted with no hesitation.

The vice-president, who was to be my boss for several years to come, said, "Well, I'm damned glad to see that! Most of the men that I interview give me a cock and bull story about how they don't drink and then we find out that they are lushes! You're up front with it and I like that! My men might not be on top as far as achievement is concerned, but by God, we can out-drink any of 'em!"

I was hired that night with a salary that I had never dreamed of and a company car, all because I had had a drink! I know now that the main reason that I accepted that position was because of what he had said about his men "out-drinking them all." Like the decision to join the Navy was based on throwing beer cans, my decision to take this job was based mainly on the statement about "out-drinking them all." The decision was made in my alcoholic mind.

It was as if my alcoholic mind knew that it had just been given all the time in the world to enjoy alcoholic freedom with no restraints or consequences. I had been affected once more in a *"mighty peculiar way."* I fit in. I was special. I felt whole and complete.

I can recall now that even then, from time to time, my mind's normal mind would know and point out to me that all of this was built around alcohol and that it would all crumble in time. That I would fall some-day.

I was fired from that company about ten years later, in El Paso, Texas, which is about twenty years ago as of now. I was earning about thirty-five thousand dollars a year and was fixed for life; family, security, career, retirement and prestige—-, I thought. Then suddenly it was all ripped away. I was hopelessly addicted. The ol' fingernails had grown out and were now a major problem. It was *"DONE HERE!"* My alco-holic mind told me that I had simply cracked under pressure and had had a nervous breakdown. Why, I hadn't been fired, I had QUIT!

I was hauled to a treatment center the night that I was fired from that job. Sue and our pastor put me into the back seat of our station wagon, kind of like a dog being taken to the vet, and hauled me off to a place called Sun Valley in El Paso. I spent the next twenty-eight days there in that treatment facility for alcohol and drug abuse, convinced that my problem was nerves.

I was in a "one flew over the cuckoo's nest" syndrome. I figgered that when this was over, I would begin anew by moving back to Georgia with my family. Get a better job, quit drinking and soar to new heights! My alcoholic mind even had me convinced that losing my job was the best thing that could have ever happened for me.

As I look back now at the overall picture of my acceleration into alco-holic addiction, I can see that it was in Sun Valley that I first experienced the mysterious feelings of real fear and loneliness that come with being an alcoholic, feelings that would accompany me from here on to the end of my journey into addiction.

It might have been a few days or even a week after having been admitted to Sun Valley and gotten accustomed to my surroundings and having been dried out, when, after the activities of the day were over and the TV was turned off and we patients made our way to our rooms for the night, that the real impact of that loneliness hit.

I was the only occupant of my room, so when I entered and the big wooden door with the number on it and the handle instead of the knob gently closed behind me with a slight thud, I was alone.

There was a picture window in my room and I could see the activity outside and I felt a twinge of desire to be out there in it. I thought about what might be going on at home and wondered if the kids understood why I was here. The light through the window was enough for me to be able to see very plainly the hospital bed with it's stark white sheets, one blanket, one pillow, the metal frame——, higher than a normal bed. I had a few things hanging in a small space next to a sink attached to the wall.

There was one of those table/tray combination things that could be rolled into a position that placed the table surface across the bed and on it was some fruit that I had saved from a couple of meals just in case I got hungry during the night. There were no flowers. Everything seemed so white, cold and impersonal. I also saw there my shaving kit and I thought of the many, many places that it had gone with me on business trips.

Then came the very clear and cruel realization that it was all over, that I wouldn't need that kit anymore, that my career was gone, that it was over. I'm sure that I also knew that it would only be a matter of time 'til I would also lose my wife and children. I wasn't a high-powered, awesome, brilliant engineer and father anymore; I was in a hospital room, alone, because I had become a sick drunk and needed help.

We were twelve to fifteen hundred miles from home and I was without a job and in those few minutes I knew stark, cold fear like I had never known before in the realization that it's "done here!" I hadn't counted on this.

Being alcohol free at the time, I was motivated to learn all that they could teach me while I was there, to come out of there a new man, to break loose from that old lifestyle and change. And I meant it! In my street mind, I meant it, but my alcoholic mind prevailed. It knew that it wasn't over yet. "Let him feel righteous while he's here!", it said. "I'll get him when he can drink again!" And it did! In effect it said, "We aint studyin' no shit as 'at, right now!"

There was, however, the time on down life's road when I was to call upon all that I had learned in good ol' Sun Valley. It had all made its way to my memory bank, thanks be to Jehovah.

We did move back to Georgia, I got a new job and bought a new home. I was on my way back up, the family was happy and I was doing all that I had planned, except that I had begun drinking again. I needed to feel good about myself, to cover up what I really was and all of those things that had recently happened to me. Then came that print out, "Alcohol will do it!"

So, I found those people and began doing those things and going to those places that would again take it all away from me. This would be the second job that I would be fired from because of my addiction to alcohol.

Alcoholism had now taken my family from me, but as I drove away from that new house in my pickup truck with my stuff in the back of it, I looked back and my alcoholic mind told me, "You showed HER! Won't SHE be surprised when she learns of your ascension to the top! You can seek fame and fortune anywhere you chose now, no limits! This is truly a wonderful thing that has happened for you!"

My disease shattered our family that day. The wedge had been driven deeply enough by now to cause the family bond to split. From that moment each of us would have a void in our lives that could never again be filled. We would all be deprived of the total family experience.

It breaks my heart even now to think of how they must have been gripped with fear, bewilderment and uncertainty when one whom they had relied upon for so long as a mudsill of the family had suddenly been ripped from under them. I just wasn't there anymore.

I fell under a pitiful illusion that I could stop this erosion. I was convinced that the big breakthrough was just around the corner; that I could fix the family thing. But it was too late to fix anything on my own.

I went into a coyote-roadrunner cartoon syndrome. I would get clobbered in some way by alcohol; jail, fired, car wrecks or something, and in the next scene I would be concocting another scheme or building another trap or gadget to try and catch the good life again, never even suspecting that alcohol was at the bottom of all of my problems. I was trying desperately to steer things in the right direction, but I couldn't do it.

I had to have alcohol now to hold me up and I still didn't know that I had to have it. I was to learn in time, that the "craving phenomenon" set in with the first drink. I had, by now, reached a point when the "first drink" would set off a long period of weeks, or even months, where my craving would be continuous. Then a drying out period would come. Then, that "first drink" again.

My first drinks were now separated by significant periods of time and those periods got longer and longer. My last "first drink" kept my craving going for several years. My alcoholic mind even had me convinced that if I didn't have alcohol, I probably wouldn't survive at all. Talk about reverse psychology! So my cover up was becoming more and more difficult. How does one explain gracefully, how he has lost a family and two jobs all in less than a year's time?

It sort of reminds me of the phone calls that I have gotten from time to time from bill collectors or a probation officer when other people were in the room. A good drunk knows about these things.

I would try to talk to him in a way that wouldn't reveal the nature of the call and it could be quite embarrassing. I couldn't just hang up. That would draw attention and he would only call back, but I couldn't respond to his comments without revealing the nature of his call so I would splutter and stammer and promise to call him back, anything to get off the phone. Then I would hang up and make some flimsy comment or whatever to smooth my perplexities over as if they were nothing, trying to cover them up.

So I tried to smooth them all over as those tragic things befell me as if they were nothing, like those phone calls and all the while a feeling of desperation was growing within me. A fear of something about to happen, but what? I was scared, but of what? I had no idea.. I know now that alcohol had me down for the count before I even knew that I was in a fight.

So my cover up continued as the result of my responding to my craving for alcohol. As it grew stronger, I had begun to justify my actions and their consequences for myself, not just for others, because my mind knew that there is absolutely no reason for consuming alcohol. By any standard it is not good to do, but I couldn't stop, so I had to justify, to explain, my mind's alcoholic mind for placing me in a situation that had no reason for existing. I had to make up reasons.

My alcoholic mind would, figuratively speaking, reach out, grab the lady's ass and leave me standing there looking like an idiot again and again, trying to defend my integrity, trying to keep my withering domain intact.

I see now that my cover up was about as effective as a friend of mine's attempt to cover up the fact that he had picked up a dose of crabs once. (Crabs are body lice usually associated with activities that we for DAMN sure don't want anybody else to know about!) The owner of the local drugstore was a mutual friend of ours and Tom told years later of having once gone to Howell's store to get himself some blue ointment to kill them crabs with. Of course, he didn't want to be obvious with it, so he picked up a few more items such as cotton balls, mouthwash, band-aids and such, so as to camouflage the blue ointment.

Ol' Howell was at the cash register when Tom checked out and of course, as Howell rang him up they chatted about the weather, their wives, their children's well being and such. Howell presented the bill and Tom paid and started toward the door at the other end of the store with his purchase, relieved that Howell hadn't noticed or at least hadn't said anything about the blue ointment. But just as Tom pushed the door open and started out, ol' Howell, loudly and clearly, hollered out; "Hey, Tom! If that blue ointment don't work, come on back and we'll see if we can smother them pesky little shit-asses!"

Now Tom didn't describe his feelings or comments to me about that, but I'd be willing to bet a hundred dollars to a hole in a donut that he said, or at least thought, "SHIT FAR!"

And so it went. I found other jobs, always at a lower salary. My reputation as a drunk spread throughout the industry. Personnel agencies would tell me up front that they couldn't help me and I would wonder why. By this time I had been fired from two more jobs because of alcohol and alcohol-related arrest, but still I wondered why they wouldn't handle me. I know now that I might as well have been trying to get a supermarket to sell rotten vegetables or meat.

I was now down to working in a lumber warehouse filling orders and loading the goods onto the customer's trucks. It's hard for me to believe now, but I remember thinking to myself that it wasn't all that bad. No responsibility, no brainwork required, all this lifting was keeping me in shape and they didn't care if I drank a little on the job, and on Saturdays I got paid time and a half! A man couldn't ask for more than that! God-a-mighty! I'd have to be two people to be dumb enough to believe that those things were outstanding benefits!

But every now and then, my mind's normal mind would flicker and let me know that all was not well with me and give me an inkling of why it wasn't.

One of the thoughts that I would have from time to time was of that "phenomenon of craving," but it would still be awhile before I would want to explore the meaning of this phrase. I wasn't sick enough yet.

If I ever doubt the total control that my alcoholic mind had over my behavior I think of how I reacted to the two most saddening events of my alcoholic years. The first was the death of my mother from cancer. Dad and we children all witnessed her pain for a long time.

During her last days we took turns sitting with her around the clock to do what little we could to try and make her a little bit comfortable. I was the last of us to see her alive.

It was my turn to be with her and among other things, to hold a little pan for her and to wipe her mouth when she had to vomit. Her mouth was so raw from the continual vomiting and wiping that it caused her agony even for us to wipe her mouth and it hurt us to do it because we knew that we were hurting our mom. We all loved her and either one of us was ready to take on her suffering if there had been a way to do it.

That abrasion in the corner of her mouth was still barely visible through the makeup as she later lay in her casket, a reminder for us that she he had been in sheer agony. I had heard her several times, during the ordeal, ask God to allow her to die.

Our aunt Johnnie, mom's sister, was a retired nurse and was helping us with those things that required nursing skills. She came in to do some of those things for mom during my watch and asked me to step out of the room for a few moments. I never saw my mom alive again. Even though I was at what I truly believed to be the pinnacle of human sadness, my alcoholic mind locked in on her suffering and her death as reasons for me to drink alcohol. I cheated her. My alcoholic mind grabbed these happenings as the ultimate of good reasons to satisfy it's craving under the guise of easing my own pain. I'm glad that mom wasn't aware of that and that she didn't know me in my really bad times. I'll ask for her forgiveness anyhow when I see her again.

The second event was when I was informed that my eleven-year-old son, Alan, who was living with his mother, had been diagnosed with leukemia. At that time, I thought that it meant certain death for him. I didn't know anything about modern treatments. I was devastated by the news as much as I thought a human being could be, but again, my alcoholic mind changed the event and the genuine sorrow that I felt, into a justification for satisfying my mysterious craving for alcohol. My alcoholic mind produced behavior that I now look back on as being utterly despicable, yet I did it. Alan has totally recovered and I know that he forgives me for that.

Again, I was, in my mind's normal mind, asking the old question, "Why?" I knew that my basic morals and basic values did not stand for such behavior. I was above such. What, I asked myself, could have caused me to drink during these times with mom and Alan? There was not and never could be, any justification for it. I stole from them. I used their suffering for my own benefit and I can't forget that.

I asked myself those same questions when alcohol took me into infidelity. When Sue began to lose her affection for me, I tried in every way to give myself the right to cheat on her, but I could never stop knowing that no matter what she might say to me, how she might refuse me, what she might criticize me for, or if she would avoid me, or whatever reasons; extramarital involvement was wrong. Yet I did it. There were times when a rendezvous had been arranged and I, while waiting for whoever it might be, would wish that she wouldn't show up. My basic moral values were screaming, "NO! NO! NO!" but my alcoholic mind would prevail. I didn't want to do it. I loved Sue, yet I did it. I wondered why I couldn't just not do it.

In the same light, I can also remember, more than once, holding a bottle of booze in front of my face and asking it, "Why must I drink you?" Then, while vowing in my street mind that I wasn't going to do it, my alcoholic mind would offer that ageless, irresistible compromise; "Just finish this one and then quit." Then again, I would suck the fiery poison into my body. I had to be more than I was, I couldn't stand me and alcohol could——- "fix it."

My lover, alcohol, was in total control by now and she was unbelievably powerful, cruel and merciless. Yet I continually turned to her for comfort and assurance that I was O.K.. "The fingernails were out there now," it was "done here!" I'm sure that an accumulated awareness of these type things brought me eventually to the realization that I had become a very defective human being. I didn't want to be one. I didn't want to do it.

I look back now on my acceleration into addiction and am always amazed when I realize that my first and second arrests for driving under the influence of alcohol were about seven years apart. Yet the time between my eighth and ninth arrests for the same thing was a mere three days. Acceleration ain't no name for that!

When this first occurred to me, I thought of a story told by the late Junior Samples, of "Hee Haw" fame, about how he was fishing in a pond once when a friend walked by and asked him, "How long you been fishin' in that pond Junior?" Junior replied, "'Bout thirty years I reckon." The friend, rollin' his eyes in disbelief, said, "Don't you know that that water is stagnant? That there ain't never been no fish in there?" To which Junior replied, "Yeah, I started suspectin' somethin' like that about fifteen years ago!"

So, when someone finally said to me, "Don't you know that you're an alcoholic?" I could have truthfully said, "I started suspectin' that several years ago." But when I would start suspecting, my alcoholic mind would go into high gear to prevent me from "studyin' sech shit es 'at."

I tried desperately to come up with an answer for myself as to why I was staying on the ride. Why was I swimming into the fish basket deeper and deeper with each drink while things that were happening were screaming out to me, "GO BACK! LET GO! JUMP BEFORE IT'S TOO LATE! THE WRECKING BALL IS HURTLING TOWARD YOU!" But my alcoholic mind would continue to convince me that I was O.K. It would let me win another round. Like the old town crier, my alcoholic mind was saying, "It's twelve o'clock and all's well!" when in reality, it was late in the evening of my life and all was far from well. It was like my second drinking experience when my alcoholic mind made me believe, "It tastes good now, don't it?"

Somewhere along the line I must have realized that my defensive system was no longer effective and I had to then search for something sho' 'nuff beyond my ability to control. I hoped that I was either crazy or that I had had a nervous breakdown, but I couldn't convince myself of either. I was being pushed toward exploring the "phenomenon of craving." Maybe that was it. It is obvious to me now that no one can survive with this sort of force within him or her. It must be harnessed somehow, some way. It is frightening now to know that for all those years, I lived with such a deadly mental condition.

So I'm an alcoholic—-. I just go insane when I drink—-. OK—-, I'll just not drink. Now the real dilemma reared its ugly head. I couldn't not drink—-! **NOW WHAT?** I couldn't drink, yet I couldn't stop. Damn! What a tense way to live!

In my acceleration, I learned a lot that I really didn't want to know: how to get into a police car gracefully, that the police really don't want to carry on a conversation with me about the weather or anything else on our way to the jailhouse, how to play the legal system to the hilt before facing the judge——, one routine postponement, then arraignment and plead "not guilty," and agree to a bench trial. Then, just before that court date, demand a jury trial to delay it even longer.

I learned how to be a convincing liar and how to function with severe physical pain. I've often wondered what a normal drinker or a person who didn't even drink would do if they woke up with a hangover like I usually had. I'm sure that they would call 911 and get someone to rush them to the hospital emergency room, but us drunks, if we still had a job, would go on in to work and make stupid statements like, "I almost stopped in at the funeral home on my way to work!" Or, "The only reason that I get drunk is to see how really good water is!" Or, if we no longer had a job, we would, as quickly as possible, drink some more of what made us feel like warmed over crap to start with.

I also developed nerves of steel. I remember particularly the ninth time that I stood before a judge for driving under the influence of alcohol. I knew that I had eight other offenses. I also knew that if he knew of the other eight and I lied to him about them when he asked me, that he would not look favorably upon my lie. I also knew that if he really only knew of this one and maybe one more, I would get off pretty easy; but if I panicked when he asked and told him of the others, that I would be voluntarily kissing my ass good-bye for a long time.

The big question finally came. He said, "Other than this current charge and what I see in this printout, do you have any other arrests for driving under the influence of alcohol?" I put on my most innocent look and replied, "No, Your Honor." The time lapse before his next words seemed long enough for ol' King Tut to be born and die and be discovered all over again! Thank God, he didn't know of the others, but *"SHIT FAAAAAAR"* what a tense way to live! Them Top Gun pilots don't know nothin' about making split second decisions under pressure!

I can now look back and imagine myself in the center of a circle. The circle being made up of my problems, bad health, the legal system, no family, no decent transportation, no driver's license, no car insurance, no job, no money, no pride or self-respect and on and on. A fuel line seemed to run from me, in the center of the circle, to each of the problems. When I poured the fuel, alcohol, into me, it flowed to each of those problems and gave them more new life. The more I poured into me, the healthier the problems became. It was fruitless to try to eliminate them separately. I might get one or two or more under control for awhile and maybe even think that they had been eliminated, but as long as they were fueled from the source (me) in the middle, they would come back stronger than ever, bringing new ones with them!

I had seen a John Wayne movie about putting out the oil well fires in various places. It was obvious that them boys didn't go after the flame shooting out in all directions because they knew that once the source was cut off, everything else would have to die from lack of fuel. So they went after the source at ground level. I knew, but worse than that, I

KNEW that I knew that if I were to survive, I would have to cut off the source, alcohol, but how? I had tried to stop and couldn't stop. Could this have something to do with that cussed "phenomenon of craving," whatever the devil that is? I was gittin' ready to give "sech shit es 'at" some thought.

My best understanding of that phrase, after some research was that when an alcoholic takes a drink, he or she, for some reason, must take another and another and another.

Now, I had to admit that somewhere in my journey along the road of addiction, I reached a point when I never stopped with just one drink. I also realized that on some occasions if there was only one drink available, I didn't want it and I remembered times when I had even refused a drink or two at a cocktail party or social hour before a business meeting or something like that. I was getting nervous now because I was getting pretty close to the bottom of this thing. I was beginning to know that the reasons for not taking a drink when the supply was limited were not fine noble Christian reasons, or because I was in such control that I could just refuse one lackadaisically. It was because my alcoholic mind was thinking, "Not now! The supply is limited! Wait until there is enough to satisfy me!" Like the old song; "All or Nothing at All." (If this book ever becomes a movie, it'll have to be a musical!)

These thoughts caused me to dig deeper and I recalled times, even though I was now a full-fledged drunk, when I had been separated from alcohol by being in jail or a treatment center for a significant period of time and realized that the desire to drink wasn't there right then, and I was acting and functioning like a normal drinker or a non-drinker. I would even daydream of an alcohol free life from that point on, not because I had a problem with it, NO WAY! HA, I knew what craving was and I'd never done *that*! I was acting normal because I hadn't had that first drink for awhile that always demanded more.

So why not just not drink anymore? Simple! I was thinking normally because my alcoholic mind was not connected at that time. I was void of alcohol. There was no craving, but sure enough, when the booze was again available and I logically, rationally, intelligently (in my street mind) decided to have "just one," the "new me" connection was made and I was off again.

I couldn't ignore the fact that time after time after time in my life I had been perfectly normal and life was going good, but that insanity started with the next first drink and my alcoholic mind laid back and soaked it up like a giant parasite and left me once again wondering, why—-? what happened—-? Why have I done it again? It had grabbed the lady's ass again and left me wondering why?

I think that the "craving" thing was driven home in my mind when I thought about the times that I had refused a cocktail or two (what a stupid name for a drink of alcohol!) because my alcoholic mind knew that it would be the first drink and that it would set off the craving and also knew that I couldn't follow it up with more. But then on the other extreme, there had been times when I, having had that first drink, might run out of booze and would drive unbelievable distances to get more. On more than one occasion, I went through trash to find empty bottles to pour up that last drop or two from each bottle that I found and would maybe accumulate a tablespoon full.

I had to know that that wasn't social drinking and was sho' 'nuff a tense way to live! I had to know that something was wrong! If there wasn't enough, I didn't want any, but if I had started and ran out, I would do anything to get more.

It was getting scary now. Could I have such a thing in me as a "phenomenon of craving?" Could this be what momma was trying to tell me, but couldn't possibly have known enough about to get her message across? I didn't like what I was thinking. The real me was trying to stand up.

The picture was clearing up some, but there was that part of that "phenomenon of craving" stuff that my alcoholic mind was trying to scream at me and that part was; "It is only in the mind of the alcoholic!

You don't need to study *"no sech shit as 'at!"* But I had thought myself into a corner. I couldn't ignore the facts any longer. It was as if I had been jumped three times in one move in a checker game! It was simple: if I was beginning to recognize a phenomenon of craving within me and if my behavior and actions had virtually proven that it was there and if it only exists in the mind of the alcoholic---------------, *THEN I MUST BE ONE!*

OOOOOOOOHHH NOOOOOOOOOOOOOO NO! NO! SHIIIIII-IIIIIIIIIIIIIIIIIIIITTT FAAAAR, NO!!!! I need a reason for being a drunk, but not *THAT!!!! PLEASE NOT THAT!!!! "Any *#!X~@!*#X!*thang but that!"* I begged whatever powers were in control to let me be crazy! Let me be retarded! Let me be just plain sorry! Let me be anything, but not THAT! Not that; please not that! Not an alcoholic!

I wasn't aware of it at that moment, but my core had been melted down. I couldn't deny the facts any longer. I knew now that I was addicted to alcohol, but it would be some time yet before I would come to the point in time where, in my mind's mind, I would know that I knew. This revelation didn't come to me all at once, but once the phenomena seed had been planted, there began to be a realization of the truth.

Even though I started suspecting the truth before the end of it all, it would be several years before I could see my alcoholic mind as a loose cannon or a source of un-harnessed deadly power that when I poured alcohol in and activated it, there was no way to predict what was going to happen.

It was as if I chose to take a drug that would induce temporary schizophrenia in me, the most feared of all mental illnesses. It was like playing the lottery except that I won every time I played. The only problem was that the prizes that I won were always prizes that I didn't want. They ranged from simple bad taste to hangovers, losing jobs, family, career, spending time behind bars and on and on. I'm so glad that I didn't win the grand prize, my own alcoholic death or even worse, killing or maiming someone else while I was drunk!

I couldn't yet admit that I was an alcoholic even though in my street mind, I knew it. My alcoholic mind was still too alive and well. There were more prizes to win yet. I wasn't ready to study *"no sech shit as 'at."*

I was to try for many years yet to prove to myself that I certainly was not one of "them," but I was getting closer to the day when I would enter into the struggle "to the death" with my alcoholic mind. One of us would have to go!

I thought back on the times that I had to drive a car in the Dominican Republic. My first words of advice from a Dominican company worker were, "Don't ever look at the driver that you are meeting or racing to the intersection because once you acknowledge his presence and he knows that you have seen him, you've automatically given him the right of way."

I had acknowledged the presence of my phenomenon of craving. It had the right of way now. There were to be no more excuses or reasons for my drinking alcohol. I would know from here on that I had just come too far to give up my charade. I had been lifted up too far now to let go of that rope of addiction. I had to maintain the imitation me. I couldn't make the adjustment to the real me. I couldn't settle for just that. I didn't even want to have even a little glimpse of the real me. The fall would be too long to survive. I had gone too far into my make-believe world to turn back. I was hooked and I had swallowed the hook deep. I had to hold on to the image, the masquerade, the imitation world that I had created and my alcoholic mind continually printed out, "Alcohol will hold you up!"

So came the vicious cycle. As my kingdom crumbled, I would try to patch it up in my mind with alcohol and with each succeeding drink, I swallowed the alcoholic hook a little deeper.

I was to learn, in time, that my alcoholic addiction is a disease, but unlike other diseases, is not considered an acceptable reason or an excuse for my actions and my behavior. A person who is disabled by cancer, depression, or diabetes, even schizophrenia or by any other recognized diseases can say to the world "I am the way that I am because I have a disease" and the person suffers no ridicule because of it. In fact, hands and hearts go out to that individual, but the alcoholic or addict has no excuse or reason to offer for his or her condition.

Even though I was to realize, in time, that something was wrong with me beyond my own ability to understand, I couldn't say, "I am the way that I am because I have the disease of alcoholism." I've learned, in recovery, that the alcoholic cannot believe, let alone accept that, until the reality of it is absolutely forced upon us and then, in most cases, it's too late. Then, even if we are lucky enough to find recovery, the wreckage of our past is extensive and most of it is permanent and we can only try to build upon what we have left from it.

So as my addiction continued to consume me and there was no acceptable explanation, reason, or logic that I could provide for my lack of a defense against alcohol and for my behavior because of it, I became like the snake that buries it fangs and pumps its venom into it's own flesh when things seem hopeless. I turned on myself and proclaimed to society; "I have no excuse! I am a sorry drunk and you have the right to ridicule and punish me in any way that you see fit."

I remember, in my "high flying" years, having been approached on several different occasions by bums obviously needing a drink, begging for money. Yet some would be dressed in a worn out, smelly old suit and some would even be wearing a tie. When one of those approached me I would wonder, "Who is he trying to fool?"

Now I know. They were trying to fool themselves. They were trying to hold on to whatever was left of their pride and whatever was left of their dwindling domains. I, too, was to come to that kind of self-deception.

Chapter V

IF YOU'RE GONNA BE DUMB, YOU GOTTA BE TOUGH

Once, when we lived in Connecticut, I was lounging out on our back deck enjoying a little peace and tranquility when all hell broke loose as our little dog Susie came tearing up the steps from the yard making all kinds of weird sounds. I could see right off that something wasn't right with her. She had that *"helllllp me!"* look in her eyes as she looked at me while racing back and forth yelping and bumping her rear end on the deck floor with every other step. I had never seen her move that fast.

She scampered across the deck and back two or three times doing that wild lookin' stuff before I finally caught her and looked her over and discovered that a yellow jacket had lit on her ass and that she had instinctively clamped her tail stub down trapping him there, on that tender spot, to just sting away at his pleasure. It was a sight to behold and a sho' 'nuff tense situation for ol' Susie!!

After I had extracted that varmint, I told Susie what my brother David had once told me; "If you're gonna be dumb, you gotta be tough!" I would recall those words often in years to come.

Well now, what a revoltin' development my situation had turned into! I could no longer justify my alcoholic actions even to my own satisfaction, let alone for others, yet I knew that I couldn't stop drinking alcohol. I couldn't change my direction. So my alcoholic mind convinced me that if I couldn't change the direction that I was headed in, that I really didn't want to change it. Like the old Fox and Grapes fable, "If I can't reach them grapes, then I don't want 'em anyhow!"

So I began to accept, in my own mind, the fact that I was a drunk, and in an attempt to hold on to some semblance of dignity, I tried to convince others that I wanted it that way, feigning indifference. I cringe sometimes even now when I hear someone say, "Man, I'm gonna get drunk this weekend!," or "It's Friday, I gotta get drunk and I shore do dread it!," or something stupid like that because I know that I used to sound just as dumb, but then if you're gonna be dumb, I guess it's gonna show!

So my struggle to hold onto a little respectability started. I became like the stray cat that one of us kids, as my momma would've said, "drug in" once. That cat was bad to excrete its bodily waste on the floor and of course we wanted to teach it some manners. After all, that cat was living in a high-class place now and we figgered that it ought to act respectable.

Our plan was that whoever discovered the cat "mess" would find the cat, rub his nose in it real good and throw his ass out of the nearest window (we didn't have screens back then)!

Know what, that cat was a fast learner! It soon got to where every time that "booger" would shit on the floor, he would immediately turn around, rub his nose and face in it real good and then jump out of the nearest window! He was obviously a very smart cat, but he just kept missing the point! Like me, I guess he held on to some self-respect by doing it to himself since he knew that it was coming anyway! If you're gonna be dumb, you've gotta be tough!

Another classic example of how we try to hold on was told by a friend in recovery, of a time when he had been arrested for drunk driving. The officer had just put the handcuffs on ol' Bo, who was still bent over the hood of the police car, when he made an alcohol-induced, dumb, smart remark to the officer. The officer must have already taken enough of ol' Bo's sass for he grabbed a handful of Bo's hair and smashed his head down into the car hood one good, swift time.

Well, now ol' Bo, being a goooood typical drunk and trying to hold on to a little of his self-respect, said, "Let me show you how to do that!" He then proceeded to bang his own head into the car hood three or four more times!

Ol' Bo must have been sort of like our cat, he completely missed the point! Yep, if you're gonna be dumb, you gotta be tough!

Another friend in recovery told of being stopped by the police while driving drunk. The officer had Neil touch his nose with each forefinger, say his ABC's and stand on one foot. Now, Neil knew that he was failing these sobriety tests dismally so when the officer said, "Hop five times on one foot!" Neil casually smirked, "Hell, I can't even do that when I ain't drunk!" Yep, the next stop for ol' Neil was the jailhouse!

The finest example of indifference, at least my favorite, came from a correctional institution. It was during the Christmas season and some of us from the outside were inside for volunteer work (I can do that now—- from the free side of the table.) As we sat around and chatted with the inmates, we could hear the traffic outside, which was exceptionally heavy and one of them said, "Man, I'm glad that I'm in here and not out there in all of that Christmas traffic!" I remember having had thoughts as ridiculous as that at one time.

So, I would hit a new bottom and again lower my standards and my alcoholic mind would convince me that my new lower standard was very comfortable.

When I was fired because of alcohol for the first time, I was earning around thirty thousand dollars a year. My next job paid twenty-five, my next one paid twenty-two five, my next one, twenty. Then, I went back up to twenty-five and then all the way down to four dollars and seventy-five cents an hour and even lower still to sixty dollars a week for unemployment, and then thirty dollars for cutting a man's grass when it needed it and that was during a long, dry summer!

Yet, each time, I adjusted to my new low standard and at each lower level, I would believe that I was still king of my domain. Even during the times that I was cutting grass and waiting for it to grow out again, I was putting together a million-dollar lawsuit against the last company that had fired me. I was going to show them sons-of-bitches! I was in control! How could I have been so wrong? My alcoholic mind, at that time, was still in total control and was always "hooked up."

So, as I hit new bottoms and lowered my standards again and again, I would convince myself that things were exactly as they were supposed to be. After all, aren't we drunks the only ones of God's creatures that will be so incapacitated that we can't even stand up and will still talk down to whoever might be trying to help us up, as if they are the ones with the problem!

A friend of mine, a small feisty man, told me of the time when, after several weeks of serious drinking, he had to be admitted to an alcoholic treatment center and was so drunk when his wife and some friends got him there that he had to be taken inside in a wheelchair. Some big, burly orderly usually pushes these contraptions, you know. My friend related, "As I was rolling down the hallway I was cussin' that son-of-a-bitch that was pushing my wheelchair, threatening to kick his ass, if he didn't turn that *@! #X*@#@* thang around and git me outta there!", "'Cause," he said, "This place is for drunks and I don't need to be here! I'm fine! I'm only drunk because I wanna be!" He also added to that story that if he hadn't have been stopped during that drinking binge, that he would not have lived through it. Alcohol is indeed a merciless mistress!

So, as I began to feel the hopelessness of my dilemma, I began to try to remain the master of my little world as it dwindled and as it did, I tried desperately to convince myself that everything was exactly as I wanted it to be, while frantically holding on to my latest foothold.

I began to defend my status with anger when someone would dare indicate to me that I was less than acceptable in the normal scheme of things. Such as, "If you keep this up, you're going to get fired!" To which my reply would be, "Who gives a damn? I was looking for a job when I found this one!" Or, "Isn't your blood pressure a little high?" "My blood pressure is my own damned business!" "Here you are, half-drunk again—-!" "Yeah, I ran out of money!" Or, executives that I worked for coming to me and saying; "We read about your arrest in the paper and we're going to have to let you go." My reply would be, "GOOD! It's the best thing that could ever happen for me, I've been planning to quit anyhow!" and then, my wife, Sue—-, "I've made an appointment with a lawyer, I want a divorce!" "FINE" I would say, "I thought you'd never ask!" "You are a really sooooorry human being!" She would say. "Yeah and you are just like your damned self-righteous friend!" I would snap back.

She was right, but neither of us could know then that the appropriate word for my condition was "sick."

I even began to be comfortable in jails. They came to know me there. In fact, at one time in my life, my most noble ambition was to be the horseshoe-pitching champion of the county prison work camp where I was confined! I can now imagine how ridiculous I would have been having come home from there and proclaiming to all my friends and family that I was the new "chain gang" horseshoe pitching champion. God-a-mighty! If you're gonna be dumb, you gotta be tough!

Sometimes, when no one is around, I'll turn the television on to the "rasslin." I like to watch it, I think, because it reminds me of myself so much when the referee asks the rassler who appears to have been beaten down almost to death, if he is ready to give up and the poor victim weakly replies, "No, not yet!" Or when the beaten down one is lying on the mat, looking helpless and the winning one is up on the ropes about to jump onto his beaten opponent, who lifts his arms saying with his gesture, "Come on! Jump on me! I can take it!"

I finally reached the point where I was saying, in effect, "Come on! Hit me! I can take it! I'm supposed to be this way! I don't care!" I decided that if I couldn't win, that I'd show the world how much I could take! Yep, if you're gonna be dumb, you gotta be tough!

Then I started seeing the indifference in others when I would attempt a feeble explanation for having gotten drunk and done something stupid, or trying to explain why I smelled like I did. It became obvious that they weren't interested in any explanation. They already knew!

I was in a conversation with a man recently who was trying to find his way out of his addiction. I knew of his escapades, arrests and all and as he was telling me more about himself, he said very sincerely, "Momma don't talk to me or cry anymore when she gets me out of jail!"

Now as we go through life, we sometimes hear or read little things that especially make an impression on us. One of those little things for me was the story, told by an ex-drunk, who had lost the caring and compassion of every human being that knew him, except for his mother. He could still depend on her for love, understanding, even pity. So one day, while he was drunk and had decided to "cry awhile," he called upon the last fragment of his domain, his mother, and opened his heart to her, seeking pity. "Momma," he said, "life has been so cruel and I have sunk so low that I think I'll just kill myself!" He said that after a few seconds of silence on the other end of the line, momma replied to his utter shock and dismay, "Well son——, I guess that would be the best thing for everybody——." That was his bottom. He sought help after that.

In a last ditch effort to at least go down in a blaze of glory I placed myself on a plateau with a man whose name is known by everybody, one of the most famous men known to the world. I was going to be proud of myself. I was going to try to justify my situation, so I came to a very convincing conclusion that Judas Iscariot had been chosen by the Almighty for his role in history and if Judas had indeed been chosen by God himself for the role of betraying Jesus, the most dastardly deed known to mankind, then he obviously could not have changed his destiny. He had no choice, but to go through with it.

So it seemed obvious to me that my destiny had been charted and that I couldn't change it. That God had indeed chosen me, as well as Judas, to be examples of the heartache, suffering and shame that come to those who go against his will and in my case, those who drink alcohol, and that I had no choice in the matter.

I could then see my body lying in it's casket, when death will have finally come, as the multitudes file silently past. In my mind I could hear them murmur, as I watched from heaven, "If this is what it's done to you, I'll never take another drink!"

I was so proud! God has chosen me for this role! What else could it be? And since He has chosen ME and I really believed that He had, then I would act it out——. **BRILLIANT!** I was proud to be God's humble servant! I was proud of my part in God's plan for saving mankind! My alcoholic mind had me convinced that this was pretty close to gittin' up onto a cross myself.

In reality, I had me a real good excuse to keep on drinking alcohol; trying to satisfy that incessant, merciless, yet subtle craving that was raging within me. Yep, if you're going to be dumb, you got to be tough!

Chapter VI

HERE'S WHERE YOU "GIT" OFF— DEAD EYE

Hallelujah! Some are called to preach and some are called to be alcoholics. Now I understood. I had been ordained as God's servant and hadn't even been aware of it. I had been serving Him all along and now I could really throw myself into this unlikely calling with assurance that I would indeed receive a heavenly reward when my pitiful end would finally come.

What a relief! All of my fears were suddenly dispelled! I was goin' to heaven! I was on God's train to glory land! In the meantime it appeared, with the way that things were shaping up, that I might have even been selected to have the honor of being imprisoned for the Master in order to have a great prison ministry to bring hundreds of lost souls to Him that way, before my train arrived in paradise.

Why couldn't I have seen these things sooner? They were as obvious to me now as the nose on my face. I should have known that people of my caliber, background and moral values just didn't become drunks. Only sorry, low life people like those that I hung around with became drunks. The Master had obviously chosen me. I was supposed to be this way. I had been predestined to lose my family, my career and my health. I was supposed to be in this mode. *YES! YES! YES!* My newly found humiliation was beginning to make Mahatma Ghandi look more like Hulk Hogan by comparison!

It's no wonder that I couldn't get saved in that electric chair church service. God didn't want me that way. He already had more than enough born again Christians out there working. What He really needed out there in this ol' world now to get His message across were some actual examples of "the wages of sin." I was deeply honored to know that this is where "Dead Eye Gilmer" comes in—-, thank you Jesus!

So I set out on my mission. I began to want to be that poor, helpless, addicted drunk waiting for the great tragedy to befall him that would convince millions (well, maybe hundreds) to turn away from the evils of alcohol; but when the big event didn't seem to be getting close, I started thinking; *"WAIT- A -MINUTE!"*

I hadn't stopped to think that while I was marching to martyrdom life was still going to be miserable, even for one of God's servants. Hunger would still hurt, cold weather would still hurt and there would still be the embarrassment, humiliation, degradation, mental anguish and all of those miserable things that come with being a drunk.

So I started thinking, "It's hurtin' pretty bad now. Please God, go ahead and take me!" I would ask and wait, but the big event just would- n't happen. I kept on waking up alive, not in paradise. I thought of the sister, Caroline, in the movie, "Little Big Man." Having been captured by the Indians, she was sure that the Indian braves would viciously and repeatedly rape her. She waited tensely for them to come and take her, but they just wouldn't come and do it. This led Little Big Man to remark, "Caroline never did have much luck with the boys!" I know how she felt because I wasn't having much luck with the Grim Reaper myself.

When I finally realized that I was not actually in God's service by being a drunk, it was as if they had stopped the glory-land train out in the middle of the desert and said; "*Here's where you git off Dead-Eye!*"

SHIT FAR! I couldn't even be a good "doomed" drunk. It became obvious to me that I wasn't going out in a blaze of sacrificial glory. My exit from this life, in fact, wouldn't even be noticed way out there. In fact it would probably be looked upon as————————; *THE BEST THING FOR EVERYBODY!*

This had indeed become a "revoltin' development!" Reality's chill was creeping over me. I was learnin' that I had been "whanged"! I knew that I had come too far to turn back, so I started thinking in terms of ending it all. If God wouldn't do it, then I would have to do it myself.

First, I began to pray that I would just go to sleep and simply not wake up again. I started off with something simple. I never was a brave soul so killing myself violently was out of the question. Then I began to pray for the house to burn up with only me in it, of course. Or when I would stagger and fall in front of a parked car, I would pray that the driver would come back and run me over before I could get up. Alas, nothing was working!

I often thought of driving into the path of an oncoming truck. That would be fitting and it would certainly fulfill the prophecy of old church days——, or maybe a train. I had once heard a fellow tell of how he had kept an old junk car in running condition for years so that he, if he ever got brave enough to do it, could drive it onto the railroad tracks for his train suicide. I certainly had the proper equipment for that. I passed up those opportunities though because I figgered that I might just get mangled. I didn't want to just get hurt——, I wanted to die.

There did come the time when I began to seriously consider taking my own life. I believe that one thought that kept me from doing it was of the financial burden that it would impose on those who would feel an obligation to give me a decent funeral. Another reason was a realization of the legacy that I would leave behind. I couldn't stand the thoughts of being remembered for what I had become.

As I see it, whether one takes one's own life or not is secondary: the most significant part of this for me was the fact that circumstances had come together in a way to cause me to think about doing such a thing. One has to be a state of severe desperation to have an inkling of a desire to die.

It was at this point that I had to consider the gnawing question, "Am I crazy—-? I must be crazy to even think about such a thing! Has alcohol messed my mind up enough to cause me to want to do myself in?" In my street mind I knew that I had more smarts than that, but I was afraid that my alcoholic mind might indeed be powerful enough to print out that I really wanted to die. After all, hadn't I followed the stages of addiction perfectly thus far? First, becoming addicted, then acceleration into it, then, becoming indifferent to it. The next stage was acting out the role and I was very much aware that the final role for the alcoholic is to die and that the alcoholic's death is usually a violent one!

Had I come too far to change my course? There was no more of this thinking that I was God's servant in the role of a martyr. No more of this being like Judas—-! I wadn't studyin' *"no sech shit as 'at"* now! This was serious. This had become more serious than that ol' hog trying to walk on a sheet of ice!

All of those things that they had said might possibly happen to me if I got hooked on alcohol were actually happening! The rest of the things on the list, that included my own death, weren't just possibilities anymore; they were very, highly probable!

My mind suddenly plunged all the way back into it's archives and activated that primal instinct to seek again that first serene feeling of warmth, protection and comfort that was indelibly etched into our minds in that instant after we were un-ceremoniously pushed from the warmth, familiarity and security of the womb; being rudely thrust into this world instinctively terrified. Then we were comforted in being quickly nestled to our mother's breast in her warm, tender, calming, loving and sheltering embrace.

I mentally screamed, "Momma," "**MOMMA,**" *"MOMM MAAAAAAHHH!"*

I was again in Donna's restaurant one day when I received another message, in a roundabout fashion. My sister Betty, the schoolteacher, came in and joined some of us for afternoon coffee. As we chatted, she announced that the Sea Turtle was on the list of endangered species. My cocky reply was, "Well, I reckon *I* can git along without 'em!" But once again, I was being affected in a *"mighty peculiar way."*

I had never been too involved in, nor even thought too much about, endangered species, or any other creatures having become extinct. After all, hadn't we done all right without the dinosaur? "What's the big deal?," I thought, until that moment when it became clear to me that I, myself, personally, was an endangered species, that Dead Eye James himself was about to become—-; *EXTINCT!!!* Those things suddenly became vitally important to me! God does reach us in mysterious ways!

I was sort of beamed out of that restaurant scene as my mind became submerged in thoughts of my first meaningful experience with the death of a human. It was my grandfather, my Dad's Dad. He had lived alone for many years since the death of my grandmother. She died when my Dad was only twelve. I remembered visiting Grandpa often at his mill village home in New Holland, after we had moved to Buford. I always loved visiting him there. One reason I liked going to his house was because it had an inside toilet that had been built onto the back porch of the old house and I felt sorta' rich going inside of the house to use the toilet!

Back in those days, the deceased's body was brought home to, what they called, "lay a corpse," and Grandpa was a well-liked and highly respected man in his community, so on that late afternoon, there were lots of folks at the house paying their last respects and for the "settin' up." Folks always brought lots of good food on those occasions and someone always "set up" with the departed loved one all night back then. It all seemed a bit festive at first; the food, the people, the talk, and lots of other kids to play with. I had just turned ten at the time.

After awhile, it became necessary for me to go into the bathroom. Of course I was all alone in that little room and it was very quiet in there. I remembered seeing the various shaving articles and lotions that Granddaddy had used and I noticed the towels all folded and in their places. I remembered thinking that Grandpa had been using those toilet articles when he was alive and that he had stood, alive recently, where I was now standing and he had placed those towels there, that his living hands had put them there and the shocking realization had come to me that he would never, ever again use those things or put another towel there. I remembered that, in that unlikely place, for the most unlikely reasons, I cried for my Grandpa. My thoughts cut right through all of the people, the food, the other kids and went straight to the fact that, in spite of the suit and tie and the mortician's makeup on him, that person in the casket, my Grandpa, was not just asleep and waiting patiently for Jesus to come——; *HE WAS DEAD!* He wouldn't be back! No matter how much it hurt me, it couldn't be changed. Life was over for him.

It was like waking up from a horrible nightmare as my mind zoomed back to the restaurant scene with a jolt and I was very acutely aware that on my present course, I too would soon be in one of those caskets! I had already estimated that I couldn't live for more than five more years.

Being honest is not always a voluntary, noble act. In fact, being honest in most situations is something that is often forced upon us. There are lots of self-service grocery stores, gas stations, pick-your-own berry or bean farms and so on, but I have yet to see a self-service cash register. I must conclude then, that honesty is not one of us humans' finest virtues. I especially believe this to be true when it comes to admitting one's own faults or failures or weaknesses.

I now had been forced to admit to myself that everything that I had done for the past thirty years had brought me to this station in life. I had to change——-, or die. It was "done here!" Now I said change or die, not stop drinking or die. There were a few more options, but the choices were dwindling rapidly. I was pretty boxed in by now.

So, as I sat there in my room, on that thirty first day of January, nineteen hundred and eighty-six, my alcoholic mind began again to come up with yet another scheme to evade, or at least postpone, events that were inevitable and about to occur! There was no stopping them. They were in my face. They were "**done here!**"

As I sat there, "drinkin 'n' thinkin," my alcoholic mind began to print, fueled by the alcohol that I was consuming. It came up with a brilliant plan! My logic was that on that day, I was probably going to jail for at least a year, maybe five. I didn't have any real responsibilities and even if I did, I couldn't live up to them in jail. Jail was certain, but if I ran, I might make it through this ordeal. There was a slim chance.

I was like the Christian that had been caught eating a loaf of stolen bread back in the days of the Roman Empire. He was arrested, tried and sentenced to either be boiled in oil or to fight a lion in the arena on the day of the games. Now he knew that the boiling oil was certain death, but that he just might be able to whup that lion so, of course, he chose to fight the lion. In other words, he and I, though centuries apart, each chose the lesser of two horrors. At least we each might have a slim chance.

I decided that I was going to take what little I had, about twenty dollars and some clothes, just enough to do, and get in my little Volkswagen Rabbit and go as far westward as it would take me. Then, I would bum my way on to California and start back up the ladder of respectability by becoming a migrant fruit picker. I could lose myself among them until the heat was off. Then I would establish a new identity for myself and in time, come back home, a new, changed man, healthy, wholesome, successful and free from alcohol. This would be after the statute of limitations had run out on my legal transgressions, of course.

I also considered the alternatives (my alcoholic mind was still struggling to stay alive!). The alternative was that if I couldn't change and ended up on skid row, at least it would be warm in California. Absolutely brilliant!

I was on my way out the door when my eye caught the telephone. The thought occurred to me that it would be pretty rotten of me to leave the family, my children and all, with absolutely no knowledge of my fate, so I decided to call Tanya, my daughter, to tell her and her only, that I was leaving and that I would always carry some identification on me in case I ever got clobbered so that she would be notified. What a plan! A new life was about to unfold for me!

When I told this story years later in an AA meeting, a lady there followed it with a story of her own that was very similar. She even went so far as to have her name, next of kin and social security number tattooed on her ass. Yep, if you're gonna be dumb, you've gotta be tough!

I couldn't get hold of Tanya, so I called my youngest sister, Sue Ellen, to give her the honor of being the bearer of these wonderful tidings. As I was laying out my magnificent plan for her and saying my good-byes, she interrupted me, not to try to talk me out of going, but to tell me that she had to take a cake out of the oven and would call me back in about five minutes.

Well, #*X!@~*#!~X*! Here I was at my lowest ebb in life, pouring my heart out to her and she was worried about some #*!@~#*! @~ cake! I said I'd wait even though I didn't much appreciate my new beginning being put on hold for no damned cake!

So, I went back up to my room with my bottle to wait for her @#%&*&*%#@ cake to get taken care of and of course, to do some more drinkin 'n' thinkin.

Now, THIS was a "revoltin' situation!" I couldn't get hold of somebody to tell of my magnificent plan. I was so sure that they would be so thrilled with it too, if I could just find somebody to tell it to!

As I continued on with my drinkin 'n' thinkin, time flew by and before I knew how long it had been, I heard the sound of tires on the gravel in the driveway. I looked out to see Sue Ellen's husband, Art, coming into the house. She had lied about the cake (God love her!) and had sent him to stall me. As I look back, I see her actions as nothing less than a miracle, because I know that in my state of mind that day, I would have started out to California, had I not called her.

Thinking back on my state of mind and the desperation that I really felt that day reminds me of the ambitious and very promising young 'rassler' who, having just gotten started in the "rasslin'" business, wanted to make a name for himself quickly, so he asked his manager to arrange a match for him against the very popular, but aging state "rasslin'" champion.

The manager reluctantly agreed to do it, but warned his protégé that it was an all or nothing shot and that if the older, more experienced champion were to get him into his famous "pretzel hold," that it would all be over because no opponent had ever escaped from the "pretzel hold" to win against him.

The match was finally arranged and when the time for the event finally came around, tensions ran high.

As the match progressed, the young "rassler" was discovering a few weaknesses in his opponent, and becoming more and more confident of his ability to beat this guy, he decided to finish him off quickly with a flyin' drop kick and really make a name for himself

Choosing the most opportune moment, he ran with all of the stamina that he could muster up across the ring and with reckless abandon, staking everything on this stratagem, threw his entire body weight into the ropes, using their recoil to hurtle him back across the ring and giving him the momentum that he needed for the mighty leap and devastating kick that would deliver his coup d'état!

Alas, the champ wadn't studyin' *"no sech shit es 'at,"* and in the twinkling of an eye, the young challenger found himself grimacing on the mat—-, hopelessly, excruciatingly entwined in the dreaded "pretzel hold."

The crowd cheered wildly out of respect and admiration for the old guy, but cheered even more hysterically when, to their utter amazement, the young challenger, with a burst of unprecedented speed and determination, busted out of the infamous "pretzel hold" and pinned the stunned champion for the victory.

Back in the dressing room, after the pandemonium had died down, the reporters pressed the new champion for an explanation of how he had accomplished this supposedly impossible feat. He answered, very candidly—-;

"When I realized that I was in that pretzel hold, I knew that I had to either give up or get out of it and do it right then because number one; I knew that if I didn't git out of it, all was lost for me and I would probably never rassel again, but the main thing was the pain! I had never hurt like that before. It was hurtin' so bad that I thought I was gonna die! Then in a flash, I realized that the one remote possibility of gittin' out of that quandary was right there in my face and that it was now or never!

"So, out of desperation and rememberin' what I had heard about that pretzel hold, even though I knew that it might have been just a little unethical, I bit down as hard as I could on as much as I could, considerin' the space that I had to work in, of that mass of human body that was smothering' me—-.

"Well you saw it, but rest assured, I'm just as amazed as you are at what a man can do when he bites his-self in the balls!!!"

So, ol' king alcohol had me in a "pretzel hold" when Art came up to my room that day and without fanfare told me that my three sisters would like to see me before I left, just to say good-bye. He assured me that it would only take a few minutes of my time so I benevolently agreed to go with him. After all I was starting a wonderful new life, I could at least give them a little of my valuable time. They surely couldn't improve on my plan and it was already in cement anyhow! Everything was to be cool from now on! We arrived at Betty Ann's apartment. I went in and sat down. Betty, Donna and Sue Ellen were all there.

They started out by saying that they were going to miss me. Then Sue Ellen, the one that I had called, "threw the monkey wrench into the machine" by asking me if I remembered promising her once, after a pretty bad bout with Ol' King Alcohol, that if I ever drank again that I would allow her to put me in a treatment center. I replied that I remembered. Yes, I had promised her that. And then she asked me if I would honor that promise. She added that she had talked to the folks at the mental health center, there in town, and that they would see me right then, if I would talk to them. They were ready to put me into treatment that day if I would consent to it.

"Well, dammit," I thought. "I can't break a promise and I'll still have time to git along if I don't like what I hear. After all it's still **MY** choice. I'M still in charge here!" I was like any other good drunk still trying to control what little fragments are left of his domain. As I said earlier, I'm still convinced that us drunks are the only ones of God's creatures that will be so impaired that we can't even stand up and yet we will talk down to anyone who is trying to help us. So I gallantly consented to talk to them, not only to keep my promise, but by now inwardly hoping that if I got into a treatment facility, I wouldn't have to face the judge that day!

HOPE! Another scheme! I was open for anything now! So brother-in-law dear took me to the mental health clinic for a quick evaluation. A counselor was waiting for me.

Now, us drunks also learn to be the world's greatest actors and I went into my actor persona. I was putting on such a good performance about how pitiful I was and of all the pitfalls of my life, that I had the lady counselor blubberin' before I was done! She came to the conclusion that I didn't have a drinking problem. I had simply been flipped the fickle finger of fate and was not drunk enough for detoxification or treatment. She concluded that their outpatient program would be just the thing for me and that I could begin next week.

OOHHH NO! I had overdone it! This wasn't the way I had planned it a'tall and court time was getting close! Scratch another scheme. I had performed myself right back into the ol' "pretzel hold," and time was runnin' out!

Now while all of this was going on, other forces were at work. My sister, Donna, had called the court officials and asked about my coming fate. Based on what they knew, they said that I would be fined and released. She didn't tell me this, so I was still petrified with fright when I went to court. I was still leery of how much that judge knew, but I went anyway.

They were right. I was fined the mere three hundred dollars and Donna had provided that money for me before I went because she already knew how much it would be. She told me it could be a down payment on the total fine.

So I was released and told that the State of North Carolina would send for my license. Man, oh man! What a relief! I had survived this battle, but the war was still raging and the biggest battle was yet to come: facing another judge for that ninth arrest for driving under the influence of alcohol at some future date. It was an empty victory. I had only changed seats on the Titanic, so to speak.

As Art and I rode home, another miracle happened for me. I was definitely relieved by the judge's decisions, but I was also in an extreme state of exhaustion, not physically tired, but just submissive; tired of holding on. I was tired of it all——, I was tired of that lifestyle, the judges, jails and schemes. I knew then that I wanted to let go of it all, but that the fall would be too severe. I wanted someone, something, somehow to rescue me and at that point in time, I would have said yes to anything that Art might have suggested. I didn't feel like I had enough sense left to make a right choice. If he had said, "Let's go to the lake and sit for awhile," I would have said, "Let's go." If he had said "Let's go and talk to the preacher about this situation." I would have said, "O.K." If he had said, "Let's go get a beer." I would have said, "Sounds good to me." But of all of the things that he could have said, he chose, "There is a meeting of Alcoholics Anonymous at the Buford hospital in about thirty minutes. Would you to go to it with me?"

I replied, rather un-excitedly, "Yeah, let's go." Up to that point in time, I didn't have any idea that Art was an alcoholic in recovery.

Now that was not my first AA meeting, but it was the first one that I had ever attended with a genuine, innermost desire to stop drinking alcohol and turn my life around. I believe that by now I knew, even in my mind's mind, that even alcohol couldn't make me believe that I was anything more than a low life drunk. Even my alcoholic mind could no longer print out "A drink will fix you!" I couldn't be fixed, I thought.

After that meeting, Art took me home. I went into the darkness of the house alone. Dad was in his room as usual, asleep by that time of night. I tried to be as quiet as possible. I didn't turn on the lights or the television or anything. I just went to my room. The moonlight, shining directly and brightly through my window, was enough for me to see by.

All was very quiet as I sat down in the same chair that I had been drinkin 'n' thinkin in earlier that day. I was as alone as any human has ever been, with only my thoughts. I was to learn, in recovery, that that feeling is known as "the chilling vapor of loneliness," that only an alcoholic can know.

I then began to have some "hot horseradish" thinking. I realized that every time that I had drunk alcohol, even from the very first drink of it, that something bad had happened to me. I remembered that it had started with the bad taste and then had gone on to the hangovers. Next came the family problems, then the job problems, the health problems, social problems, the divorce, fired from a job, fired again and again.

I realized that in spite of all of my goals and ambitions, my education, having come from a highly respected family in our community, having had a Christian upbringing, having been a father in a model American family, having worked hard at what I did for a living and in civic affairs, having become the best at what I did for the company that I spent most of my working years with, I had become nothing more than a despicable, low life drunk and I wondered——; "How? Why? Why couldn't I have seen this alcoholic wrecking ball coming? How could it have happened to me?"

The physical pain, the discomfort of the jails, the heartache of losing jobs, the divorce, losing my relationship with my children and all of those other horrible reactions that had come as a result of my addiction to alcohol were only memories now. I couldn't feel them as vividly as I had felt them as they were happening, but the indisputable fact that these things had happened to me, that my alcoholic mind had raped me so unmercifully, that this merciless obsession had turned me away from every wholesome moral value that I had ever possessed, the fact that I had become what I was and that I was continuing to deteriorate, brought on an unspeakable mental anguish. I knew then that I had to be free from alcohol——, one way or another. I was at my bottom.

The only feeling I can remember that comes close to the feeling that I had that night was when I was a lad of eight or nine years and my Dad had brought home two beautiful Beagle puppies for us kids, a male and a female. We named them Jack and Jill. The female took a special shine to me and Jill became my dog.

There is no deeper love than that of a boy for his dog. It is simple and pure and uncomplicated. It is probably the first exchange of true commitment with a living thing in a man's life, his commitment to his dog and his acceptance of his dog's commitment to him.

My dog was with me all of the time except when I was in school of course, but she was always waiting for me when I got home. She would always go with me to milk the cow and she would listen very attentively as I milked while singing to the top of my lungs. I just couldn't keep from singing when I got that two handed milkin' rhythm down good.

I found out later that Jill wasn't my only audience. Mr. and Mrs. Kelly, who lived across the hollow from us, said that they too enjoyed my singin' and hollerin' when they were sitting out on their back porch in pretty weather and I was milking the cow outside of the barn.

On our way back from the barn I would always pour some fresh warm milk in a pan for Jill. She had grown to be a sleek, pretty dog.

One day my dog and me went over to my grandmother's house for a little visit with her. Of course we walked most everywhere that we went in those days.

My grandmother lived about a mile from us and to get to her house we had to walk most of the way on a dirt road and then go up a path alongside a bank. There we crossed a railroad track on top of the bank and of course went down on the other side. Then we crossed a two-lane gravel highway, right in front of Grandma's house. There weren't very many cars in the area that we lived in, in those days, so we didn't have to look for them; we could hear one coming a-half-a-mile away and could usually tell who's car it was by the way it sounded.

We visited with Grandma for awhile. I had a piece of pie, which was really the main reason that I went and then my dog and me started our journey homeward. Jill was a few yards ahead of me as usual as we approached the road.

I don't know why I didn't hear it or see it before the speeding car hit her. I ran to where she had rolled into a ditch hoping to find her just shaken up a little, but when I saw her I knew instantly that she was dead. I still remember, even now, how suddenly that hurt came and how deeply it plunged into my throat and chest as the full realization came over me that my dog was dead. The finality of it was crushing

The car hadn't stopped so I was all alone with my bewildered, help-less feelings. I struggled to gather her in my arms, to begin my long walk home. I was sobbing, hardly able to see through my tears, with my dog hanging limply across my arms, her head swinging slightly in unison with my labored steps. A slow trickle of blood was coming from her mouth intensifying my agony even more because I knew that she must have suffered intense pain for an instant before she died.

The thing that I loved most in the world, at that time in my life, was suddenly gone. It had been destroyed and I couldn't understand how or why it could possibly have happened. In my adolescent mind, I could see no possible way for me to ever overcome this devastation. My dog was such a huge part of my life at that time and she was suddenly gone, she just—- wasn't there anymore.

Like all of my dreams and aspirations, I suddenly knew that January thirty-first night, that they too were just—- all gone; family, lifestyle, career, self respect—-, they just weren't there anymore and at that moment I knew that those who had loved me had suffered intense pain as they, out of necessity, had been forced to let me go. I again could see no possible way to overcome the devastation. The pain was deep.

Such were my feelings as I sat there in that chair on that night. It all finally cleared up for me that night. I could now see the unquestionable cause of it all. At that point in time the mental anguish that had come from drinking alcohol, far outweighed the desire for the feeling that it gave me and my innermost self must have cried out; *"NO MORE! PLEASE NO MORE!*

The scales had finally tipped. I wanted no more of it. After thirty years, alcohol was on the same level with Ex-Lax, electric fences and hot horseradish. I couldn't stand anymore of it, yet I knew that I couldn't just stop pouring it into me. In spite of wanting no more of the way that I was living, I knew that I would need much, much more than human help to change my course. I knew, that I knew, that I KNEW, that I was hopelessly, chronically, unmercifully addicted to alcohol.

I was, at last, being honest with myself. It was indeed "done here." I was at the famous "turning point", "crossroads", "hour of decision", or whatever you wish to call it. By any name, it was "DONE HERE!" I knew then, that in some way, my alcoholic mind had to be stopped. I couldn't go on like this. I was as serious now as ol' Susie dog was with that yellow jacket under her tail! I was ready now to study *"sech shit es 'at!"*

I also compare my feelings that night to the way that I felt when I was five or six and wanted very badly to learn to swim. I was spending lots of time paddling around in the shallow end of the swimming pool, in the mill village recreational center that we called "The Building" in New Holland.

I would try to learn in the shallow end of the pool because I knew that I could stand up in the shallow water when I started sinking, but sometimes I would venture out into the water that was a little over my head, but always holding onto the poolside. I just didn't believe that the water would support me and I couldn't bring myself to let go of the side or to just plunge in and do it.

One day I was sitting on the side of the deep end of the pool with my feet in the water, watching the big boys dive in and swim back to the side, get out and dive in again. They pushed each other into the water with no fear of it, laughin' and hollerin'. How I longed to be doin' that, too.

I was dreamin' of being part of that fun and was submerged in my dream when suddenly, I found myself in the water! A big boy walking by had noticed me sitting there and had nonchalantly placed his foot against my cute little ass and kicked me off of the side into water that was eight feet deep! I was much further than an arm's length from the side and I was suddenly on my way to the bottom of that pool!

I didn't have time to try and decide if I should use the backstroke or the Australian Crawl, the breaststroke or the scissors kick or any of them other strokes that I had heard about, to save my life. I could only think of water all around me swallowing me up and I certainly didn't have time to analyze the situation!

During all of this confusion, I felt my feet touch the bottom of that pool. I instinctively pushed upwards as hard as I could and to my amazement, I went back up to the surface of the water only then to discover that there was nobody or nothing to grab hold of.

I again acted on instinct. I took a deep breath and began to kick and frail the hell out of that water with my arms and legs and to my surprise, I stayed afloat! I didn't realize that the deep breath had made me buoyant. I began to move toward the poolside and was finally close enough to grab hold. I was safe!

I got my breath back, recovered from the terror of the experience and THEN, I began to analyze the situation. The water had supported me; I had been swimming, not very gracefully, of course, but it had really happened. I certainly had been, **UNEXPECTEDLY**, but *most GENUINELY* MOTIVATED TO LEARN TO SWIM and I have been able to swim ever since.

At that instant in time, I really, truly, inwardly wanted to learn to swim in a way that transcends my own understanding and even my awareness; and that was manifested in my doing, not just in my saying.

On that January night I knew that I had been swallowed up by alcohol. I had sunk in it and I wanted to survive. I was motivated and my mind had recorded enough data to know what to direct me to do. So, setting all other business aside, I instinctively did what I had to do to survive.

Alone in my room on that January night, after many years of spiritual skepticism, I instinctively yielded to my mind's "normal" mind and walked over to the side of my bed and got down onto my knees for the first time in many years and asked God, because I knew of no other word to use, no other name to call upon, to please take away my craving for alcohol and to salvage whatever He would of the rest of my life. If nothing more, I asked that He would allow me to just be able to live my life out without drinking. I asked to be allowed to just be me, whatever that was to be.

I had surrendered. I really, truly, deeply wanted to survive in the way that transcends my own understanding and even my awareness; and that is manifested in my doing, not just in my saying. I was playing my very last card. I was exercising my very last option. This had to work.

I stood up finally, but to my surprise I didn't feel any differently. Nothing divine had shown itself. There was no heavenly host nor spiritual glow or even a divine wind. I must have stood there in the glow of the moonlight for a long time waiting for those things for I remember, in that stillness, hearing the hum of the refrigerator's motor running. I even heard the icemaker dump a load of ice cubes into its tray. I heard a car go by. The electric heater in my room shut off and I heard it pop and crackle as it cooled down. A train rumbled along in the distance and blew its whistle as it approached the crossing. The railroad was about a mile from our house.

The moonlight was casting shadows of the tree branches and their leaves, framed by the window's opening, into that room which was, by now, what my once vast, glittering, all fulfilling domain had dwindled to. I stood and watched, in numb bewilderment, for awhile as those shadows danced silently on the walls and on the bed covers as the wind stirred them intermittently outside.

It was late into the night by now and except for those few sights and sounds, the place was uncannily still and deathly quiet. I felt desperation in thinking that nothing had changed. I remembered that feeling from my youth and finally saying out loud to myself, "God still doesn't want me and I don't know of anything else to do." It all seemed totally hopeless.

Everything that had ever been precious to me was gone. I was scared. I felt that agony of defeat. I felt that chill of loneliness and hopelessness. I suddenly understood those words once written by Lord Byron toward the end of his life, which he had supposedly spent primarily in pleasure seeking; *"My days are in the yellow leaf—-. The flowers and fruits of love are gone—-. The worm, the canker and the grief—- are mine alone."*

I took off my shoes and outer garments and got into my bed expecting, as usual, to toss and turn all night. I really didn't want to sleep because I knew that morning would come too soon and I would have to face another day. On the other hand, I didn't want to stay awake because by now my every waking thought, day or night, had become sheer torment.

I again wished that I could just go to sleep and not ever wake up again. I was beaten. Everything seemed hopeless. I couldn't stand life as it was any longer. It all had to end somehow.

The sounds of the night continued as I watched the trees outside, through tears of hopelessness, loneliness and shame, as they swayed gently in the wind. I watched the silent fluttering of the shadows of their branches and leaves on the seemingly compassionate walls of my room, which was by now my only reasonably comfortable place of refuge and seclusion, as I drifted off to sleep.

Thoughts of the events of that previous day were beginning again to tormentingly whirr in my mind as I began to awake from what I thought had been only a short doze. I was puzzled when I realized that sunlight was pouring through my window instead of moonlight. To my amazement, my next conscious thought was, "It's morning!" Then I realized that I had, for the first time in a very long time, gone to sleep and I had slept peacefully all night long. I also had a mysteriously pleasant feeling.

I didn't have any inkling of any idea yet that those tears that I had shed the night before were to be the last tears that I would ever have to shed because of my addiction to alcohol.

I didn't know yet and wouldn't realize for some time to come that my miracle had taken place, that the change had happened; that in those few moments the night before, I had been set free from it all——, that I had come to a point where I couldn't hold onto that alcoholic rope that was taking me to destruction any longer and I indeed had fallen——, but not to destruction——! I had fallen into the loving hands of my Creator.

I didn't know yet that I had, that night, been touched by the master's hand. That having been as honest as I could bring myself to be and having asked as humbly as I could make myself ask, and having wanted and asked for spiritual help without any reservations, I had been healed of my merciless craving for alcohol. I haven't had a drink of anything with alcohol in it since that night!

I didn't know yet that my alcoholic mind had been caged, that I was free, that it was over, that I had suffered my last tormented thought and had shed my last tears and had had my last lonely moment because of my addiction to alcohol. I didn't know that I, without any fanfare, had unknowingly stepped onto that mysterious spiritual plateau, the step that I for so long had thought would be impossible for me to take.

I was to learn in time that I had found God there. How can I know that now? Because I not only haven't had a drink of anything with alcohol in it since that night, I haven't even wanted one.

As theatrical as this next statement might seem to some and would certainly have seemed to me in times past, it was as if God had been waiting there for me.

When I recall that night, I think of the night of John F. Kennedy's election to the Presidency. The race was very close between him and Richard Nixon. I didn't watch all of the voting returns, but just before I retired for the night, I tuned in to hear the latest results. The tide had turned in Kennedy's favor enough to insure his election.

The newscaster was telling the country that John F. Kennedy had already gone to sleep and was unaware that he was indeed becoming the next president of the United States. The commentator went on to say that, "Even as our next president sleeps, secret service men are taking up their places around him and their vigil to protect him." He didn't know yet that his protection and safekeeping were already in their hands.

Just as surely, as I slept the night of my deliverance from my addiction, my protector had taken up His vigil. I didn't know yet that I wouldn't have to live the alcoholic life any longer, that the hell of it all was finished. That it was over. It still boggles my mind to think of that night!

I later began to think of it as if another mind, my innermost mind (the one that has the final word), took over and subdued my alcoholic mind. I sort of see that mind as one similar to the mind that controls my vital organs. I know that my heart beats, that I breathe, digest food and all of those things because my innermost mind knows that my life depends on those vital functions; they happen without my even being aware of them. I likewise believe that my innermost mind caused me to know that my life was at stake and caused me to see very clearly my choices: spiritual help or total destruction.

I was not in any sort of trance, nor was I experiencing any sort of an illusion when I asked for spiritual help. I remember very vividly my choices. It was probably the clearest mental moment in my life. It was up to me! I could have gone either way.

I'm glad that my mind's normal mind contained enough good data by then to provide the right printout for me: " LIVE! LIVE! LIVE! LIVE!"

Now back to the story about the Christian and the lion:

The day of the games came and finally it was time for the Christian to fight that lion. He was escorted by the Centurions to the center of the Amphitheater and was placed in a standing position in a hole that had been dug neck deep for him. All but his head was then covered up with dirt, as the teeming crowd watched this seemingly insignificant event rather indifferently. The half-famished lion was then released.

That lion was a huge, ferocious looking beast, as I'm sure all of them would look especially in a situation like that. The lion began to stealthily circle around the Christian and after carefully analyzing the situation, realized that a tasty morsel had been placed before him.

The lion finally aligned himself with the poor fellow and charged with the intent of taking that Christian's head clean off of him in one big bite, but at the last split second, the Christian, not to be taken lightly, jerked his head as quickly and as far to the left as he could. The lion missed and passed directly over him! The crowd had taken notice and now roared its approval of this Christian's gallant effort.

The befuddled lion again circled the Christian's tantalizing head, re-analyzing the situation, while the spectators by now watched in eerie silence. Finally the lion, feeling a little more sure of himself, charged again!

This time the Christian waited for as long as he dared and then jerked his head to the right! The lion missed once more and again passed directly over the Christian's head! The spectators again roared their approval. They were beginning to appreciate this lowly Christian's spunk and cunning.

Then, out of frustration and with a mighty roar and by this time desperate for his meal, the lion again made a furious charge. The Christian again jerked his head to one side and as the lion passed over him he stretched his neck as far as he could then snapped his head back to the other side, hitting the lion with a crushing blow, squarely in his testicles. The now humbled lion collapsed, rolling over into a pitiful heap, roaring in agony, unable to continue. The spectators, in a frenzied state of shock, leapt to their feet and while clapping their hands and swaying from side to side in unison, chanted hysterically ——————; "FIGHT FAIR CHRISTIAN —-! FIGHT FAIR CHRISTIAN —-! FIGHT FAIR CHRISTIAN!"

I was about to discover the wonderful world of recovery from my addiction, which didn't only include just not drinking alcohol. I was about to discover life again as it was meant to be. Yet there would be times on my journey into recovery when I would feel the frustration that our Christian must have felt during his struggle with that lion.

Chapter VII

YE OLDE COMMODE OF LIFE

A friend in recovery recently noticed that I was wearing a new pair of shoes and he commented on them. My reply was that they were a part of being sober. Guess what? He understood!!! He had been there and done that.

There are thousands upon thousands of people living happy, joyous and free lives who are not recovering alcoholics; most of them even take a drink from time to time or even more often than that. They can even get gloriously drunk sometimes because they don't have that built in mechanism that launches them into the insane orbit that I always went into when I drank.

I sometimes wonder how one of them normal folks would react if I were to approach them and say, "I have stopped drinking! I don't crave alcohol! I am not afraid of getting fired today! My wife doesn't want a divorce! I believe in God! My children love me! I don't have to go to jail today! I have money in my pocket! I'm not worried about my liver! I live in a nice home! I don't owe any taxes! I have a car, car insurance and a license to drive! I have a new pair of shoes! **GOOD AIN'T NO NAME!**"

I'm reasonably sure that by the time I got to the part about the shoes, the person would be backing away from me with raised eyebrows, wondering why I was such a babbling idiot!

It was in recovery that I would hear another one of them pearls of wisdom from one of my new ex-drunk teachers. He said, "Us addicted people in recovery from our addiction look upon things with a keen appreciation that normal folks just take for granted."

So change for us is not always from something good to something just different or better. It is from what we had become to simply back to normal. I also learned that change is easy when circumstances are right.

A friend told of being in the woods once when, as he walked along, he came upon a small stream. "The stream was just a little too wide to step across, so I had to go back a little ways and get a running start at it to jump across." he said. "I was in mid-flight, about halfway across that stream, when I spotted a snake lying where I was about to land and I turned around in mid-air and went back!" I can understand how he felt!

When I finally saw where I was about to land in my flight into addiction, I desperately wanted to turn around and go back. The realization of where I was headed wasn't sudden like my friend's snake experience. It took years for me, even after I began to see my future. I didn't have to be too smart to know that those things that I had been warned might happen to me in the alcoholic arena weren't only possible, they were happening and they were indeed destroying me. I was in my future. It was almost over for me. I've learned that for me to drink again would indeed send me back to my future!

I personally believe that recovery from addiction, like becoming addicted, is very much like the ol' fingernails-growing-out syndrome. I really didn't know that recovery was growing in me, I just sort'a realized one day that it too was "done here!"

I heard one of my new teachers talking once about the great Alaskan pipeline and how different grades of petroleum were moved through it. He said that the batches were separated by a dye being pumped into the lines between the batches. Of course the dye would mix into the old batch in front and into the new batch behind and as the oil flowed, the dye faded out and the new batch would eventually flow clean and pure. It took time and during that time the old and the new would be mixed for awhile. But in time, the good and pure stuff would be "done here." Recovery from my addiction was somewhat similar to that pipeline; there were plenty of times when I wondered if the dye of my alcoholism would ever fade out. It finally did.

About thirteen years prior to that January thirty first night that I took my last drink, we were living in Connecticut and I had come home from work one day to find Sue and a man from Alcoholics Anonymous(whom she had invited to visit me), waiting to greet me. It was called an "in-ter-ven-tion." I will be eternally grateful to her for inviting him, because I believe that the dye was dropped into my recovery pipeline that day. I know that recovery started for me right then and there.

Sue left us alone, which seemed odd to me. He talked for awhile and then he gave me the famous alcoholic questionnaire, which, by the way, I made a *goooood* grade on! Then he invited me to an Alcoholics Anonymous meeting being held that night. I accepted, but only out of curiosity and courtesy, I told myself.

The time for the meeting drew near so I drove on down to the town of Shelton, Connecticut and following the directions that he had given me, I found the church where the meeting was to be held. It was a cold looking, old gray stone church. Of course, the meeting was to be held in the basement, as AA meetings usually are. I made my way down the cold, dark steps and finally stepped into my very first Alcoholics Anonymous meeting room. I spotted the coffee pot with several people standing around it drinking coffee. My attention was immediately drawn to two priests who were mingling with that group.

Now, based on my Pentecostal up-bringing, I would never have *dreamed* that a priest, or any other person of the cloth, would ever even *think* of takin' a drink of likker, let alone become an alcoholic, so my first reaction to their being there was "God-stuff!" I was thinking of slipping back out of that door to avoid the lecture that I assumed was to come and to sho' 'nuff not be around when they broke out them little cookies, when suddenly from out of nowhere, my visitor from earlier that afternoon came out and greeted me before I could make my "git-away."

He introduced me around, got me some coffee and we took our seats at a table that was arranged with some other tables to form a "U" shape. I was flabbergasted to see the two priests sitting among us, not at the head of the table.

The meeting started and after the preliminaries: the readings, the passing a basket (for tithes and offerings, I thought) and so forth, a speaker was introduced and to my surprise, he began to tell his own story of his struggles with alcohol. Man-o-man, had he had some ever-more hair-raisin' experiences with it!

After he had spoken for awhile, the individuals seated at the tables (even them priests!), began to tell of their experiences with, and since, alcohol. The meeting lasted until everyone had the opportunity to share his or her stories. I passed up the opportunity of telling mine! I had seen others passing when it came their turn, so I did it too, Whew! However, I heard some impressive stuff that night that affected me in a *"mighty peculiar way."*

After the meeting, I left that room and as I climbed those steps and made my way to my car, my heart was singing! I was skipping along, much like Fred Astaire, or Gene Kelly, "Singing In The Rain!" I was overjoyed that I had gone to that meeting! I had done the right thing! The song that my heart was singing was; "I ain't one a' them! I ain't one a' them! Thank God-Almighty, I ain't one a' them!"

Compared to them folks, I didn't have a problem with alcohol! I was in good shape! I was employed, had a wonderful job, nice home, nice family, good income, two cars and a swimming pool. Why, I had only been in in jail once because of alcohol, and they think I'm an alcoholic?

NO WAY and on top of that, I ain't never craved alcohol! I can't be one! I got more smarts than that! I ain't studyin' *"no sech shit as 'at!"*

But wait a minute; one thing stood out in my mind like a prophylactic in a church collection plate. I couldn't ignore it——; I had just walked out of an *ALCOHOLICS ANONYMOUS MEETING—————-!* *Shiiiiiittt Far!*

I had to admit to myself that nobody goes into one of them places just for the hell of it, because most folks think that that's about as low as you can go in this world! Why back then I'd sooner have been accused of bein' a member of the Ku Klux Klan, *AS LOW-DOWN AS THAT WOULD HAVE BEEN,* than to have somebody think that I was a member of Alcoholics Anonymous!! Another brighter aspect about bein' in the Ku Klux Clan rather than in Alcoholics Anonymous would've been that at least in *them* meetin's, I could have put a sack over my head like I sho' 'nuff wished that I could've done in that AA meeting!!

I can see now that I began then to try and prove to myself that I wasn't one of them. I didn't realize it then, but my party was over. That night, the imaginary fun of alcohol would begin to come to a halt. The alcohol scene was never the same again. The dye had been dropped into my pipeline. Sort of like stepping in dog doodie——, it (the guilt) was on me and I couldn't get it all off.

It was only a matter of time from that point until I would begin to desperately try to turn around in "mid-air" and go back from what I was to see lying ahead of me, because I was to have all of the experiences that I had heard about that night.

That first meeting had a massive impact on my destiny. It's sad that I can only look back and see it now. That incident did cause me, in my alcoholic mind, to try and prove that I wasn't one of them. I would have an extra drink now to show myself that I could. I took more pride in being able to hold my liquor, therefore I believe that my efforts in trying to prove that I wasn't one of them brought me to a desire for recovery sooner. I'm grateful for that.

I sometimes will tell newcomers to AA that if they're not ready to stop drinking yet to please continue coming to our meetings because they are going to do some strange things to try and prove that they "ain't one of us," and I want to enjoy their new experiences too. Lordy, there are some mighty comical ones! Unfortunately, there are some mighty sad ones as well.

Another major impact that this first meeting had on me was that I realized there was a safe haven for me if, BY CHANCE, I were to ever need it but more importantly, if I ever were to want it. I'm grateful that I came to know that I wanted it before I won one of the grand prizes------------; my own alcoholic death or my being the cause of someone else dying or being horribly maimed as a result of my addiction.

Another impression made on me that night was that I didn't need to be anything other than myself among those people. They were real people. I didn't need to impress them. There was no rank in their circles. The highest status that one can achieve in Alcoholics Anonymous is to be sober. I didn't need to change myself therefore I didn't need alcohol when I was with them. I felt comfortable among them.

So, the dye was in the pipeline. Addiction and recovery were mixed now and for awhile I would practice both. When times were good, addiction would rule. When times got bad, it was back to AA and some more recovery. My attendance in the meetings would begin to become more frequent over the years. I was to learn from my new teachers that in AA, coming and going are referred to as the "**gnat-in-a-mule's-ass-syndrome.**" In other words, you're in awhile and then you're out awhile. I slowly began to be more in than out and little by little, the dye in my pipeline began to clear up.

I have already stated that my first two arrests for driving drunk were about seven years apart. My last two arrests for driving drunk were about three days apart. I was phasing into addiction. Likewise, my first two times in Alcoholics Anonymous meetings were about three years apart. Now my appearances there are almost every day! I'm phasing into recovery.

So for all of those years, between my first AA meeting and my hitting a real bottom, I weighed the advantages and disadvantages of recovery, or as I saw it then, just quitting drinking. Remember, I was still a member of a bunch of two-fisted drinkers. Could I give up my barstool at Mancini's? NO WAY! They would miss me too much! Could I go to them management meetings at Great Gorge in New Jersey, Doral in Miami, Ponte Vedra in Jacksonville and all of them other places and not drink with my buddies? NO WAY! Could I travel to the various plant locations; Kentucky, Alabama, Georgia, Puerto Rico, Dominican Republic, Canada and others and not drink with my working buddies there? NO WAY! Could I fly on them big airplanes without alcohol? NO WAY! I thought, "AIN'T NO WAY!" Could I have lunch with the company president and not have a drink with him? **SHIT FAR NO!**

I saw myself as ol' Jed Clampett in that Beverly Hillbillies show when, just after striking oil and facing the possibility of moving to Beverly Hills, he asked Cousin Pearl if he was doing the right thing. She rolled her eyes in disbelief at the question and replied, as best as I can remember, "Jed, y'all have to walk fifty yards through the bushes to get your water and fifty yards in the other direction to use the toilet, y'all cook on a wood stove, you've got them smelly ol' hogs right next to the cabin, y'all freeze in the wintertime and burn up in the summertime, y'all bathe in the creek or in an old washtub cause you ain't got no modern conveniences, ya'll have to ride a mule or walk to town when you even git to *go* to town, yo're closest neighbor is ten miles away and Jed—-, them's just the good things that I've mentioned so far! Yet you're askin' me if you're making the right choice, a-movin' to Californy?"

Ol' Jed looked mighty perplexed as he studied for a spell and then he finally said; "I knowed that I could count on you to be level headed about it Pearl, and you're right, a man would have to be a danged fool to leave all a-this!"

So, here I would go again, enjoying them things, people, and places that were bringing me down and all the time really believing that I'd be a danged fool to leave all of that! The thought of never again possessing a bottle of Jack Daniel's sippin' whiskey was just too heartbreaking. Yet as the years wore on, events began to convince me that there might be some real advantages to leaving off the so-called glamorous life that revolved around alcohol.

The dye was fading out little by little and the sober life was looking better and better. AA meetings were becoming more frequent, maybe only months apart by now. I had begun to give myself credit for having at least as much sense as a gnat; why even the lowly gnat knows that as unpleasant as being in a mule's ass seems, there are times when being in there is much safer, warmer and more comfortable than what the outside world and ol' Jack Daniel's has to offer!

So I began to make my way to them lowly meetings——, always around back and usually in the basement, hoping that nobody that I knew would be there. I didn't want my friends to know that I was in no "mule's ass!" The fear of running into someone that I knew in one of them places was dispelled one night when the topic for discussion was on that very subject. This is deeply philosophical so hold on! An old-timer simply said; "Bein' seen in an AA meeting is like being seen in a whorehouse. Nobody is going home to their wife or to their friends and say; "Guess who I saw at the whorehouse last night?", because the reply will be; "I don't give a damn who you saw——! What the hell were **YOU** doing there?" Scratch another good excuse for not going to meetings!

So, as unpleasant as them meetings seemed, I was coming to grips with my need to be there, yet not wanting to go there. I compared it later in life to a time when I was sixteen or seventeen and was driving mom and dad somewhere when, just after dark, we went by the Spradlin's house. The Spradlin's were members of mom and dad's church. Mom was in the front seat with me and dad was in the back seat, not saying much as we drove along.

Mr. Spradlin had married probably a year or two before this time after his wife of many, many years had passed away. I know that it was many years because they had about twenty children and their youngest one was now in his teens.

Anyhow, the story goes that a friend of Mr. Spradlin's, Harvey, an old bachelor around town, had arranged a marriage for himself through one of them Lonely Hearts clubs, but when his bride-to-be arrived, she was way, way too ugly. We tried to tell him that ugly was only skin deep, but Harvey said, "Damn——! She's got mighty thick skin!," and he backed out of it, but Brother Spradlin saved the day. (Brother and sister being the way that the Church of God folks addressed or referred to each other——I never did earn that title!) He decided to take her, ugly as she was, for his own and he did just that.

So, as we were riding by their house that night, mom noticed that their lights were all off and innocently remarked, "Well, I see that brother and sister Spradlin have already gone to bed."

Now, this is a basic southern observation in a small community such as we lived in. There were no implications at all in it, especially coming from my momma. However, after a few seconds of thinking about that statement, Dad's voice broke the silence. He said, "Now, that's one "thang" I'd put off just as *loooooong* as I could!"

My mom burst into a hysterical, crazy frenzy of laughter——, not lady-like a'taaaall! Of course we all got tickled then. I was thinking that same thing, but I was afraid that I'd git struck dead if I'd said it.

Now I've already indicated that momma was a genuine, straight-laced, devout, saintly Christian woman and I had never heard her say a bad word against anybody, but at that remark from Dad, she lost her cool and for years after, it was just as funny when we talked about it.

So, I was putting off recovery for *as loooooong* as I could, but as time passed I had to begin to ask myself, "Do I want this recovery stuff, or do I want what I've got?" The dye was fading out, but I still needed more convincing. It was to come in abundance!

Now if you have raised kids or are raising kids, you know the help-less, frustrating feeling of going into the bathroom, doing whatever you went in there to do, flushing the commode and watching in horror as the toilet bowl, instead of flushing down, fills up and overflows because some kid has put too much paper, or maybe a Dixie cup in there before you came in. No feeling is worse than that and the sickening, sinking realization of the fact that YOU must now clean it up!

I think of the events caused by my addiction as the overflowing of "Ye Olde Commode of Life." I was having that feeling much too often! I was having to clean up much too much.

So on that night of January thirty-first, the overflow was too much. I couldn't stand anymore. I said, in effect, "I want that recovery stuff!" With that honest thought, the dye started clearing up and I had indeed entered into recovery. I didn't know it yet, but I was in! I had asked God, as I perceived Him then, to take my craving for alcohol away. He then caught me in mid-air, turned me around and started me back to safety.

I was about to begin a real life education and I would get it from real people who would pass on the wisdom of the ages to me, having learned it themselves from those who had gone before them.

My teachers wouldn't wear caps and gowns and only one of them, Larry, would carry books around with him, but he had a good reason. They would be Carpenters, Butchers, Plumbers, Builders, Retirees, Professional Sportsmen, Painters, Ex-burglars, Ex-prostitutes, Maids, Train engineers, Entertainers, Police Officers, Housewives, Company Presidents, Politicians, School Teachers, Welders, Doctors, Nurses, Bikers, Rich folks, Poor folks, Bartenders, Waiters, Waitresses, Airplane Pilots, Military personnel, Sign makers, Secretaries, School students, Tile layers, Convicts, Priests, Senators, Preachers, etc. etc. Probably, the only occupation that I haven't seen represented in some Alcoholics Anonymous meeting, or other, is the presidency of the United States! I'm sure that some of them need to be there. My teachers were certainly a most unlikely lot!

Now, I don't want to imply in any way that all who attend Alcoholics Anonymous meetings are pillars of strength and guidance for others. That ain't just a no; it's a big **SHIT FAR NO!** It must be remembered that we draw from the "nuts" of the world—-! I can say that now 'cause I'm one of 'em!

We have the destitute, the unloved, the sex fiend, the sexless fiend, the con artists and the homeless among other specimens of humanity. There are male and female specimens of all of the above. You name 'em, we've got 'em! Some of us appear to be just plain ol' mentally retarded. In fact, my AA group even has a large, in house trophy that we award when someone tells an exceptionally bizarre story!

So not all who come are real alcoholics who have found what we real alcoholics need and want and who are truly enjoying and are grateful for deliverance from our dilemma. Some are there to bum, con, find sex, or just ain't accepted nowhere else, but those of us who mean business surface sooner or later. In fact, some of the future pillars of our Alcoholics Anonymous society are right now in jails or treatment centers, homeless shelters or mental institutions, or more than likely sitting in a bar somewhere. Some are probably wondering where they will sleep tonight

Some of my lessons were to be deeply psychological, theological, philosophical and intellectual. I first of all learned that not taking a drink is as easy as falling off a log. There is nothing to it! Now how do I know that? Because as of this very moment, I am still an alcoholic and there is absolutely nothing that would stop me if I decided to go to the liquor store right now, buy a bottle of booze and drink it. But I'm not going to do it. It's simple! I'm just not going to do it! It's easy!

I walk by a truckload of beer every time I go into a grocery store, yet I don't buy it! Now here is the mind-boggling part: if I don't have it, I won't drink it thus—-, I won't get drunk—-! Amazing, ain't it? How did I ever miss that point? It's easy! I learned that from my new teachers.

So new stuff started being programmed into my computer. A slow change started coming over me. I started thinking with my mind's normal mind instead of it's alcoholic one.

I often recall how I worried, in my street mind, about my craving coming back on my thirty-first day without a drink. I had been alcohol free for thirty days once before, twenty-eight days in the Sun Valley treatment center (thank God for it, I don't know if I would have survived without the seeds that were planted in my minds there!) and two days out, but never for thirty-one days and I just knew that the uncontrollable impulse would come on the thirty-first day. I still believed that it controlled me. Day thirty-one came and went and my mind's alcoholic mind couldn't command me to drink. Good feeling ain't no name!

I learned that no two thoughts can occupy my mind at the same time from them ex-drunks. Then I "figgered" it out: if I wasn't thinking about a drink, I couldn't possibly be wanting one and that I can choose my thoughts!!

Simple—-; mind-boggling, ain't it?? A craving is a thought. If I ain't thinking about alcohol, I can't be craving it. For instance, I don't recall ever thinking about how good a drink would be while I was standing in front of a judge waitin' for him to decide what my future was to be. There was way too much other stuff goin' on to occupy my mind! It would have been easier for me to think about wantin' a drink while lookin' at a big ol' coiled rattlesnake fixin' to git me, than it would have been to think about wantin' one while standing in front of one of them judges! That's proof enough for me anyhow, that I can't think about but one thing at a time. So if I ain't thinkin' drinkin', I can't be wantin' to do it.

So I learned that if I ever drink again, that it will be because I want to do it, not because I have to. Now that's deep psychology! I started suspecting that doctors and psychiatrists probably know all these things, but don't pass it on to patients because it is priceless and patients can't afford to pay for it and of course, they would lose patients too quickly, because we wouldn't need them as long! We do eventually get that good stuff in AA meetings for about a dollar a meeting if we've even got a dollar by the time we get there. And if we don't have one, then it's all free!

My teachers never tried to tell me that cleaning up the garbage of my past was easy. In fact, they said that that job would be hell and it was! They said that being a drunk is easy and being sober was easy. It's the switch that's a bitch! Now, that's intellectual stuff!

My college trained mind jumped right on that one and it came to me that I had spent much of my young life milking cows and many times have had one of 'em step on my foot while maneuvering for her position at the feed trough. Now, having the hoof of a twelve to fifteen hundred pound animal on my foot hurt like all damnation, especially if she would just stand there on it and I'm convinced, by the way that she would look at me, that she knew that the choice to stand there or not was, of necessity, being left to her discretion. Then, I recalled that when after lots of hollerin', beggin', cussin' and pushin', I would finally get her to move, my foot still hurt like the devil, but **OOOOOH LORDY**, did it feel better! So much better in fact, that the remaining pain felt good! Now, that is *deeeeeep* psychological stuff!

So I started seeing solutions for my problems and they started feeling better. Just seeing them not get no worse was sheer joy! Now that's *DEEEEEEEEEEP!!* I was getting smart!

I also learned that choices are not always between something good and something bad, but sometimes between something bad or something worse. Later, I came to know that our choices are often between something good or something even better!

I heard the term "shit storm of life" (that's the Latin term for depression or frustration, things going wrong, the problems of life, etc.) and from that, I came up with an original saying of my own, namely;

"Sometimes in the shit storms of life, you gotta jump in front of a little turd to keep from gittin' clobbered by a big 'un!"

Eat your heart out, Norman Vincent Peale! Deep psychology ain't no name for that! Maybe I'll become famous for that as my contribution to mankind like Admiral Farragut or some of my favorite philosophers; Plato, Aristotle, Socrates and of course Junior Samples did for some of their sayin's!

I also learned that shit does happen, but if you have some shit to handle, don't handle it while it's fresh—-, it'll get all over you! Now that one has become invaluable for me! It works! Just let that shit (problem) get cold and dry and hard and then you can move it around in any way and to any where that you want to move it. It's still mighty unpleasant, but it's manageable. Deep philosophical stuff ain't no name for it. I wish that I could take the credit for that sayin', too.

Being in meetings with these seemingly unlikely people (of which I am one now, too!), became to me like panning for gold. We go through a lot of silt, but usually come up with a little of the glitter every time we look for it. I figgered out one day recently, with my ol' college mind, that if I went to one AA meeting each day, I would hear at least three-hundred and sixty-five different topics discussed each year. If there were an average of ten people at each meeting, I would hear thirty-six hundred and fifty different opinions on them topics. If only fifty percent of the opinions were worth a damn, I would have had one thousand, eight hundred and twenty-five good inputs from people who know about recovery and have found a way out of their addiction. Now this sounded like a vast source of wisdom to me when I look back and realize that before recovery, I had only one source to go to: my own alcoholic mind!

So I was getting along just fine not drinking, however cleaning up the past was beginning to look pretty awesome; but wouldn't you know, God sent me wisdom through my teachers. Here is some more of the deep and advanced psychology that they taught me, in some "*mighty peculiar ways.*"

I had been sober for over a year, but was still having difficulty with lots of the problems that I had created in my drinking days. This time, I was being sought out by the officials for back child support and was hiding out and living with a lady friend while working my ass off, literally, to accumulate the money to catch it up. I was a fugitive.

I was helping a friend who was trying to start a wholesale vending supply business and the work was very strenuous and at times involved loading, hauling and unloading drink vending machines and believe me, them devils are heavy! It must have been moving them machines around that did something to cause the pain and irritation that caused me to think that I was developing a case of hemorrhoids.

My suspicions were strong enough to motivate me to ask some of my new teachers if they had ever had this problem in their recovery and if so, to describe the symptoms, since I had never had the experience.

I had heard that after this particular surgical procedure, one can look forward to having the most absolutely horrible, excruciating, painful experience known to mankind upon having that first call of nature.

I remembered having once heard an aunt of mine tell of how painful the ordeal was for her. She said, "I'd rather give birth to all five of my babies one right after the other than to have that hemorrhoid experience again!"

Fear's icy fingers again wrapped themselves around my heart. I remembered what my wife had gone through having our children and I've heard other women tell of the hell that they went through having babies and I had seen that Murphy Brown TV episode when she was having her baby. WHOA!! Yet here was a woman saying that she had rather have five babies in a row than to have hemorrhoids again!

OH MOMMA, MOMMA! Terror wadn't no name! This was taking on hot horseradish proportions! Suicide began again to look like a viable option for me!

Of course, in my quest for knowledge about this dreaded experience that I anticipated having myself, I heard some more pretty hair-raisin' stories from those who had had it or been close to someone who had. People in recovery are experts on everything and they all jumped on this one with gusto, especially when they noticed that I was walking around like Fred Sanford of the Sanford and Son TV show, yet they turned it into a valuable lesson about recovery for me.

One friend told me that when he was a boy, his daddy had had the hemorrhoidectomy and had suffered the usual pain and agony before leaving the hospital. He had gone home with instructions from his doctor to eat only soft foods, jello and such as that, for the next week so that his healing would be far enough along for him to be able go through the breaking in period with, let's just say, *BEARABLE* pain. Well, wouldn't you know that on his first night home, his wife cooked country fried steak, creamed gravy, biscuits, green beans and mashed potatoes for supper for the rest of the family and some oatmeal for him. Well, no real good country boy could just sit down to a table with all that good stuff on it and eat nothing but oatmeal, and he was no exception. He reckoned that, by God, he felt fine and that a little pain in the ass tomorrow (that he could certainly handle with no real sweat, he thought) wasn't going to keep him from enjoying this delicious meal, especially after all the crap he had been eating in the hospital. So, he chowed down, throwing caution to the wind.

Well, sho' 'nuff, my friend said that the next day, he happened to see his daddy head off to the outside toilet and that he didn't think much about this routine occurrence until a few minutes later, when he heard a blood curdling scream pierce the atmosphere and he figgered out what was happening! My friend must have been a college man! He said that the sounds of agony continued periodically for about thirty minutes and finally he saw his dad return from that place of torture, looking physically abused and beaten. He said that his dad didn't eat much for awhile after that. Of course, this didn't help much with my anticipation of coming events!

Another teacher that I asked for input on what I thought was my impending doom, said that he, himself, had had it and that the surgery itself wasn't all that bad. So I asked about the experience afterward. He reported that he was at home when he was faced with his first post-operative encounter and since he was out at the barn, he had to find an out-of-the-way place in some bushes outside to meet this dreaded challenge.

In his own words, he recounted the experience and ended with: "I can't speak for anybody else, but when it was over with, I was about fifty-foot from where it had started!"

My teachers were brutally honest it seemed, and the clouds were gathering quickly on my horizon.

Of course, my fear of this thing was ballooning, so I went to my Alcoholics Anonymous sponsor, feeling sure that he could console me (an AA sponsor can handle anything!) .

He told me about his Uncle Amos having had the operation back when the city hospital wasn't much more than a good sized chicken house sectioned off into rooms and offices with no security, so anyone could come and go at will, so my sponsor decided to drop by to see Uncle Amos after work, which happened to be shortly after the operation had been completed. The anesthesia hadn't even completely worn off yet.

Uncle Amos was back in his room, feeling proud of his decision to have those damned things cut out when my sponsor, Edwin, came in and asked him how he was feeling. Uncle Amos, still numb from his local anesthesia, started boasting of his decision to have it done and talkin' about how he wished now that he had done it years ago; about how good he felt and that he had had very little pain and discomfort and how anyone who would put up with hemorrhoids for as long as he did, or even for just a little while, was just a fool! "Hell," he said, "I was awake when they done it!" He went on to say that there was nothing to it and that he was anxious to get out of that hospital the day after tomorrow and pick up where he had left off. He said he felt like a nineteen twenty-eight model with a brand new rebuilt rear end and that he was ready to go home right then, but they just wouldn't turn him loose.

So Edwin left there that day, surprised himself at how well things were going and glad that Uncle Amos was in such fine fettle and he figgered that since Uncle Amos would be there through tomorrow, that he would stop in again since it was right on his way home from work.

The next day, when Edwin stopped by to see Uncle Amos, that excruciating event from hell had happened—-, more than once. Unknowingly, Edwin strode happily into the room and cheerily asked, "How you doin' today, Uncle Amos?" Uncle Amos, dazed by his gross misconception of the far-reaching ramifications of this undertaking, stared at Edwin absently for a moment with that "what happened?" countenance.

His eyes were weak and filled with bewilderment. His face was pale and drawn when finally with a pitifully weak, trembling, almost pleading voice he replied————————-; "GGAHHHHODDD *DAAAAAAAM, I WISH I HAD 'em BACK!*"

Of course, in time Uncle Amos did return to normal and was happy to have done it after all.

As it turned out, my situation was not hemorrhoids, but just a condition caused by moving them coke machines; but my pain felt real good compared to what had been described to me. It was sort of like the pain and problems that I now had in recovery, compared to the way that they had been when I was a drunk. My problems were wonderful problems now and there was a solution for all of them.

So my new teachers were teaching me some valuable lessons now and they didn't even know that they were. I was gittin' educated by just listening to them talk. They were assuring me that my recovering from alcoholic addiction is very much like them folks' recovering from their hemorrhoid operations. In the early days it was wonderful discovering that I could go for some days, weeks, or even months in a sublime state of mind; folks proud of me and me proud of myself, wonderin' why I hadn't done it sooner! But then I had to face that first painful cleaning up of the wreckage of my past and it was painful, to be sure. It is so painful in fact, that some of us, like Uncle Amos, do wish that we had the old lifestyle back; it was hell, but it was familiar and some of us do take it back since we do still have that choice.

The obstacle course between an alcoholic or a drug addict and recovery is tough—-, so many problems and situations present themselves that would have been such excellent excuses to drink or to use over before, that only a small percentage of us make it through to recovery.

Another story about the hemorrhoidectomy (that has nothin' to do with recovery from addiction, it's just extra) was told by a gentleman who had had it. He had discovered, in his early recovery time, that it was even too painful for him to squeeze enough to prevent that insidious curse that plagues us all. That truly great equalizer of mankind that emanates from kings as well as peasants, from the most profane to the icons of righteousness. Even the pope does it—- and invariably for us all, it happens at the most awkward times. Surely another of Gods mistakes in His creation—-, the passing of one's flatus.

This gentleman said that when he felt one of those horribly embarrassing, abominable happenings coming on, that there was absolutely nothing that he could do to stop it! In fact his painful attempt to squeeze it off only put it under more pressure and made it sound off even louder!

Now if he happened to be alone when he knew that one was breaking, he could do it with gusto, even be creative with it such as synchronize the sound with a command to "FIRE TORPEDO NUMBER ONE—-" , or if he was in a store or some other public place, he could retreat to a safe spot and hold onto his self-respect as his dilemma passed privately. But on this particular occasion, he had been pressured by his wife to sit in for an absent member during a gathering of her bridge club.

When the inevitable terrifying gas alert was sensed, he knew that he had to act fast. He couldn't just jump up and run out of the room nor could he defile the dignity of the occasion by saying to the ladies, "Excuse me, I must go and pass some gas!" In fact, there wasn't time for either of those solutions so his brain started whirring and he worked out a brilliant diversionary tactic (a college man, of course!).

He would drop a card, slide his chair back to pick it up and fart as the chair was makin' a racket while skiddin' across the floor, thus camouflaging the incriminating sound. Then all of their dainty eardrums would be spared and there would be no condemning moment of silence by the group and their refined indignity would have simply been his own foregone, yet embarrassing assumption.

"Alas," he said, "my timing was off and on top of all of that, I had to squeeze a little to try and synchronize the two sounds and my squeezin' effort only made it louder!"

When my really tough times started, I was about to be sent to the county prison camp to pay society for my ninth and last conviction for "drunk driving." I had been sober for six months by this time, so as my friend Perry from old camp days had once said, I wasn't scared, but I was highly uneasy. In seeking the council of my new teachers in recovery, I was being told to take it easy. *"REE-LAXXX,"* they said. "It'll be alright."

As they were offering me their comforting words of encouragement, my mind plunged once more into it's archives and swept me back to a time and to memories of a doctor who had, many years before this time, found it necessary to comfort me with those same exact words——. He just happened to be, at the time, fixin' to give me my very first rectal examination with a proctoscope!

I hadn't figgered on that examination because he had, a few days earlier, already done a basic physical exam on me that was required and paid for by the company that I worked for and he hadn't included the proctoscope part of it. I figgered that was routine. I was simply back in his office on this particular day for the results of that earlier examination.

The results of that basic exam were all excellent so I had become totally relaxed in his plush office chair and a little jubilant as he read off the glowing results of the various tests, in being assured that I wasn't about to die anytime soon and especially in knowing that my virginity was still intact having escaped the dreaded proctoscope exam.

I had heard some awful stories about that examination so I laughingly, sort of knee slappingly, remarked to the doctor, when I thought that he had finished his report, that I was sho' 'nuff glad that he hadn't found it necessary to do that damned proctoscope thing.

I could now vividly imagine a picture, although distorted by time, of that doctor's leering, grinning face as, in my mind, he had suddenly sat upright and said, with an hideous crackling voice, "Oooooh yeah, I'm gonna do that now!!"

SHIIITTT FAAARR! I was trapped and I had "done it!" He had appeared to have forgotten about that procedure and I had gone and reminded him of it—-!! Another one of them times when my mouth just opened up and the wrong words came rollin' out!

I had, in reality, almost fainted, having been caught totally off guard! I remembered feeling all of my blood cascading to my feet and realizing that my knees were weak, as he then escorted me into the torture chamber and instructed his nurse to "git me ready" for the ordeal. I was walking bravely under my own steam, but I know now how Marie Antoinette felt as she was being escorted to the guillotine! I couldn't run; it was too late; it was done here!

Now picture this: I was, back then, really up there on that doctor's table on my hands and knees while he was talking to me, holding that gleaming instrument of torture that I was about to be mercilessly impaled with. It looked like a six-foot long spear to me.

He then tested the little light bulb on the end of it and it was working fine. When I saw it flicker I made one last feeble attempt, for my own relief, at injecting some humor into this truly revoltin' situation by saying, "But doc——, I wanted a Miller-lite." The doctor and his nurse were laughing hysterically at that as he walked around to position himself, like a matador for the kill.

His first thrust with that instrument was a dismal failure (we don't need to go into the reason's for that!). So it was as he was about to try again to do that thing of unspeakable horror to me, that the doctor said those renowned words; *REE-LAAXX,* take it easy, it'll be alright."

My exact, and by now desperate reply to him was, "ARE YOU KID-DING ME, DOC? EVEN WHILE YOU'RE TRYIN' TO SHOVE THAT @#*# %*#@* HARPOON IN MY ASS YOU'RE TELLING ME TO REELAXX! HAVE YOU EVER DONE THIS TO ANYBODY WHO WAS TRULY COMFORTABLE and REE-LAXXED, LIKE THEY WAS TIPPY-TOEIN' THRU THE @#*# %*#@**#@* TULIPS, IN THIS PREDICAMENT!?!?!? If you want that @#*# %*#@**#@* thang in there you'll just have to push har-*DERRRRRR!*"

He had already come to that conclusion and had almost pushed me clean off of the table with his very successful second thrust, while I was raisin' hell. I felt like the bull in the bullfight arena as my mind suddenly reverberated with the imaginary roar of thousands of imaginary bull-fight aficionados repeatedly screaming "OLE!!"—— in adoration of their matador.

So, what had started out to be a pretty good day had plummeted all the way down to that; I was hung-up——, like a dog!

It was a mighty tense few moments, but a little more good training in handling all of them sudden, horrendous changes that were waitin' for me on down life's road.

As my now impending imprisonment approached all of these years later, my terror was much the same as my terror had been back then, except that I could now vividly imagine a judge in that doctor's place, as

he appeared in my mind, before me; his helpless trembling victim having been prep'ed and placed upon what was now the table of justice on
my hands and knees like the hunchback of Notre Dame on public display; my eyes agog with fear as I awaited my fate.

In my mind I could picture that judge wringing his hands together
with glee, like an executioner anxiously awaiting the kill, as he was
about to plunge this "proctoscope of justice" thing of equally unspeakable horror up my ass. In my mind I could hear his wicked evil laugh
and see his lips as they spoke those words that my new teachers seemed
to be chanting, in chorus, to me now—-; *"REEEEEEEEE—
LAAAXXXXX, TAKE IT EASY, IT'LL BE ALRIGHT!!"*

So, my early time in recovery was as tense as the proctoscope examination was for awhile, but somewhere along the way I knew that a feeling of freedom from my addiction was coming over me and that it was
happening with seemingly little effort on my part. I had thought that
this recovery thing would be a gargantuan effort and that my chances
would be slim, but it was actually happening!

That brought to mind a true story that I had heard in a small
Kentucky town that I had traveled to fairly often in my engineering hey-
day. It was about a young lad of nineteen or twenty who had fallen in
love with a woman who was in her mid-thirties.

The lady already had three children from a previous marriage and
she, because that marriage had ended in divorce coupled with a few
more wrong choices that she had made involving matters of the heart,
was forced to endure a repute that was considered by the more "Hoity-
Toity" of the community, to be—- hmmm—- shall we just say, something less than pristine.

The young man announced his plans to marry the lady, much to the
chagrin of his father, who was quite aware that this was an exceptionally
fragile matter and immediately undertook a very tactful campaign to
try, in his benevolent way, to gently thwart his son's perilous course.

After having spent several arduous days of trying to convince his son that their age spread was too great for a lasting marriage, that her kids would be a terrific burden on him for many years to come, that he would need much more income to support them and after having delicately spelled out all of the other various good reasons that he dared to use for their not going through with this union, ol' dad began to realize that his efforts had been fruitless. He was forced to consider those questions from that old song that Anne Murray made famous; "Are you not seeing things to clear? Are you just too in love to hear? Is it all going in one ear and out the other?" He had to concede to himself that his son "wadn't studyin' **no sech shit es 'at!**"

However, unbeknownst even to himself, dad's mind's mind, aware that time was running out, had already reached all the way into the arsenal and was poised like a coiled snake, ready to use the one remaining reason that his street mind had gingerly evaded.

So pushing all gentility aside, his mind's mind took the situation in hand and as the last desperate measure, it very rudely, emphatically, unmercifully and irretrievably catapulted out of him the "Crown Prince" of all good reasons for this madness to desist—; "**D-D-D-Damn it son! She's been in a bed with just about every man in this damned County!**"

The son, enchantingly enamored with a love that surpasseth all understanding and steadfast in his decision to take this lady to be his own, cooly replied, "Well daddy, this ol' county ain't really all that big of a place!"

So things started happening for me to let me know that my dilemma just might not be as big of a thing as I had feared after all, and that I was indeed recovering from my addiction.

I started feeling sure that a change of some sort was coming about. I was on my way to a noon AA meeting one day when I realized that I hadn't even thought about alcohol for that entire morning. What a feeling of release that was! I was talking to a friend after a meeting one night when another friend came up to us and simply said, "I believe that ol' Dead Eye is gonna be worth savin'!"

J.D. will never know just how much that simple comment boosted me up and fortified my confidence. So even if things didn't seem to be gittin' a whole lots better right then, at least they weren't gittin' no worse.

So I began to realize that recovery was happening for me. I learned that I wasn't sorry nor was I crazy. I had expressed my fear of each of these possibilities to my new teachers and I was again and again assured by them that I was neither sorry, nor was I crazy. I learned that I was simply an alcoholic and that we, together, could fix that. They also assured me again and again and again that it really wouldn't be all that big of a job.

I was unaccountably changing. I could feel it. However, there was still that little area of doubt in my mind as I went along, as to whether this miracle was genuine or not. In other words, can I now go through life's heavier situations, that I knew were to come, without running back to the drink for comfort and escape? Is there a flaw or weakness in what I feel? Is this newfound thing powerful enough to take me through anything without my having to rely on alcohol? Will the new wear off?

It's sort of like putting a new roof on a house; we can't know for sure if we did a good job until it rains.

The year nineteen hundred and ninety-one would be the year of proof for me.

Chapter VIII

THE YEAR THAT THE RAINS CAME DOWN

I had moved back in with Dad in July of nineteen eighty-five. It was between then and January thirty first, nineteen eighty-six, that I was arrested for the eighth and ninth times for drunk driving and on that January thirty first that I had my last drink. So it was while living with Dad that I began my new sober life.

It was during nineteen ninety and nineteen ninety-one that Dad began his demise. He had already been diagnosed as having prostate cancer.

Our relationship had gradually changed from one of my dependence on him, to one of his dependence on me, but as we moved along, we were developing a strange sort of bond. Not just a father-son bond but also one of dependence on, and sort of friendship with, each other.

Dad was pretty comical in that last year of his life, but then he had always had a sharp wit. I remember a time when he owned a small café and a customer ordered coffee without cream. Dad cheerfully replied, "Sorry sir, I'm all out of cream. You'll have to have it without milk!"

I finally had to take dad's driver's license from him because folks around town were calling him Mr. McGoo. He had come to believe that buildings had been put there to stop his car when he had reached his destination, and that other cars were on the road in front of him to stop him when he was approaching a traffic light that had turned red.

We lived close to a busy intersection where dad knew that accidents happened fairly frequently. One day he asked why I took his license away from him. I told him that it was because he was having too many accidents. He asked how many he had in the last year and I reminded him that he had had a total of six. He replied that there had been that many accidents at the crossroads every week. "Yep," I replied, "that's true; but there are different drivers involved every time!" I think he got the point.

Another time I was driving him home from Donna's restaurant. We were coming out of the parking area and at the street Dad said, "Turn left here!" Then at the first traffic light he said, "Turn left here!" On our journey there was a dead end where we had no choice but to turn right, but he said anyway, "Turn right here!" I was getting a little aggravated by now.

At the next stop sign, he said, "Turn left here!" That took us to the street that we lived on and there he said, "Turn right here!" Now, I was sure that he figgered that I could make it the rest of the way without his help because after all, we lived on a dead end street with only three driveways on our side. Ours was the middle one. I was sure of that, I thought. I slowed down to make the turn into our drive and as I started to make it, he said, "Turn left here!" "SHIT FAR!" I thought.

One of my favorite memories of those comical things was a time when he was filling me in on a little gossip about some of our neighbors. Keep in mind that he didn't remember by now that I had grown up in that neighborhood. Anyhow, we rode by the house of one of the women in our community who in years past had admitted to being gay and had indeed left town with her female lover.

Now, this had happened before being gay was "cool", so this news was the talk of the town for some time. In that age of morality, it had been even more earth-shattering than someone gittin' "saved, sanctified and filled with the Holy Ghost" all at the same time, and dad was telling it to me as if it had happened only yesterday.

Dad wasn't familiar with the meanings of all of the terms that signify one's sexual persuasion these days such as bi-sexual, transvestite, heterosexual, nympho-maniac and the others. Why, he thought that bi-sexual meant to speak two languages; but he had pulled together in his mind what he could and in amazement he cried, "*Looooorrd* help my time, she run off with a *homosexual MANIAC!*" At which I muttered to myself, "Now that would sho' 'nuff be a tense way to live!"

I took Dad many places; we watched alot of television together: ball games, cowboy movies and such. If a movie had a horse in it, he liked it. I'm a train man myself. I took him to Donna's restaurant for most of his meals. Those meals that she didn't provide for him, I prepared for him at home. Toward the end, I had to spoon-feed him. He wasn't able to feed himself. I'll always remember, with much pleasure how, between spoonfuls of food, or after a swallow of milk or tea, he would say, "That's *goooooood!* That's *goooooood!*"

Another thing that I'll always remember about Dad is that, as long as he was physically and mentally able to do it, he would, in the privacy of his bedroom, get down to his knees every night, as his last act of the day and pray. Many times I would peek in to see if he was asleep, yet he would be on his knees by his bed, obviously praying.

When I see him again, I'll tell him how having witnessed his very personal and private relationship with God as he understood him, planted a spiritual seed in me that germinated when I began desperately searching for help.

Donna and Betty lived nearby and they started helping with him when it was obvious that I couldn't carry the whole load. They took on a large chunk of the responsibility, but I lived in the same house with him so it befell me to be with him most of the time and almost all of the nights. It finally became necessary for me to bathe him, shave him and in time, to change his diapers. I had to carry him in my arms to the bathroom and to do the necessary things for him when he needed to go. I used an old Debra Kerr line from an intimate movie scene on him once as I was bathing him from head to toe: "When you speak of this, please be kind!" I enjoyed knowing that he felt good after I had bathed, shaved and fed him.

I remember thinking, before he became helpless, of how I would dread taking care of him like I eventually had to do and of how despicable it seemed that I might have to do those things for anyone! But as this human being, having once been such a robust man who had now lost down to around eighty pounds, became totally dependent, physically and mentally, on me and my sisters, I was amazed at how ready and willing I was to do those things for him. To my surprise, I felt a strange pleasure in being there for him. I found myself changing into the kind of person that I had always wanted to be.

Being free of an alcoholic mind, true feelings and emotions could now surface, and for the first time I became aware of the real power of the family bond; of the intuitive caring for a member of my family. I discovered that I loved my dad and instinctively became ready, willing and even wanted to do those things for him, while expecting nothing in return for it. The family bond had held fast. He was my father and even though he didn't know who I was most of the time, I discovered that I loved him. I wish that I had told him that more often. I was becoming aware of the changes happening within me and I liked them.

Dad had to go into the hospital once again and there a lady told us about a place called Our Lady of Perpetual Health that was operated by some nuns who had chosen, as their service to God and the world, to care for terminal cancer patients. We applied for Dad's admission there when it became obvious that we couldn't give him the care that he needed at home. They called about two weeks after we had applied to advise us that they could take him right away.

The appointed day came and I packed up what they said that we should bring for him. Dad and I then went on our last trip together. It was on a Monday and I knew that it was to be our last ride together. I think that he sensed it too.

He was pretty talkative as we rode along. He was amazed to see all the new skyscrapers in the Atlanta skyline as we approached the city. The nuns received him with open arms when we arrived. I knew that I was leaving him in good and loving hands. It was a lonely journey back home and a very empty house when I got there.

The following Sunday was Father's Day, nineteen hundred and ninety-one. The five of us siblings, Betty, Donna, Sue Ellen, David and I went to visit him. He seemed to know us all. It was a good, special, close day for all of us as we rolled him all around the grounds in his wheel-chair. It was to be our last time together with our father.

The next morning, Monday, one week from when I had taken him there, the call came. Dad had taken his leave of this life during the night. He died very peacefully, they said. The nurse who was with him said that she turned away from him for just a moment and when she turned back, dad had just simply slipped away.

I had heard somewhere, at sometime in my past, that the son doesn't truly become a man until his father dies. I grasped the meaning of that when I learned of his death. I was very glad that he had had some time to be proud of me.

I went through Dad's demise, death, and funeral; and all without using any of it as an excuse to drink. A drink of alcohol hadn't even crossed my mind. I was keenly aware that my alcoholic mind had been unable to use this event to cause me to want to do that.

I was very pleased and somewhat surprised that it had been unable to do that, but I was still not sure of how strong I was in my recovery. This was my first trial run and I thought that after all, Dad was eighty years old. We all have to go sometime. "Will something more powerful cause me to want to drink?", I wondered? "Is my recovery complete? Have I left anything out? Will it stand up to anything now?" More rain was to fall soon.

It was July eighth, nineteen ninety-one. Sue and I had been divorced for about eight years by this time. Our relationship hadn't been good during those years but I still felt a tie to her. After all, we had shared such a huge part of our lives together. We had been devoted to each other in times past. We had produced children together. The marriage, the family bond, was still stronger than even I realized.

Sue had developed cancer about five years after our split up and had deteriorated steadily. Finally she had to be moved to her sister's house to be cared for, back to her hometown, very close to my hometown where I now lived.

She had lived in Albany, Georgia during most of her sickness, the town where we had come to live when we had moved back from Texas. Albany was about two hundred miles from her family and from Tanya, our daughter. I hadn't seen her for a long while and not at all since she had become bedridden because I had been informed that I wasn't welcome to visit her there. I kept up with her condition through Tanya and Alan, my youngest son, who had moved in with me after Sue had been moved to her sister's house.

There had been no hope or desire for reconciliation between her and me. She had been smart and I had been stupid; she had seen how the jigsaw puzzle was coming together and I had been concerned with only one piece of it, my own vanity. However, there was still something there that prevented my acceptance of total severance from her while she was still living. Tanya told me later that she also indicated an inkling of that feeling and that sometimes, during her sickness while she was sleeping, she would call out my name.

I was out doing some business on one particular day. On my way home I was thinking about her and felt an overwhelming urge to visit her. Even though I knew that it might be awkward, I was compelled to go.

I was very tense as I entered the driveway and as I walked to the door of her sister's home. I was glad that her sister's husband, who had always treated me cordially, greeted me at the door. After welcoming me, he pointed the way to Sue's room.

I knew my way around the house, so I very quietly made my way to where she was so that if there were to be a confrontation with anyone, maybe it would be out of Sue's sight and hearing.

Until now I had thought that this was going to be a simple routine visit, sort of a courtesy call out of respect for our past. Little did I suspect what I was about to learn about life. The real maggots under the rock of addiction were about to be exposed.

As I approached her room, I could see Sue's mother and two of her aunts there with her. When they recognized me their faces showed that they were pleased that I had come. Sue's sister wasn't around anywhere that I could see. I later learned that she was in another room catching up on some sleep.

I could only see Sue's hospital bed at first. I then stepped nervously to just inside of the doorway and stopped. I really didn't know what to expect from that point on.

The room was naturally very quiet and still. I could only see the white socks on Sue's feet from where I was standing and then her mother kindly invited me to come closer to her bedside.

I was stunned as the scene unfolded before me, for lying there unconscious was a frail facsimile of the person who at one time had been my healthy, vibrant partner in life. She had been reduced to almost nothing now by her cancer. Then the sound of her labored breathing reached me and then came the stark reality, the one that I had tried to avoid believing; the reality that she was actually going to die crashed down upon me.

Before I knew what was happening, a sob that seemed to come up through the floor and the soles of my shoes, a sob that felt as big as a basketball, welled up through me and spilled out of my throat and my soul. I couldn't stop it. Even if I had had more time, I wouldn't have wanted to stop it. I was experiencing true, genuine emotion, untainted by an alcoholic mind.

"Why," I wondered, "in addition to what I put upon her, did she have to suffer this agony? No living creature should have to go through what she must have suffered to come to this condition!"

Feelings suddenly came pouring out of me with that sob that I had suppressed with alcohol; new relationships, my career and feigned indifference since that day, eight years earlier, when I had arrogantly driven away from that house in Albany, Georgia leaving there the ones that I loved most in this world. I could now see and feel the raw, gaping wound that my alcoholic sickness had left as it ripped our family apart.

I stepped into a nearby hall bathroom to try to regain my composure and after having done that as best I could, I returned to the side of her bed. After a moment or two, even after all of those years, I became aware that I was touching her feet. I didn't care who might see me touch them or even that I, myself, till now, would have considered that gesture a weakness in me. I had changed! I was becoming the real me. I felt all of this. There was no insulation between these feelings and me.

As I looked at her, my anxieties and uneasiness vanished as my mind again reached deeply into it's archives and produced that feeling that had been stored away there for so long and that I had experienced so often in our good years together; in having been close to her, in watching her do her things when she was unaware that I was watching, in touching her, in being as one with her——, all before alcohol had taken it's toll. I suddenly felt comfortable there with her. I felt, during that short time, that I was where I belonged. Not anything or anybody else mattered during those few moments, for I had been granted a wisp of time to be close to her and to touch her once more. I wanted to seize every fleeting second of that time. I couldn't waste any of it.

I became oblivious of anything around me as I looked at her. It was as if the wind had started blowing across the pages of my memory, turning them back one by one in rapid succession. As each page turned in my mind, I could see pictures from our past. I saw the happy and the sad ones as well. I saw how she and I had started out; two young college students falling in love, vibrant, eager to take on the world. The happiness that surrounded our graduations from college, our wedding, the beginnings of our careers, her's as a teacher and mine in Civil Service. How thrilled we were when we learned that she was going to have our first baby, our little girl, Tanya.

We were in love. We worked together to establish a good life for our baby and the two that were to follow. Our second child was a son we named James Jr. Now we had one of each; a boy and a girl! How happy we were! The third one, Alan, was to come along seven years later.

I saw our growth together as a twosome and as a family; our moves, our adventures, the laughter and the painful times. We were sharing an adventure together.

Our family unity was strong, but my alcoholic mentality somewhere, at some time along the way, had already begun to eat away at my love and logic and cause them to begin to give way to my addiction. I also saw how she had tried to help me in the latter years to see what my addiction was doing to us. And I saw that sad day when she realized that her efforts had been fruitless, that my addiction to alcohol was too powerful and that she would have to salvage what she could of her and the children's lives; that alcohol had driven the wedge too deeply between me and them. I also saw the tragic courtroom scenes where we became enemies. I saw her tears.

The pages of my memory continued to turn revealing to me that this human being, who at one time had chosen to love me more than any other in the world; who had known only a little of the good, but all of the bad in me and was about to leave this life having been dealt devastating pain by me, the one in whom she had placed, without reservation, her total trust and commitment.

I knew in that moment, that she had been stripped of all choices other than to believe, until she had taken her last conscious breath, that I was only the bad that she had come to know and that I had inflicted the kind of pain that comes to most who are involved in an alcoholic's life upon her intentionally. In those few moments by her bed, I came to a full realization of the merciless, devastating power of the disease of alcoholic addiction. I realized that even though I had been the addicted one, she had suffered from it even more than I had.

The word commitment kept coming into my mind and I began to realize that I had missed the point in the commitment concept. I had always thought in terms of the importance of my own commitment to another, but now I became aware that even more sacred than my commitment to another is the responsibility that I take on when I accept the commitment of another's trust, friendship, dependence, emotion, love and intimacy to me. I know now that that person will have delivered their most precious possession—-, their innermost self—-, into my care for safekeeping.

I should have been with her through all of this. I, at one time, had made this vow to her. I was suddenly, sensitively aware that I had failed in that vow. It hurt deeply to have that veil that I had used to conceal the reality of it all from myself in my mind, ripped away and thus to become so suddenly aware of the tragic course of events that my addiction had brought to us, especially to her. I had been the afflicted one, but it had all been thrust upon her. There was only one very plain bottom line now; I had handled Sue's commitment to me very carelessly.

I never wanted to or planned to do it, but my alcoholic mind trumped every card that I played. "How," I asked myself, "could I have allowed it to happen? How did it happen to us? No sane person could have planned it or wanted it this way!" My God, how totally awesome the power of an alcoholic mind is!

I recalled that somewhere in some school, we students either did an experiment or saw the results of one where two pieces of metal had been bound together and after a time of some significant length, a cut away section of the two pieces clearly showed that the molecules or particles, or whatever, had begun to flow from each piece into the other and that they were indeed becoming as one piece. They had melded together to a point where total separation was impossible. Yes, they could be ripped apart, but there would be some of each left in the other.

I knew then that our union had started that way. That for years, she and I allowed the initial attraction for each other to grow into a total, loving commitment both physically and mentally. There were no reservations by either of us. We were becoming as one. Then the children were born into the commitment. Their dependence on us made our bond, we thought, totally indestructible. They automatically became part of our melding process. Our characteristics, physical features, personalities are blended together in them. **We are them. They are us.**

I realized that she and I, having been mentally and physically intimate to the fullest in many of our years together and that having shared each others innermost selves, could not help but still possess some of each other. I wanted somehow to tell her that I was sorry; that I didn't want to and didn't mean to do it, that I simply couldn't make things go where I wanted them to go with an alcoholic mind.

I knew that my sob had been a release of my true feeling in realizing that the five of us; Sue, me, Tanya, Jim and Alan; had become closer to, more dependent upon, more loving of, more open with, more enjoying of, more concerned for each other than for any or all of the other creatures on earth. We had committed to each other. Yet, my disease of alcoholism had unmercifully blasted our seemingly indestructible family bond apart.

Again I wondered; what happened? How did it all come to this? This wasn't the way that I planned it. My mind flashed back to when, as a lad, I had watched a controlled explosion from a very safe distance, of course. I remembered my surprise when it took some time, after I had seen the blast, for the thunderous sound waves from it to reach me. I suddenly realized then that even though our devastation had happened many years before now, the waves of pain from it were finally reaching me.

So my feelings for my family became again as I recalled having felt once at a time in our early life together. We had found a puppy for Tanya, our only child then. That puppy became part of our family, but after a year or so it became critically sick and was obviously in much pain. I decided that the humane thing to do would be to put it out of its misery.

I was pretty good with a rifle and one well-placed shot would do it painlessly, I thought. I reluctantly fired that first shot and was suddenly plunged into a sudden and agonizing realization that I had over-estimated my ability.

I had only wounded our pet. Instead of giving it relief, I had heaped incredible pain onto this living creature that I had cared deeply for and I couldn't take it back.

My feelings of guilt, failure, and frustration in having inflicted that grotesque wound by over-estimating my ability to handle it, and in having done it all wrong, were beyond description. My tears blurred my vision as I was then compelled to fire the second and fatal shot.

So, as I stood there by Sue, I wondered how I could have been so wrong for all of those years; so totally blinded and deceived by my alcoholic mind as to what my actions were bringing upon my family until after those punishing deeds had been done to them. I stood there wishing, hopelessly, that I could take them back, that I could erase the pain that I had inflicted upon her and upon my children. The agony of it all was finally where it belonged. It had come home in those moments there with her. The pain was with me now and I would have to bear it for the rest my life——, alone.

I felt a helpless aching to say something or to do something to let her know that I was now very much aware of the devastation that I had brought upon them and in doing or saying that, something to convince her that I didn't mean to, or want to hurt them.

I came to know in those few moments that I, for a long time, had not only deeply wanted, but had also deeply needed to hear her say to me——, "I forgive you——," but because of my innermost fear of facing the reality of being responsible for it all, I had waited too long. It was too late now for me to ask that of her, for I knew that she was dying. I realized in that instant, that she probably would have enjoyed living with the real me, but that alcohol had forced her to live in darkness as to the true nature of the one whom she had chosen in good faith to be her husband.

I became totally aware for the first time, as I stood by her bed that night, of the devastating, lasting effect on each of us when that alcoholic wedge ripped our once powerful melding apart, and left us groping desperately for loving wholeness in a family bond that none of us could ever totally know again.

I wished that I could talk with her. If only we could start over. If only we could do it again. Even if, for whatever other reasons, we couldn't have made our marriage work, at least we could have parted without the hurt. Even though her cancer was inevitable, at least she could have lived out her life knowing that her commitment to me had been handled with care. But it was too late; those things couldn't be fixed now. I alone would have to live with these realities.

I know now that I found myself touching her feet because some of the bond was still there, because I wanted her forgiveness, because I was groping hopelessly for a chance to say, "I'm sorry," and as I felt that chance slowly slipping away, I wanted it all to be just a bad dream that I was about to wake up from. I wanted our time all back to do again and to do right, because deep in that infinite array of acts and feelings encompassed in that phenomenon that we call love, had been stored away the now glaring reality; that I still loved her. I ached to say to her; "It's me——, It's James, your husband——, I'm here——, I'm alright now——, could we start again please——?" But I was too late.

I wanted to at least fulfill part of my marriage vow by sharing part of this suffering with her, but I was painfully aware that alcohol had taken away my right to be with her or her family, the family that had once been my family, through this most intimate experience that a loving family must share, the death of one of it's members.

I had no place there now. All that I could cling to now was in hoping that if she could have known that I was there, she might have found some inkling of comfort in knowing that I had come.

Rather awkwardly, I expressed my sorrow to the others and said my good-byes not fully knowing yet how deeply affected by all of this I had been. As I walked to my car and on my journey homeward, I regretted that part of my life. I remembered with wish that I could live it over and live it differently. I wondered, "Why couldn't she have known me before alcohol or why couldn't we have at least gotten acquainted after alcohol? Why was I only allowed to show her the alcoholic me that really wasn't me at all? She never really had me after all." This realization went deep within me. I had known the real her. She had given me all that she was capable of giving yet she couldn't make it go in the right direction either. My alcoholic mind stopped her.

She had only known the alcohol-tainted me. There would be no more of that "she was at fault too," in an attempt to assuage my guilt. There was only the "gut-wrenching" reality that the tragic, alcoholic devastation had actually happened to us. I was painfully aware now that, by virtue of the fact that I was the addicted one, the responsibility for it all rested squarely upon me. Above all other things, I pray that I will never again be found guilty of being careless with another living creature's commitment made to me.

James E. Gilmer

I will be eternally grateful for that powerful urge that I had to go to her that night, for early the next morning Tanya called to tell me that Sue had died quietly during the night. My personal comfort in having gone to see her on that particular night has been immeasurable.

I had been free from alcohol for about five years by then, but even though it had torn my family and me apart, I discovered that the bond with my children was still there. I was asked by them to help with arrangements for Sue's funeral, so once more I felt that, or at least pretended that, we were all together again. Sue, in death, but she was the focal point. She was there in our minds. I like to believe that she was somewhere, aware of and happy with this final reunion of the five of us.

With my children's permission, I attended her funeral; it was held in the same church that we had been married in those many years earlier. Out of respect for her family, I tried to enter the church unnoticed by them. Afterward I went to the cemetery to watch the graveside service from a distance.

When that service was over and everyone except for the funeral director and his workers (who were to complete the interment) had left the cemetery, I made my way to the graveside. As I approached, I could see the workers loading those folding chairs and going about their task with total indifference toward whomever they might be doing this final service for. After all, it was only a job for them. I was struck with how very inappropriate it seemed that her last vestige of existence on earth should end in such an impersonal way, with only people around her that she hadn't even known in her lifetime. The funeral director, after I had introduced myself to him, kindly instructed them to stop their work for a few minutes to allow me a moment to say my good-byes.

As I approached her coffin, resting on the device that would lower it into its steel vault to be forever sealed away, I suddenly found myself in one of those windows in time when a person seems to be taken out of the normal scenario for an instant and, in that instant, all that we see and touch and hear and smell and feel become so very formidable.

During these times those basic things that we normally take for granted become so very precious; the air, the ground, the blades of grass—-, they all seem to demand recognition of the significance of their roles in God's scheme of things.

We become very much aware that our own existence, even in that instant, is contingent upon another heartbeat; another breath of air that God is allowing us take. These times bring us, all alone, into the presence of our Creator. These times have a way of humbling even the most agnostic of us and of giving us a desire to clean up what we can of our past and to not squander anymore of our allotted time in this life.

Suddenly, as I thought about when Sue and I had fallen in love and all that had been ours; the happy, but sadly also the bad, from then 'till now, I became aware of the tremendous significance of that coffin's role as a merciless sovereign of irreversible, irrevocable closure on our unfinished portrait that might, but for alcohol, had turned out to be such a beautiful portrayal of the way that God meant for His families to be. It was looming there within an arm's reach of me, containing the lifeless remains of the one who had once done me the honor of loving me more than any other and had trusted me with her total commitment and had shared twenty-one years of her life with me as my wife. She was the other half of each of our children, the one whom I had failed.

That coffin seemed to proclaim: "Things could have been different, it shouldn't have ended so asunder, there'll be no mending of it now!"

The last fiber of the flimsy thread of hope that I had un-admittedly clung to, since my alcoholic avalanche had begun, hoping for a retrieval of the good life, as it had started out for her and me was now severed—-. I hadn't included anything like this in my plan.

During that short time I prayed that God would take her aside and explain my alcoholism to her and tell her that I was not, in reality, the person that she had come to know. That I had been sick with a disease and that I truly didn't want or mean to hurt her, or to be the way that she had come to know me in the latter years of our marriage. I then took the liberty of staying there with her until her interment had been completed and she was completely at rest. That's as close as I could come to making amends to her in this life. I'll ask for her forgiveness personally when I see her again.

After the people, the cars, the workers, the tools and the trucks had left, I was there all alone. The cemetery had settled quickly back into its peaceful, serene setting. The only evidence of what had taken place there were the flowers and the funeral home awning that sheltered the grave. The floral arrangements rustled and the awning strained slightly against its tethers and flapped softly in the breeze that seems to always be in a cemetery. It seemed as if they were resting after having finished an arduous task.

As I drove away from there, winding my way through those hundreds of headstones, I felt the magnitude of our loss to my disease and an acute sense of loneliness.

So quickly, again, I had been thrust into the depths of genuine feelings and had come up again with assurance in my recovery. New feelings had been awakened. A new awareness of my love and caring for my children, that I was learning had been there all along but had been suppressed by my alcoholic mind, had emerged from it all. These mixed emotions had surfaced in me, yet I hadn't once considered using any of it, not even my awareness of my betrayal of Sue's commitment to me, as an excuse to drink alcohol; but again I reasoned that Sue and I were, after all, divorced. Would it have been different if we had still been together, still intimately in love? Would I have been compelled by my alcoholic mind to turn to alcohol for comfort? I wondered.

So, life marched on. I was living sober, feeling sober. Things were coming back to normal in every respect. I was becoming the person that I had always wanted to be. Still there were those nagging questions in my mind; Is there something even more powerful out there that will make me drink again? Must I forever be on guard against that craving that mom once described as one that I could never be rid of? Am I still vulnerable to it? Is it lurking somewhere? I yearned for assurance that I was safe from it. That assurance was near.

Tanya, my daughter, was carrying her second child through most of nineteen ninety-one. He would be born in late October. I was happy to finally have a grandson on the way. You know that they can tell now what the baby's sex is before they are born. She called to let me know that she had entered the hospital to have the baby.

Finally the next call came, but it was not a happy call. There were serious problems with the baby's heart and there were other complications, but the doctor had given her hope that they could take corrective surgical action. We found out later that they had been very overly optimistic.

How does one comfort his own child when she has learned that her child might have severe lifetime complications or might not survive for very long? This was the most devastating thing that I had been faced with in recovery, or in fact, ever in my life. There was no logic to this. This was crushing! I couldn't bring myself to just accept this as "God's Will."

Surgery was performed on little Cameron more than once, but things didn't look promising. When I would go to the hospital to see him, he was always connected to the life support systems. I remember seeing the incision that encircled most of his side where corrective heart surgery had been attempted. Why did God allow this, I wondered. I couldn't even hold my only grandson. I could only touch him.

On December nineteenth, nineteen ninety-one, after weeks of wondering what would happen, I joined Tanya and her husband Mike, at the hospital once again. The baby's condition was not good. He was only producing urine now on his own. His other vital functions were being performed for him by machine. It was obvious a choice that everybody, especially a parent, dreads ever being faced with had to be made, so I left Tanya and Mike alone for awhile. This was something that only they should be involved in. When they called for me, they had decided in the child's best interest, to allow him to be taken off of the life support systems. I felt a powerful admiration for them for their strength.

The nurses and doctor left us four alone for a few minutes; Tanya, Mike, Cameron and me. We each held little Cameron for a moment. It was my first time to hold my grandson. I couldn't hold him in my arms because of the tubes and various connections, so I held him in my hands. He was so little. He was making that little sucking movement with his mouth that babies instinctively make. He had that baby powder, baby oil aroma that had always been so pleasant for me with my own babies. I held his tiny face against mine and I could feel his warm breath on my cheek.

I have never before, nor since, faced such stark reality as in knowing that in a matter of moments, his breathing would forever cease, that I would never again feel him close to me. He had been named after me—, Cameron James. I had planned to call him "C.J."

I finally had to hand my little grandson over to Mike, his father, and after a few moments with him, he placed Cameron in my daughter's arms.

She was seated in the rocking chair where she had rocked with him for so many hours every day during the ordeal. As she held him to her breast, the doctors and nurses removed the life giving support systems one by one. I stood there, helplessly, as my grandson's life slipped away as he lay cradled in his mother's arms—. He wasn't with us anymore—. His little mouth was still now.

She laid him back onto his little place there and then she arranged the folds of his gown neatly and brushed his hair into place with her fingers just as if she were putting him down for a nap. Then Mike, Tanya and I left that very solemn place together.

There was nothing more for us to do now. Cameron had totally become God's business. I shall never forget, nor cease to be proud of, the sheer strength that my daughter, my *own* baby, displayed that day.

We wouldn't see Cameron again. He was to be cremated and that little smattering of ashes would be scattered over a playground where he would have played. There was no conversation among us except for our saying good-bye at the elevators. What could any one of us have possibly said? So I again started a lonely journey homeward.

As I drove along Interstate eighty-five, I recalled the events of the days since Cameron's birth and I was hurt and disillusioned with this "God business." I wondered if I had been a fool to begin to let all of my weight down with what I had once considered such a "myth?" Had I again been sucked into some fantasy? Was what those preachers had told me years ago about God forsaking me been true? How could God, after I had begun to trust and rely on Him so heavily, do this to me and mine? This was senseless! There was no old age or cancer or separation involved in this! There was no warning. There was no reason, no logic to it! **WHY? WHY? WHY?** I screamed in my mind.

I took the Suwanee exit off of the Interstate to go the scenic route the rest of the way home, but as soon as I had turned off of the exit ramp onto the main road, I saw the liquor store where I had made so many purchases throughout my drinking years. In my moment of rage towards God, if there was such a thing, I turned into the store parking lot, parked, and went in.

Not much had changed over the years since I had been in there, just the new faces behind the counters and of course, the prices were much higher. The displays and the sounds and the programmed, impersonal greetings were all the same as they had been when I had bought my last bottle there over six years ago. I knew that no one in that place could know, or would have even cared that I was an alcoholic that had been free from alcohol for many years; or of the devastation that had come to me because of it and that I was about to take it all back. I was just another face in the crowd and more money in the till to them.

I selected a quart bottle of Jack Daniels black label and took it to the counter. I remember thinking,"If I'm going to do this, I might as well do it right!"

While I was waiting for the cashier, one of the most valuable lessons that I had learned from my new teachers in recovery eased into my mind. I remembered some of them, who had experienced similar pain, having said to me, "We are not excluded from God's plan now just because we are sober." That thought was interrupted by the cashier's voice asking, "Will that be all?"

I made my purchase and went back to my car with my bottle in its ever so familiar brown paper bag. I got comfortable behind the wheel and then something else that I had heard my teachers say over the years rang out in my head, "When we have done all that we can do in any situation, it then becomes God's business and God can handle His business without our help or our self-pity."

Still seething over God's treatment of me, I angrily crumpled the top of the bag down around the neck of the bottle (as we drinking drivers do), and then I removed the bottle cap so that I could take that first big, comforting, relief-giving swallow.

As I raised the bottle to my mouth, the odor of its contents reached my nostrils. The stench of it must have opened the archives of my mind once more and revealed to me the hell that I was about to plunge back into and for such a trivial reason—-, simply because I felt sorry for myself.

I suddenly became aware that there had been other babies in that intensive care unit and that some of them would also die. That I truly wasn't the only one involved in God's doin's. Then another lesson that I had learned from my teachers became clear to me "that no two thoughts can occupy the same space at the same time in my mind." That thought narrowed down to another very critical thought, and then just as if it were someone else's voice, I heard myself saying the words that I was thinking: "God help me!"

A few seconds that seemed like an eternity passed before I opened the car door a little and lowered the bottle through the opening at the bottom. I then turned it upside down and watched as the fiery, amber-colored, insidiously devastating liquid poured out in dollops onto the asphalt pavement and trickled away in now harmless little rivulets.

It was after Cameron's memorial service that I realized that even through this ordeal, a depth of sorrow such as I had never known, the indescribable feeling of watching as my grandson's life left his body and seeing the agony in my own child; my alcoholic mind could not cause me to take a drink of alcohol. Something had prevented that. I knew then *that I knew* **THAT I KNEW** that I was free! I was sure of it! There has been no more doubt. I knew then that my fortress against a craving for alcohol was not penetrable from without. Only I could penetrate it and it would have to be done from the inside.

MY RECOVERY WAS DONE HERE! Something, not of my own doing, not of this world, had brought it about. I had given Dad, Sue and Cameron all of my emotion, all of my feelings. My alcoholic mind had been powerless to take any part of those events to use as a reason for me to drink alcohol. My new roof was sound. There had been no leaks. It had weathered the storm.

I felt that my mind was now under the control of some Power infinitely greater than it, or me or anything in this world; and if that were true, then surely it——, the God stuff——, also had to be true!

I vaguely recalled some words that I had heard in church many years before that were about to become very clear for me now: "You are embarking on stormy seas. Your voyage will be treacherous, but fear not, for I am at the helm!" I knew that I was indeed safe now. Red Ryder would have been pleased. I, in effect, had took off my six guns and hung 'em up. There was peace in my valley now. I didn't need 'em any more. The word God was becoming comfortable for me now.

A desire began to grow within me to know more about this Power that was at the helm. I didn't feel like I *needed* to know; it was working fine, and even though I couldn't understand it, I was free! I just **WANTED** to know more. I also remembered having read or heard somewhere, maybe it was from my teachers in recovery, that "if we look for Him, God will reveal Himself to us."

Those words became meaningful not to long after those events, at a time when I was way up in the north Georgia Mountains and had some time on my hands between a couple of appointments. I was way back up in "them thar hills" in an area not frequented by tourists. I was on a dirt road alongside a mountain stream. I stopped the car and made my way down to the edge of the water and then clambered over the rocks for a ways upstream close to the foot of a good-sized waterfall.

That place was virtually untouched by humans at that point, and I wondered for how many centuries had this scene been there for anyone who found it to enjoy it. I stood out there on a rock in the middle of that stream for awhile, soaking in the beauty and peace of it all.

I've thought about that place often since then. I've enjoyed it in my mind many times, but I know that to enjoy it to it's fullest, I'll have to go back to it. If I want to enjoy the sounds and the smells and the color and the illimitable designs that the movement of the foliage in the wind and the seemingly endless cascading of the water over and around the rocks make there, I'll have to go back to where it is. I'll have to go back to where I found it.

So it is, I've discovered, with the joy of my recovery from alcoholic addiction. If it is to stay fresh and full and vibrant in me, then I must continue to go back to where it is; to where I was fortunate enough to find it.

My alcoholic mind, using those powerful events: Dad's, Sue's and Cameron's deaths; had tried again to regain control of me. Those things had made me waiver some, but in that time of doubting, I had been forced to mentally revisit my old life. I found myself being able to see, as if it had been illuminated for me, into what had been that dark, deep abyss of addiction that I had blindly groped my way through, stumbling into most of the devastating pitfalls therein, yet escaping by pure chance, those fatal ones by what I could now see as only a hairsbreadth. I didn't like what I saw there. This look back only pushed me closer to the mysterious Power from whence my new life indeed had to have come. I was now ready to try and find God.

My quest was to become a magnificent one.

Chapter IX

IRON WILL FLOAT! IRON WILL FLOAT!

When my three children were little and we would be on one of those family outings, we would always stop for Cokes or Pepsi Colas, or drinks of some kind to enjoy as we rode. Invariably, one or more of the kids would spill a drink in the car. We couldn't know when this spill was going to happen, so the tension was at a high level until it did; and when the inevitable spill finally came, the hollerin' and cryin' would start.

I came up with a brilliant, college-mind-type plan to ease this situation. There were five of us, so when we would stop, I would go in and buy six drinks——, one each for Sue and me and the kids and one to just go ahead and pour out into the car. Then there would be no worry, no tension, no waitin' or hollerin'!! **BRILLIANT** wadn't no name!

So I am now going to go ahead and, figuratively speaking, pour that drink out into the car and put an end to the tension by telling you that this chapter is about GOD!

Now if you are reading this book and you might have had a hard time with the God thing somewhere along the line, please don't be scared off, because rest assured as we go along, that I didn't much believe in a supernatural divine architect of the universe God thing, either. In fact, I looked at the God thing like I looked at the craving for alcohol thing, out of the corner of my eye instead of straight on. Like them Dominican Republic drivers, I didn't want to give God the right of way, either. I was like a kid who once wrote a letter to God asking, "What happens to people who don't believe in You?" The kid then quickly added, " P.S.- I'm writing this letter for a friend!" But I, like most of us, was always quick to call on God when the chips were down.

My purpose in this book is most assuredly, NOT to try and convince you of anything having to do with divine power or spirituality, nor do I mean to imply that only recovering alcoholics and drug addicts can make a God connection or anything of that nature. I am simply telling you how my recovery from addiction happened for me; of my own way out of my dilemma. Like the good fishin' hole, I'm telling you where I found it! I'm catchin' lots of big fish in it these days. You can fish in there too if you want!

I have discovered that a religious person will try to convince us that God exists and then tell us what we must do to find Him. The atheist will attempt to prove to us that there is no God and that's why we can't find Him. The agnostic will try to convince us that we aren't capable of knowing if there is a God; but most folks that I know who have been snatched back from the brink of disaster that alcohol or drug addiction brings us to, will simply tell of their experience with the spiritual and then allow us to take it or leave it. That's what my new teachers did.

Some of my teachers are even atheists (*LORD HELP MY TIME!!*), who have recovered from their alcoholic dilemma, so it works for anybody. I personally believe now that God sees what we do and not necessarily what we think we believe, yet strangely enough, when I have asked those atheists if they really are atheists, they usually reply; "I swear to God I am!" I had a friend tell me once that his atheist's group was having a picnic so I told him that I would pray that it didn't rain! He replied, "Thank God for a friend that ain't no atheist!"

So, like that kid who wrote to God, I believed because I was afraid not to believe. I had given up any hope of ever finding God, if there was such an entity; but two things happened in my life that I can't just write off without an attempt to understand.

First, I became an alcoholic; a sorry drunk and a substandard human being that did, said, and thought things that were incomprehensible even to me; and yet while I was doing, saying, and thinking those things, I didn't want or mean to do, say or think them.

It's not pleasant having to remember that part of my life with wish that I could relive it and live it differently. I certainly would not have just chosen to be that way. So I was very much surprised when I came to know, beyond any doubt, that I had become that kind of person—-,"an alcoholic!" "Where did I go wrong," I constantly asked myself. I couldn't explain how it had happened, but the word alcoholic, a word virtually impossible to define (in fact I couldn't even *spell* it before I became one), seemed to encompass it all.

So, I hadn't had any trouble accepting the word "alcoholic" as being descriptive of a way of life that I had unknowingly been driven by for many years. I was even about to make a human sacrifice to that "higher power"—-, alcohol. I was giving my own life for it and I had always scoffed at those people that I had read about or heard about who make human sacrifices to their gods, and now here I was a-doin' it myself! *LORD HAVE MERCY!*

Secondly, I was miraculously healed of my merciless craving for alcohol. I am now sober, free from alcohol, without a craving for it. I don't even wish that I could drink it. I am living a good, happy life that I had come to believe could never happen for me again. I am just as surprised that I have come to this! Now I ask myself, "Where did I go right?"

I am living sober. Even though I can't define the word "sober", nor can I explain how it happened for me other than through a Power greater than me; a Power not of this world——, a spiritual thing; the word "sober" is descriptive of my new life.

So, this higher power deal works both ways. The proof, for me, is in the fact that I asked something (all that I knew to call upon was God), to allow me to stop drinking alcohol on that January thirty-first day, and I haven't had a drink or wanted one since.

Now, I don't know of all of the psychological workings of the mind mumbo-jumbo that might have been involved, if any, and I don't care. I'm sort of like the blind man in the Bible that Jesus healed. When he was asked later by those who had wanted to nail Jesus to the cross how Jesus had done it, the man said, in effect, "Man, I don't know and I don't care! All I know is that I was blind and now I can see!" Likewise, I know that I was a chronic, seemingly hopeless drunk, fearing death soon; but now I am a healthy, useful, sober, happy camper. I don't need any other explanation!

Still, I had to get into this God stuff. I had to be reprogrammed. I must have begun to know by then, that there was truly something to it.

When I think of being programmed, I think of the time when my son, Jim, was about five or six and the family was on a little Sunday trip. I was in one of my Christian periods then. There were Sue and me, Jim, Tanya and Alan, and our choir director's little girl in the car. I just happened to be a little slow getting started when the stoplight had turned green and the driver behind us honked his horn. The kids must have had me on edge by then because I instantly whirled around and shot that driver the mighty middle finger!

Well, after the commotion had died down and the choir director's daughter recovered from her shock, we were cruising along the open road when I spotted a car in front of us that looked like the one that I had cast the middle "digit" spell upon. I remarked to Sue that it looked like the car that had honked at us earlier. Little Jim, in the back seat, heard my comment to Sue and as I proceeded to pass the car he loudly announced, "Everybody get your fingers ready!" He had been programmed.

Another humorous occasion involving his wit was a year or so later as the family was leaving on another day outing. As we left the driveway, little Jim stuck his head out the car window and hollered loudly to the entire neighborhood: "WE'RE LEAVING GLAD, BUT WE'LL BE BACK MAD!" Programmed.

So for all of my life, I had been programmed that God, if God even existed, had to be approached formally. Like those three phases: "gittin' saved, sanctified and filled with the Holy Ghost"; that God had to be talked to in proper religious language like: "O God in Heaven, Your humble servant beseeches thee to accept me into thy Bosom!" Or "Brethren" or "Sisteren" this or that, or "that thou wouldst, or thou wouldnst." Those times that I prayed back then weren't very meaningful for me because I didn't think that I could speak the language, so I just didn't bother to pray much. I reckon that I am still programmed because I expected a lightning bolt to strike me dead even as I wrote those last few lines!

So, here I was on the horns of a dilemma. The word God was very distasteful for me. That word had been crammed down my throat all of my life. I had always been instructed to accept God and don't ask questions or you'll die and go to hell! There was never any "Here's why you should believe," there was only "God will do for you whatever you need if you believe," so there!, and if He don't do it, it's because you are a sorry sinner and don't deserve it!

It was like a guy telling me once that if I followed his instructions, I would be a millionaire in ten weeks. Of course, I eagerly said, "*TELL ME HOW!*" He replied, "All that you have to do is save one hundred thousand a week for ten weeks and you'll have it!" Of course, I asked, "Where do I get the hundred thousand each week?" He replied, "*You'll* have to work out *them* details!" So, of course, in my mind, I would ask, "How do

I find God?" My only answer was, "Just do it! Don't ask questions, you'll be struck dead! Just believe!"

My dilemma was that something miraculous had happened for me; more miraculous than anything I'd ever known. I didn't need or even crave alcohol any longer! I was free from it! It was real! I had stopped drinking alcohol and it had happened suddenly! I, in that milli-billionth of a second, on that January thirty-first night eleven years ago, changed once more. I swallowed that last mouthful of alcohol and I haven't had a drink of it since and I, at that time, was thoroughly convinced that I would never be able to stop drinking it. At last, life's sudden changes for me had begun to be for the better.

What changed me from a drunk to a tee-total non-drinker? I wasn't capable of understanding that with what data my mind possessed. I couldn't just whole-heartedly begin to praise God for that. I couldn't just "commence" believing. I wasn't mentally capable of doing that, but I couldn't deny that something miraculous had indeed happened.

As I wandered along trying to figger it all out, I stumbled across the words, "psychic change." Well now, that was it! Now, I was comfortable. I had solved the mystery. Yes, sir-ree, I could handle that! If someone asked me how I had quit drinking, I would simply say, "Psychic change, man!" Then another part of my dilemma popped up: "What the hell is a psychic change?" I can't explain that either! "Damn! I shore do wish that whoever or whatever came up with all of this stuff would have made it a little more simple!"

It finally occurred to me that I would never understand nor be able to explain what had happened for me. It would always be a mystery. No matter how I tried to solve the mystery, I would always come to a point where I had to say, "I don't know!" Yet, I knew that I needed, more like *wanted*, a word or a name that, when presented, would cause my mind to embrace this new phenomenon that I couldn't understand. I thought of other words that, when spoken, read or heard, bring to mind something vast and indefinable such as

"ALCOHOLIC", or *"SOBER"*; yet there is a childlike acceptance of the vast phenomena that they represent.

The word "SPACE" came to mind: a word that I can't define, yet when I speak, hear, or read the word, my mind encompasses all of the universe that I can see: the sun, the moon, and the stars; and I can even believe that the part of it that I can't see is really there and that the solar system, gravity, the fact that there are fifty billion galaxies out there and that the most far out galaxies are fifteen billion light years away is all true! And *now* they've figgered out that there are even more universes out there that are bigger than ours—-!!!!

Every bit of that staggering information is encompassed in the word "SPACE". It is something that surpasses our understanding, yet we had to pull it all together in our minds as best we could and call it something. Why not call it "SPACE"? Thus, we readily accept what the word space implies without reservation. I've never heard anyone say that space, even beyond what we can see, is not really there.

Then, the word "LOVE" came to mind as another one that represents something so vast that it can't be defined. A word that has frequently befuddled me. There have been many times when I've said to someone, or someone has said to me, "I love you," and I've heard others say to someone, or even to a group of people, "I love you," but somehow, most of those times the words seemed to have an empty ring to them, because down deep within, I intuitively knew that the word "LOVE" encompasses so much more than just the saying of it could ever define.

I've discovered that when I say to Nancy, "I love you!", I am saying an infinite number of things to her. The word encompasses feelings ranging from simply: "I enjoy being close to you", to "I think that you are beautiful", to "I would give my very life to save yours." The range of feelings and acts represented by the word "love" is infinite and cannot be defined; yet we know that it is very real, because we have felt it.

So I have learned that one can love in ways that range from being genuinely concerned for the well-being of another to, as most of us I'm sure have discovered at some point in our lives, being intuitively willing to make any sacrifice including giving up our very life (if that were to become necessary) for someone that we can truly say that we love. The word can only be defined by what we do, not only by what we say.

Yes, man also had to call this phenomenon something, why not love? I have never tried to reason that there is no such thing as the feelings that are implied in the word love, when spoken sincerely. So, love is also something that surpasses our understanding, yet we instinctively know that it is real.

So, in my mind, I knew that something vast and miraculous had happened for me that I couldn't define or even understand. Yes, a mental or psychic change had happened, but that wasn't all. I knew that just my mental change couldn't have had anything to do with the existence of all of the physical things of wonder that surrounded me. I began to know that my mental miracle was only the tip of the iceberg, that this thing went far beyond my mentality; that this mysterious thing was all-inclusive. It was even more vast than space and love combined. It even included space and love and all of those other unexplainable things that we humans just accept at face value.

Then, if there are words such as "alcoholic," "sober," "space," "love," and others like "electricity," "nuclear," "jet stream," "lightning," "eternity" and others that represent these indefinable phenomena that we all just simply accept as part of our way of life without really understanding them, then there must be a word that when used will cause my mind to attempt to encompass and accept this vast phenomenon that includes not only the wonders of the world, but also the power to stop an addiction abruptly and enable a person in the throes of alcoholic insanity to come back to normal.

So somewhere along the way I had begun to realize that it already had a name, that for thousands of years man has called it "GOD." I knew then that I would also come to comfortably call it "GOD". Nothing else could fit for me, but the best part of it all was that I began to feel a desire to call it God. I started being able say "God" without having a funny feeling. The word God started coming easy for me. Now there was logic to it and I had been given proof, through my own experiences, of the existence of this mysterious entity.

Man also had to attempt, as best he could, to pull this phenomenon together in his mind and call it something. Why not call it God? Why, I wondered, had I, a mere speck in all of creation, in spite of overwhelming proof of this spiritual phenomena, denied it; even scoffed at it on occasion?

I began to be able to look at the God phenomenon straight on. I began to realize that I was beginning to give God the right-of-way, that I was at last getting a little inkling of what the word God implied. I was slowly coming back to normal.

"Why," I wondered, had it taken me so long? In the face of overwhelming evidence, how could I have missed it? "How," I asked myself, could I have lived this long without at least an intuitive acceptance of the God phenomenon, when I had readily accepted so many other unexplainable things; space, love, electricity and so many, many others? Why not God?

Wouldn't life have been miserable without electricity in it? What if I hadn't have known about it and how easily accessible it is and then one day I accidentally turned on a switch and discovered just how wonderful it really is; how easy and comfortable things are with it, how it can truly light up one's life! I believe that I would be madder 'n hell that I had lived without it for so long!

So it is with God. I see now just how dark and miserable life had been until I was forced to turn on the spiritual switch and now I wonder, "How could I have been so totally convinced that God wasn't necessary in my life?" And I ask myself, "How could I have lived so long without Him?"

So, I had gotten programmed early in life, but as I started into recovery I began to realize that I had already been accepted by God (hmmm, very comfortable, now!) just as I was. I had been wrong in my assumptions. I now began to realize that I could talk to God just like I talk to anybody, in plain English. I can even question God's acts! I had been programmed to believe that to do that surely meant "gittin' struck down dead on the spot!" "Why", I wondered, "couldn't they have told me the good stuff sooner?"

I have also discovered that I can bargain with God, because on that famous January night, I said to Him, "If You will let me stop drinking, I will do whatever You ask me to do, if You will only let me know somehow what it is that You want." Well, I've been alcohol free for many years and I never dreamed of writing a book about it, but here I am doing it and telling you about what God has done for me. This must be what God wants me to do. If you are reading these words, then it must be true. Therefore, I'm holding up my end of the deal.

I have been reprogrammed to know that I can be comfortable in my relationship with God without the formality. I've discovered that believing in God is easy. In fact, I believe now that from us alcoholics, God will take whatever He can get! In fact, I think that we are sort of His hobby! We entertain God, I think, trying to figger it all out and even if God is not the right name for that power, I don't believe that I'll be punished for using that name. So for me, it's God, or in some cases, simply Him.

Now I was still having trouble with some of them miracles in the Bible until I heard an Alcoholics Anonymous speaker, another teacher of mine, once say, "If you don't believe in God right now, but you really want to learn to believe in Him, for goodness sake, don't start by studying about the Virgin Birth!"

This was advanced theology at it's finest! I'll bet the Pope hadn't even thought about that approach and here I was gittin' it from an ex-drunk!

I remembered that lesson! Man-o-man, that was a hard miracle to swallow! I've tried to put myself in ol' Joseph's place and I'm afraid that if I had been him, Mary might have gone to Bethlehem by herself! I'm glad it worked out like it did! God chose the right man for that job! Anyhow, I told God as I began to pray in recovery, "I know that You know that I don't believe much in You and all of them miracles and things, so if You will, please (to start with), help me to believe." That prayer was answered on Easter Sunday morning, nineteen hundred and eighty-six.

I had been without a drink for about three months and had started going to an Alcoholics Anonymous meeting on Sunday mornings at the Federal Penitentiary in Atlanta with my sponsor, Bobby Lee. Talk about a tense way to recover! He was hauling me around then, so I was waiting at that busy intersection close to my house for him to pick me up.

As I waited, I began to notice the people going by, all dressed up, either coming back from Easter Sunrise services or going to the early morning Easter services, and I became aware that today was the day that we Christians, in the general sense of the word, observed the resurrection, which also, at that moment seemed a little hard to believe.

I was again conscious of an uneasy feeling that came from my having that inkling of doubt that I had about the resurrection and the Virgin Birth and the Creation and Daniel in the lion's den and Moses' magic walking stick, the crucifixion, the water to wine, Lazarus rising up from the dead and all them other miracles. I had forced myself to believe them (it was another one of them "am I gonna believe it, or am I gonna git struck dead" situations), but I couldn't ignore that little feeling that those things must seem pretty "far out", for other people, of course!

Then they threw in that Shadrach, Mesach and Abed-nego in the fiery furnace business, and that blew it all! I thought, "Who in their right mind is going to believe 'sech shit as 'at, just because somebody tells them that it's true?"

Suddenly I heard myself saying, "Those things don't matter right now!" I suddenly realized, with great impact, that I had, three months ago, asked God (the only name that I knew to call upon), to take away my obsession to drink alcohol and since that time, I hadn't had a drink of it. I had, myself, experienced a miracle!

My doubts about the existence of a God-like power had to be eradicated in that instant, that morning, because I couldn't deny that a miracle had happened for me. In spite of my doubts about God, the greatest miracle in the world, barring none, had happened for me!

I had read about and heard about and knew, first hand, of miraculous healings that had happened for other people whom I considered to be special in God's sight and I had wished for an experience such as that and now one had actually happened for me. I didn't drink alcohol anymore! My obsession for it, that had been the most dominating force in my world, had been snuffed out. I didn't even want to drink it anymore! I wasn't just wishing sober. I was living sober!

How could I deny that I, who had come to consider myself less than an infinitesimal speck in God's infinite galaxy, if I was in it a'tall, had been healed, and that I, too, was special to Him.

I thought of a fellow that had worked at the same lumber company that I had worked at once. He was a little on the ignorant side, like me. The proper pronunciation for our mental condition is "ignert." Probably Latin, meaning; to not have one's mental plow deep enough in the dirt.

Anyhow ol' Joe had never had the opportunities that I had "lucked" into. He had actually never even been very far away from home, so he had some stuff programmed into his computer that no words could ever change. For instance, Joe would swear with his dying breath that iron would not float. He had never seen it float. He had seen iron things sink, but he had never seen anything made out of iron float; iron bolts, iron nuts, iron plowshares, iron rods, horseshoes and so on. He had even used iron nuts and bolts for fishing sinkers. So, in Joe's computer, the data was that **IRON WILL NOT FLOAT!** No way! No how!

Well now, there was an order for a load of special treated lumber that had to be hauled all the way to Jacksonville, Florida one day and ol' Joe was afforded the treat of going along with Luther, the driver, to deliver it.

When they got back home, Luther told that as he and Joe were coming into Jacksonville, ol' Joe saw some Navy ships for the first time in his life and as they got closer to them, he exclaimed wide-eyed and with sheer and utter amazement, *"GOD-A-MIGHTY LUTHER—-! THEM BOATS ARE MADE OUTTA 'ORN—-, AND THEY'RE A-FLOATIN'!"*

In that instant, Joe had to believe. There was no room for doubt. He was forced to know that iron will float! The proof was in the experience—-, a- seein' them 'orn boats *A-DOIN' IT!*

Just as surely, my perception of a power greater than me, that I do call God now, had to change. The proof was there, There was no room for doubt. I was free from alcohol. I was seein' that Power a-doin' it. That Power had taken away my obsession for it. Why shouldn't I call that Power God? Why not? Yeah, why not? A wave of relief flooded through me when I realized that I was thinking, "It's true, it's true! The God stuff is really true!!" Finally I knew that *I KNEW* that God does exist and had already accepted me as I was and as I had been all along!

All of the doubt that had gone into my computer about God and spirituality had been displaced by one unimpeachable fact: I had asked as honestly as I could for freedom from alcohol and it had been given to me! I was free from it! The experience was proof enough. All of them other miracles were to fall into place in time. They were to become part of the God phenomenon just as surely as the galaxies are part of "space." That Easter morning experience was like getting the first olive out of the jar. After that first one, the rest come out easy!

I knew now that there were other times when God had tried to help me get that first one out. Once was in a church service. My sister, Betty, must have begun to sense that I was losing my grip on my sanity and she must have known that I was needing, and probably willing, to explore the possibility of spiritual help because one Sunday when I was home visiting, from wherever I was living at the time, I had gone to church with Dad. Sometime during the service, just out of the blue, she handed me a note with "Job 23: 8-10" written on it. I waited until I got back to the house before I found a Bible and looked it up. I was affected in a *"mighty peculiar way"* when I read:

> *"Behold, I go forward, but He is not there;*
> *and backward, but I cannot perceive Him;*
> *on the left hand where He doth work, but*
> *I cannot behold Him; He hideth Himself*
> *on the right hand, that I cannot see Him;*
> *but He knoweth the way that I take; When*
> *He hath tried me, I shall come forth as gold."*

Of course, it's out of context, but who cares? I'm sure that it gave me a spark of hope. Even though I didn't recognize it then, those words and the fact that she gave them to me just "out of the blue", made a massive impact on me. They stuck with me. I believe that this was the first major "ass kicking" that my alcoholic mind had ever taken. The dye in the pipeline faded a little that day.

There was another similar event at the same church, which was in fact the very same Pentecostal church that I had gotten saved in so many times, only now it was modern. The requirements for getting to heaven had been streamlined somewhat, but they still got into some of the *REAL* spiritual stuff, one of them being speaking in "unknown tongues". Sometimes when someone would speak in the unknown tongue, someone else would interpret that spiritual language.

I happened to be there one Sunday, visiting again shortly after the divorce. That day, the service was very intense and I was concerned about my destiny. I was bewildered, to say the least. After awhile, a silence fell over the congregation and after a few short moments, some-one began to speak in an "unknown tongue." All that could be heard was that person's voice. This is one phenomenon that happens in that church that I have a deep belief in and respect for. There is no way to fake it.

When that person had finished, there was another moment of total silence (even the babies don't cry during these times) before another person, somewhere else in the congregation, began the interpretation that was to later play such a major part in my recovery:

"You are embarking on stormy seas.
Your voyage will be treacherous,
but fear not, for I am at the helm."

That message was for me and it went deep. It was yet another event that affected me in a *"peculiar way"*, and I know it played a great part in my choice that January thirty-first night to ask for spiritual help.

As powerful as these experiences were, I just wasn't ready at these times. I hadn't gotten desperate enough yet to be forced to seek recovery through the spiritual and I certainly had no idea that I even came close to qualifying for a relationship with a power greater than myself, that I only knew of as God. I thought that I had blown that. At least that's what them preachers had told me was gonna happen to me years before this time.

Now, if this book has reached you and you are saying to yourself, "prove that these things were meaningful!", well then, here goes: I was once a chronic, hopeless drunk and wanted to die. Today, I am sober and happy and I want to live forever!

There is also a practical reason for using the word "God" for those of us who just can't say the word comfortably—-; I couldn't! Now, I don't have any idea who came up with the letters G-O-D standing for **"GOOD, ORDERLY DIRECTION."** I have heard this stated many times by others in recovery and I passed it off as just being another brain explosion of some genius, like those who came up with **S-L-I-P**: Sobriety Lost It's Priority; or **H-A-L-T**: "Don't get too Hungry, Angry, Lonely or Tired; or **K-I-S-S**: Keep It Simple Stupid! So, along with these and many others, I flushed "Good Orderly Direction" down the ol' mental toilet—-, too tacky for ol' Dead Eye!

Then one day in an Alcoholics Anonymous meeting, a lady was relating to us some experiences and feelings that she had encountered on a recent vacation trip; how she had experienced a very enjoyable, in fact, a super time, because she had learned from her teachers in recovery how to refrain from assuming the responsibility for keeping everything orderly, even to the extreme of missing out on the fishing and exploring and other activities so that she could keep the camp site clean and have everything in "order". She really had been convinced that she was totally responsible for these things. In reality, she was being a pain in the ass by keeping everything "just so" back at the ol' campsite!

But this trip was different. Her mind, for some reason, had changed; this time she wanted to join in on the fun and having done so, she had a wonderful time! She said that on one particular day, all of the family members living in the area were to gather at their campsite on the beach. The night before however, she found herself steeped in fear of the situation.

She told of how she managed to get away from her husband, the kids and dogs for a short time the night before, and she simply asked her higher power, without a lot of fanfare, to help her cope with the situation that was coming. She went on to relate how she immediately began to feel a little more comfortable about it and that when the occasion actually materialized, she realized how completely comfortable she was with the crowd and what a good time she was having! It dawned on me that this lady was painting a very clear picture to me and to the others of how, if we ask for Good Orderly Direction, it will come!

Now, I realize that this all sounds like the ol' "ask and ye shall receive" stuff that we have heard so much about in church and have said to ourselves so many times that it works for others, but it won't work for me; but the difference now is that I know this person and she is no more of a spiritual giant than I am. Her God connection was like mine. She is an ex-drunk like I am and she had told of two miracles there that day that she did not, and could not, have pulled off by herself. The belief that she had to be the one to keep everything orderly at the expense of her own and everybody else's pleasure and the fear of people that she had always possessed, had both been taken away, at least for that time.

These two old ideas and emotions that had governed her until now had been replaced by new ones without her even knowing that they had: GOD——, **GOOD ORDERLY DIRECTION.**

It seemed that my own mind was opening up as I listened to her experience and began to look back at the God that I had received without even knowing what was happening.

Those of us in recovery often express amazement at our reactions to situations; to our right decisions and our successes in sobriety. How many times have we been told to ask and believe and good things will happen, yet we couldn't figger out how to ask and believe. In fact, we were trying so hard to figger out how to ask and believe that we didn't have time to realize that the act of trying to figger out how to do it was, in fact, doing it! How often have we been told that if we have a hard time getting on our knees to pray, to throw our shoes far enough under the bed to force us to our knees to retrieve them. It took me a long time to realize that the act of throwing them under the bed was, in fact, an act of believing.

I recently was in a conversation with my brother and sisters about how we, as children, would call on Lena, one of the saints of the church and a dear friend of our mother's, to pray for our needs. Lena was a real saint of a woman, and back then we were convinced that only the most devout could communicate with God. We were talking about our lack of faith by going to her, instead of praying to God ourselves.

Suddenly, it dawned on me that, in our ignorance, going to Lena was as much of a demonstration of faith as anything that we could have done ourselves because we had faith that her faith was in something real.

Maybe some learned religious leaders are convinced that they are required to say flowery prayers and do noticeable things to get God's attention, but I am now convinced that us alcoholics, drug addicts and other forms of the dregs of humanity, can make any effort at all to reach God and He is tickled pink! In other words, from us, God will take any effort that we can muster up enough courage to offer Him.

So now us skeptics have a good, logical reason for calling our spiritual power "God", without feeling foolish. It can simply mean—-; "Good Orderly Direction." I realize now that even when I was just looking for an excuse to use the word "God" in my life, that God knew that I was looking for Him all along.

> *"As the hart panteth after the waterbrooks,*
> *so panteth my soul after thee, O God."*

So that night on my knees without even knowing it, I met what I now, without any reservations, call God. I believe that I, personally, had to do it alone, because alone there weren't any other humans around for me to try to impress.

I didn't need to prove that I had "prayed through" to the saints of the church or to anyone else. I was there for one reason and one reason only; because I desperately wanted to live and to be rid of the misery in my life. In fact, I think that it might have been easier to get down on my knees in front of someone else than it was to do it alone, because I could fool them; but I couldn't fool myself and even *I* knew that I couldn't fool God. I had to make an acknowledgment to myself as to why I was down there.

The hardest thing that I have ever done was to get down on my knees alone, in front of just me; but in doing that, it seems that my alcoholic mind was de-activated, totally pushed aside, totally neutralized and put into a cage. And then a new dimension came into being—-, my mind's new mind, that today I call "God within me."

Now the way that I see God within me working is that just as surely as my alcoholic mind would cause me to do and say things that I couldn't understand (all sorry stuff), my new mind does the same thing; but now it's usually good stuff. For instance, in traffic when I get a finger flipped at me, I can smile and wave back. I sho' 'nuff don't understand how I can do that, but I know that it makes 'em madder than gittin' a finger back! Wavin' and smiling back at someone who is risking their life to give you the finger, is like stoppin' your car when a dog is chasing it. That dog can't figger' out what the hell to do then!

I'll have to admit though that I feel a little proud about getting a finger. I like to know that I'm important enough to cause another person to get upset enough to go through the mental turmoil and the physical effort of flipping me one! I feel real special to be able to control them to that extent!

In fact, I've got two bumper stickers on my truck. One of 'em says: **"GIVE ME THE FINGER SO I'LL KNOW THAT I'M A GOOD DRIVER."** The other one says: "RE-ELECT CARTER / MONDALE."

Since I had my last drink of alcohol, I have found myself simply doing the next right thing, which has led to a series of more right than wrong things and thus, a good, happy life that I can remember with pleasure instead of regret. I might find myself being honest, when being dishonest would be more profitable. I don't understand that and when the transaction is over, I might ask myself why I had done or said that. In fact, I won't even lie now unless there just ain't no other way out of a situation! At least, I put off lying until the very last resort! I don't understand that, either! The fact is that I have changed. God within is calling the shots. **"Good Orderly Direction"**!

Another aspect of God within was revealed to me through an ex-drunk teacher when he said; "Just as surely as no two physical objects can occupy the same space at the same time, no two thoughts can occupy the mind at the same time." I had to experiment with this one, but soon discovered that he was right. Now this man is not a Buddhist monk, priest, minister, or anything like that. He was just an ex-drunk who had recovered from his situation and was simply passing it on to others in an Alcoholics Anonymous meeting room.

I learned that there ain't no way for me to think of the sweetness of sugar and the bitter taste of lemon at the same time. It can't be done. Nor can I think of being on a Caribbean cruise, while I'm fixin' to get hit by a car! I can't think of eating steak if I'm thinking of eating chicken.

So I can't think of hurting someone if I'm thinking of helping 'em. I can't think of taking a drink if I'm thinking of how wonderful it is being free from alcohol. I have learned that when that ol' sleazy alcoholic mind rattles it's cage and slips the thought of a cold, frosty beer or a sip of Jack Daniel's on the rocks or some of that new "Ice House Beer" or one of them wine coolers into my head, all I have to do is say; "God, take this thought away from me!" The split second that I even begin to form that little prayer in my mind, God within removes the other thoughts!

It's true I can't be craving something if I ain't thinking about it. So for me a craving is a thought and I don't have to tolerate it just as I don't have to tolerate any other thought that I don't want to keep. If I keep a thought, it's because I want to keep it. There can be no other reason to keep it. I possess the simple ability to say "GOD", thus invoking good orderly direction, and things change! Man, what an asset! Sorry!!— I got philosophical again!

When I look at the overall God picture, I have to also believe that God exists outside of me; so for me, God is within and without. You see my mind could never, by any stretch of the imagination, control things that already are or events that happen that are beyond my mental or physical control.

God within gives me an inner appreciation for the beauty of a mountain, or an ocean, or a song, or for the people around me; but God without had to have put them all there to begin with.

I would be quite comfortable with the theory that man evolved from an ooze of some kind that washed up onto the ocean's shore some multi-trillions of eons ago if the evolutionists could answer one question to my satisfaction: What put the ocean there and the ooze in it to begin with?

So the God data in my computer has been changed; "**IRON WILL FLOAT! IRON WILL FLOAT!** I can now believe that all things are God-created; now there is no need to doubt! I can now believe that the virgin birth, the crucifixion, the resurrection, Daniel in the lion's den, Lazarus, wine to water, healing of the blind man, walking on water, healing of the lepers, even ol' Shadrach, Meshach and Abed-nego in the fiery furnace, all happened! All of those things happened! I can believe now that they did! Just as surely, I can believe that God put the mountains, the oceans, the rivers, the trees, flowers, little puppies and fluffy little kittens and all of those things here for us.

Why can I believe them now? Because on that January night, I asked something called God to take away my craving for alcohol and allow me to live without drinking it and I haven't had a drink of it since! This was the greatest miracle of all times and if God could do this, all of them other things would be a piece of cake for Him!

So when I hear, speak, or see the word God now, all of those things are included in it. I am nowhere nearly as mystified by them miracles now as I am by the facts that I don't drink alcohol, I don't crave it, I don't miss it, I don't want it and I don't even wish that I could drink it!

So, in spite of my efforts to complicate the recovery process in order to make it appear that I was really struggling for it and forcing it to happen, the miracle was happening for me in a different way; in a way that I had no control over a'tall! I think that I was a little disappointed to find that my efforts didn't seem to be what was doin' it. I must have felt the same way about it as the young lad felt who was telling his friends about having gone huntin' with his dad. The lad said, "We killed a bear!!—-Well—-, daddy shot it." So, something greater than me was handlin' this situation!

Chapter X

HOLD ON 'TIL SUNDAY HONEY! THE DUMPLIN'S ARE COMIN'!

If I ever do begin to doubt God's existence, I just look back on some of the miracles that have physically happened for me in recovery that I couldn't have possibly had any influence over.

In looking back I recall a time, not too long after the divorce and during a long period of unemployment, when I was visiting my daughter, Tanya while she was in college. She had made some very nice friends there and one of them, Stephen, who has been one of my favorite people since then, had dropped in on us. As we talked, the discussion came around to our own economic problems and what a rotten world it had turned out to be.

Stephen was evidently a country boy and back then country folks looked forward to Sunday dinner because it was the one day of the week when we would have something really good to eat. That something was usually chicken which was either fried, baked, boiled, stewed, or chicken and dumplin's. God really knew what He was doing when He created the chicken or the egg to hatch one from, whichever He did first! Now, there ain't nobody that don't like chicken and dumplin's that's ever had 'em!

Stephen caught a lapse in my tirade about how unbelievably rotten things were and he injected a statement that has stuck with me ever since. Stephen, Tanya and I adopted that statement as our battle cry and to this day, we use it often. He simply said, "Hold on 'til Sunday, honey; the dumplin's are comin'!!"

Now, this first dumplin' story that I'm gonna tell you about might get a little complicated; not philosophical—-, just hard to keep all the events straight; so hang in there!

The day was approaching when I was to face the judge for my ninth and last arrest for driving under the influence of alcohol. This was six months after my last drink, which made it the end of June, nineteen eighty-six. I had filed my income tax return in January and was to get back around six hundred dollars for that tax year. I had been needing and anxiously waiting for that check since I had filed and hadn't received it yet, six months later.

I was already on probation for my seventh arrest for drunk driving in another Georgia county, but I had been placed under the supervision of the county that I currently lived in and was reporting faithfully each month. My probation officer would always ask if I had had any other arrests since our last visit and I would always smile, lie and say "No!" There just wadn't no other way around that lie!!!

Now, I have already mentioned that I had had two more arrests: the eighth one, which was a city court affair with a North Carolina license, so it didn't "figger" into this mess, but the ninth one, which was a state court affair, didn't just "figger," it was the major part of the equation, even though I still had a North Carolina license!

Now the eight and ninth ones had both happened in December, but the ninth one was the crucial one that I knew my probation officer was to learn about soon and it had happened smack-dab in the middle of my probationary period for number seven! I had about six months left on that probation time which meant that to have it revoked would mean six months in jail, plus whatever the judge would give me for the "secret" ninth one! Talk about a tense way to live!

Now, I knew that if that x@#*#x* internal revenue service would get off their asses and send me my money that was long overdue, I could pay off the fine in the other county and they would probably revoke the rest of the probation sentence for number seven there, and do it in time for me to be free and clear of that seventh one by the time the secret ninth one came to the attention of the probation officer in my own county, where I had been arrested that ninth time.

I knew that he wouldn't know about the secret ninth one until after I had gone to court and then off to jail for it. After that, the seventh one couldn't be part of this revoltin' drama because of the double indemnity, or jeopardy, or whatever. So every day I checked the mailbox praying for that check to come, but it hadn't come and the day of reckoning for number nine was done here!

I was to appear in court at two o'clock that day, so I left home around eleven-thirty so that I could have my last good meal before going to the dungeon and then go to a mid-day Alcoholics Anonymous meeting and still be in court in plenty of time and get it over with.

Now, the mailman had always come by eleven o'clock and I had, with flickering hope, checked the mailbox once more before leaving, but the mail wasn't there. I checked again as I left, but still it hadn't come.

I know now how Gary Cooper had felt in the movie "High Noon," except mine was 'High Two O'clock' and the big clock was ticking! Fear was mounting because I didn't know if this judge would know about the other eight convictions. If he did and found out about my probation, too, then woe was me! My future hung on the extremely remote possibility that the tax refund check might have come, but it was nowhere in sight! *Ooooohhh, Shit far,* **Shit far,** *SSHHHIIIIT FAR!*

After the AA meeting, I looked at my watch. It was 1:10 p.m. It was about fifteen minutes each way to home and back and I "figgered" that I could make the round trip in time for court, so in desperation, I decided that I would run back and check the mail box one more time. My Rabbit and me hit the road.

For some reason, when I arrived, I drove into the yard instead of driving up to the mailbox. I guess that subconsciously I wanted to delay the finality of my impending doom as long as I could. I was praying that some miracle would happen.

I walked over to the mailbox and with only smoldering hope by now, stood ready to open it. Lordy, that mailbox looked mighty formidable; demanding my respect for its importance now in God's scheme of things for me! It seemed to be saying, "I know what the future holds for you, big boy!!!"

Tense wadn't no name as I eased it open. It was like striking my last match to get a fire started out in the wilderness where there wouldn't be another chance if it went out.

Well, now! There was some mail. The mailman had run late. Maybe this was an omen. The good mail was mixed in with the circulars and junk stuff so I started nervously flipping through it. The white envelopes were bigger, but between two of them big ones there was nestled a small brown envelope.

My heart stopped! I was afraid to look too close. I mumbled a little prayer; "Oh God; your sho' 'nuff humble servant beseecheth thee not to play around with him, right now! Please don't let this be none of that Publisher's Clearinghouse or Reader's Digest shit! I ain't got time to wait around for that even if I've won their sweepstakes! I'll give all of them future millions (please sir!) for that six-hundred dollar tax refund check right now!"

I was about to collapse as I realized that the return address on that brown envelope was for the United States Department of Internal Revenue and that the mailing address showing through the little window of the envelope had my name in it! *YES—-! YES—-! YES—-! THERE IT WAS! IT WAS HERE!*

Never before in my life had anything like this ever happened for me! My knees were actually weak! *IT WAS HERE!* I was transfixed! I was experiencing a genuine, physical miracle! *IT WAS HERE! IT WAS HERE!* God himself must have been carryin' my mail that day!!

I swore that I would never ag'in sin in any way, shape, form, or fashion. I said, "God, if you're trying to tell me something, you've got my undivided attention!!" I could feel it in my hands. I was trembling when I took the check out and saw the amount. It was for a little more than what I needed; don't tell me there ain't no God! **IT WAS HERE!** Thank You, Jesus! Thank You, O God of Abraham, Isaac, Jacob and Dead Eye Gilmer! Thank You, Holy Spirit! Thank You, Peter, Paul and Mary!

I called quickly to find out how much the balance on my fine was, rushed to the bank and cashed the check. They knew dad so they cashed it for me on his credibility. I then rushed to the post office, got me a money order and a prepaid envelope. I made out the money order for the balance of my fine, addressed the envelope to that probation department and dropped it all into the out-of-town mail slot.

There!! That felt good!! Even them indifferent, impersonal, slow as the vapors risin' off of a fresh pile of cow shit on a frosty mornin' probation department public servants ought to be able to process that payment by the time I get out of jail!

Next I rushed back to face the judge. That was probably the happiest trip to anywhere that I have ever taken, and I had twenty-four dollars left over that would come in handy in the slammer for Little Debbie snack cakes and Bugle cigarette rollin' tobacco! I might never win the lottery, but boy howdy!—- I sure know how it feels!

Of course, the judge only knew of one of the other eight arrests, so I was only sentenced to twenty days in a county work camp of which I only had to serve ten. But after those ten days, I had to see my probation office who, by now, knew of my secret arrest. He reminded me that I had lied to him. I assured him that I thought that when he asked me about any other arrests, that he meant in the same county.

He laughed at my lying attempt to smooth it over and had me thrown back in jail and later that night, transported to the jailhouse in that other county, chained like a mad dog, to serve the remainder of that probation time—-, he thought.

What that no count excuse for a law enforcement officer didn't know was that it had already been cleared up while I was in jail for the ninth offense, and that that dear sweet lady, my probation officer, the epitome of law enforcement in that other county, would tell them to let me go the very next day. I had been tried, sentenced and had served my time for the most recent offense and that dirty, rotten, home county probation officer couldn't do nothin' more about it! (Double jeopardy or indemnity or something legal sounding like that). Bobby Lee, my AA sponsor, said that he had never seen nothin' that slick! Believing in God was gittin' even easier now but there was more to come!

When I entered that correctional facility to pay for that ninth D.U.I. offense, I was again thinking about what my friend Perry had said: "I wasn't scared, but I was highly uneasy!" I had heard about some of them *"mighty PECULIAR"* sexual things that go on in them places and I was aware that even I could be mighty *pretty* to some of them sex- starved long timers in there!

Sweat popped out on my brow as we newcomers were being processed in and as I nervously surveyed that menacing horde of society's debauched misfits, I too felt like the sheep when she heard the Shepherd walkin' through the flock wearin' his rubber boots! "Who among 'Les Miserables," I wondered, "will defile me?"

Fortunately, I had met a guy named Jack who had been processed in with me and Jack was not a newcomer to the prison system. Jack had been in and out of prison so many times that he could predict the day's weather by looking through the skylight in the ceiling.

I soon found out that he knew most of the old-timers in there and he cordially introduced me to several of his old acquaintances. Jack helped me through those first fearful moments of prison life. He helped me to round up a cup (a precious commodity in prison) so that I could get me a cup of coffee and such.

I was very happy to be able to hob-nob with Jack and the good old-timers that he knew because my acquaintance with them and my *"I don't take no shit"* charade just might discourage any perverts from botherin' me and just might make them believe that I was an old-timer too! Then hopefully, they would fear me!

I had certainly come too far along in life by now to be *gittin'* *"boogered"* by Bubba, and then I had a *sho' 'nuff* terrifying thought; "What if I was to like it?" *SHIIIITT FAARRRR!* That was definitely a new trick that this old dog didn't even wan'na try to learn!

OOOOOOOHHHHHH MIGHTY DELIVERER OF THE HEBREW CHILDREN please deliver thy humble servant from this abomination and I will promise to keep your commandments forever and forever more; even until the end of time!!!!

Even though I knew Jack and had made some wonderful new friends, I slept with one eye open that night! My fears were unfounded however, as I soon discovered that most of the inmates were like me; just good ol' innocent boys.

We new guests were issued our new prison fashions, read the rules and then were shown to our new home; a bunk in a big room full of bunks with a drawer welded underneath it that would contain all of my necessities during my stay, mostly Little Debbie snack cakes and, of course, the Bugle tobacco.

My bunk number was one hundred and forty-four and it was an upper one. I thought, "What a coincidence! That's the same number that's on my two new shirts and two new pairs of pants! Well, it wadn't no coincidence!! The numbers matched so that the laundry could be crudely thrown back onto the right bunk and to my surprise, not even pressed or folded!

Anyhow, a top bunk is not conducive to sitting; your feet don't reach the floor and the guy beneath you don't want your feet dangling in his face, and sho' 'nuff don't want you sitting on his bunk, especially if he is in for a long time (and he probably is if he has a bottom bunk). A long timer has already done some home decorating and has made his bunk into a paradise all partitioned off with towels, pictures and a crucifix hung in a conspicuous place. Jail is a very religious place, you know! (Like I said earlier, I've been saved—- through the bars—- more than once!) Anyway, it's amazing how beautiful those long-timers can make their bunk; turning it into their own home away from home!

Besides your bunk, the only other place to sit is one of the television benches. Now, these don't have backs to them and they are rather low so your feet reach the floor too quick and your knees are in your face. Couple this with the fact that the television set is mounted about eight feet high on the wall, and you've got yourself a pretty painful situation after a program or two. So there was just no comfortable place to sit, even to tie your shoes, except for some few chairs that I noticed scattered around. None of them matched so I figgered that they had been scavenged somehow. I soon found out that they belonged to the long timers and were not to be touched by anyone, except maybe close buddies, and I sure didn't know anybody besides Jack, and certainly didn't want to stay there long enough to climb the social ladder!

Now, I had entered the facility on Tuesday or Wednesday and it was Friday now and I was needin' a place to sit—-, BAD! I also knew that the weekend was here and I would be without a sittin' place from that afternoon 'til Monday morning. At least on weekdays, I had a break from it in the auto shop where I had been assigned to work. I knew that it was going to be painful before the weekend was over. Imagine living with absolutely no place to sit down and lean back!

I was definitely getting uneasy about this revoltin' development! I was really scared! I didn't figger that God would want to fool with this sort of thing, but with the tax refund check in mind, I asked Him for a chair anyhow.

In the performance of my work duties in the shop, I had found it necessary to go up onto the area over the offices where tires and other things were stored, and I had seen some stackable chairs up there (like those you see in government offices), so I decided to ask my civilian supervisor if I could use one of them over the weekend. He told me that he would ask his boss and let me know. Well, I waited, asked again; waited, asked again and again. I began to get that "Gary Cooper, High Noon" feeling because quittin' time was fast approaching. "Damn!", I thought, "I wish that God would get a watch!"

In my nervous state while I waited, I looked for something to do and began to re-arrange the work uniforms that were hanging on a rack in the washroom. To do this, I had to push them all together to one end of the rack and when I did I discovered that the uniforms had been con- cealing a single fiberglass stackable chair, like those that you find in a waiting room.

It seemed to appear as if by magic! Suddenly, there it was! I wouldn't have been surprised if it had still been smokin' from God having put it there so quick! The only problem was that it was split up the back (evi- dently the reason it had been discarded), but it looked so much better than nothing! I grabbed that baby and went off in search of the supervi- sor to ask him to ask his boss if I could borrow this one. Time was flying and I knew that the chances of his finding his boss were growing slim, but as I came out of the washroom with the chair I almost ran smack into his boss! God had sent HIM to me!

Nervously I spluttered, "Can I use this chair?" He looked at it and simply said, "Yeah, go ahead. It ain't worth nothin." I sure wasn't going to waste any time telling him how much it was worth to me—- he had said it was O.K. and that was enough! **I HAD ME A CHAIR! THANK GOD-A-MIGHTY, I HAD ME A CHAIR!**

And that ain't the end of the story. A guy from the paint shop was close by and he saw all of this (he and I had become acquainted during the last couple of days, so he knew by now that I wasn't a murderer or a rapist or a child molester). He looked the chair over and motioned me into the paint shop for a minute. Before I knew what was happening, he had smeared some stuff onto that split in the back, let it harden for a few minutes, ran a sanding tool over it and presented me with not only a chair, but a good chair!

I've never seen a piece of furniture before or since as beautiful as that one, and I've been to the Biltmore Estates in Asheville, North Carolina! There was only one more obstacle: getting it into the main cellblock.

Quittin' time came and I walked very nervously out of the shop with my chair. I made it across the yard to the main prison building without any problem. I guess that I was expecting a shot to ring out from one of the guard towers like in one of them prison break movies. I was with three other inmates, so I was probably not very noticeable.

We entered the front door with no problem, walked down the hall and arrived at the locked door of our "bullpen" where we were to be searched. I sat my precious chair down and waited tensely for the words that finally came from one of the guards searching us:"Where'd that damned chair come from?"

I almost said that I had taken it to the shop that morning to fix it, but I figgered he would know that as a new inmate, I wouldn't have had a chair to start with. He would have caught me in a lie and then definitely wouldn't let me keep it. *DAMNED TENSE WAY TO LIVE!!!* So I told the truth, at least as close to it as I could. I said, "The shop manager told me that if I fixed it, I could have it." Then came his dreaded reply—-, *"You can't take that in there!"*

My heart broke, but without any comment I just moved the chair to an out of the way place. I then waited for the search to be finished and when it was completed, the door was unlocked and opened for us to enter. Just as I started in, the guard pushed my chair over to me with his foot and muttered, "Don't tell anybody that I let you keep this." I wanted to kiss him!

I stepped through the door holding my chair. It had really happened! I had me a chair! I was the envy of a lot of the inmates at that moment. I borrowed a magic marker and put my name right on that baby along with bunk number one hundred and forty-four. Now it matched my shirt and pants, too!

Nope, them Top Gun pilots don't know nothin' about pressure and don't tell me there ain't no God!

I used that chair in every way that a chair can be used. I watched TV in it. I used it on my bunk for laying back to read "The Executioner's Song" of all things, but it was the best book to read in the prison library. I sat on it to tie my shoes. I took it with me to visit other bunks to socialize and play cards and sometimes, I just enjoyed looking at it. It was sort of like having a new car. Sometimes I would just sit in it for no reason a'tall.

I hate to admit it, but I think that after I found that chair, I enjoyed the rest of my time there. In fact, one of the guards must have been noticing that I wadn't actin' too miserable and finally asked me what in hell's name was I doin' in there to start with!!

After a quick look back down the pathways that I had traveled to come to this moment and place in the saga my life, I replied (choosing my words very carefully), "Sir---, It was all a BIIIIIIIIIIIIIG *MISTAKE!*" I didn't bother to add my next thought: "**And *I was the one that done it!***"

Another miracle had happened! How could I doubt it? When I left there, I felt good that I could leave my chair in good hands. I gave it to Jack the night before my release. What a touching moment.

But that ain't all. When I was released, the last barrier between me and full time employment—jail time—was gone. So I began to look for work. I knew that I would need to have a little money coming in before I could even begin looking for a good engineering job and it was obvious that the thirty dollars for cuttin' the grass job wasn't going to do it for me; there would only be about three more months of that anyhow. So my college trained mind kicked in. I thought, "God is doing real good now, I'll ask him for a job!", and I did just that. Then I put out some feelers—-, well, one feeler.

A friend, also in recovery, was a partner in a construction type truss making business and I figgered that he would know of some construction people that could use a "go-fer," or something like that (that's somebody to go for tools and stuff for those workers who know what they're doin'). So I asked Kirby to keep his eyes open for me and he said that he would.

I saw Kirby again later in the day and he informed me that one of his workers had quit since we had talked and he offered me that position. Thank You, God, Jesus, Holy Spirit, Peter, Paul and Mary! I started my first job in my new life the next morning. The position was driving nails into two by fours for trusses.

But that still ain't all. My poor Rabbit by now was fading fast. I already had black pepper in the radiator to stop the leaks and my sponsor, Bobby, a good mechanic, was keeping other things patched up, but finally the ol' Rabbit died. Repair estimates came to around five hundred dollars, so I sold her for fifty dollars to be used for spare parts. I also got a set of speakers worth about fifty more dollars out of the deal. One never knows when one might need a set of speakers.

I drove Dad's pickup truck while I worked on a way to get me some decent transportation. It was almost as far gone as the Rabbit was when it died so I had to get me some new wheels fast and that was one hell of a challenge with no money and, by now, absolutely no credit.

The search had gotten desperate for a car cheap enough for someone to lend me the money to buy but I finally found one that seemed remotely possible. The price on it was one thousand, nine hundred and fifty dollars. It was worth it but to me the price might as well have been a million.

The word of my search was out among my friends in recovery but nothing else had turned up yet so I was going to have to see if I could borrow the money from someone to buy that car. I knew that God didn't lend money but with the timely tax refund and the jailhouse chair and my new job in mind I asked Him for it anyhow.

On this particular day I attended the noon AA meeting where I had been going for about eight months now. I was going to the bank after the meeting to see if they might make a mistake and lend me the money. Man, I dreaded the rejection!

For some reason, some of us got into a conversation after the meeting and for the first time ever I stayed for almost an hour longer. I finally told my friends that I had to leave and as I went out the door I was greeted by another recovered friend hurrying across the parking lot who said, "I'm glad you're still here! I've found a car for you!" I had never before stayed after a meeting for that long.

As it turned out he had just left his sponsor's house in a neighboring town and that very day his sponsor had decided to sell his nineteen seventy-seven Buick LeSabre that he had been driving up until several weeks before but his crippling arthritis had rendered him unable to drive any more.

My friend took me over to see the car but I was very disappointed when we arrived to see a big old Buick covered with leaves and pine needles from sitting in one spot for those several weeks. I immediately rejected that car, in my mind, as a big pile of junk. We went to the door to get the key to start it up but the owner and his wife weren't there. I thought, "Thank You, God!" Then as we were walking back to my friend's car to leave, the couple drove into the driveway. Of course, they had the key with them and they insisted that I drive the car. Out of consideration for their feelings, I did.

To my surprise that awful looking thing started up like it had been just waiting there for me to show up. I brushed the leaves and pine needles off of it and backed out of the driveway and went on up the road.

Man, did she drive and ride good! She had my attention now, so I pulled into a store parking lot to look her over real good. She was downright beautiful! The maroon, vinyl interior had been immaculately kept. I realized then that the outside would have looked just as nice if the owner had been physically able to take care of it. I hadn't even considered his physical condition as being the reason for the cars not having been moved.

I knew that I had found me a diamond in the rough and that I sure would love to own this car, but I was just as sure that they would want at least three thousand or more for it. It was newer and nicer than the one that I had already picked out. I drove back prepared for the disappointment that I knew was to come when I asked them how much they wanted for the car that I was already so much in love with. I was once again absolutely floored when Darrell, who was also to become a guiding light for me in my recovery, said that he needed at least a thousand dollars for it.

OH FATHER OF DAVID, DIVIDER OF THE RED SEA, CREATOR OF ALL THINGS, You've done it again!!! I wasn't sure that I could get up even that much money, but I told them that I would be back the next day to pick up the car. I knew then that God would get me the money on his own credit; and I knew by now that He had *sho' 'nuff gooooood* credit!

I tried a long shot. I called good ol' Kirby (I had been promoted to night watchman by now) and told him the whole situation and bluntly asked him if he could see his way clear to sign a note for me for the thousand dollars, holding the title on the car as collateral. Then I waited for his "NO!"

He asked me a couple of questions, paused and finally said, "Meet me at the AA meeting room tomorrow at twelve o'clock."

The next day at twelve o'clock sharp he walked into the room, came over to me, put ten one hundred-dollar bills in my shirt pocket and simply said, "Pay me back as you can."

Don't tell me there ain't no God! I got my new used car, took her home and cleaned her up. She was absolutely beautiful! The first car that I had ever had with a blue high beam indicator light! I drove it to work that night and every few minutes I would go outside, look at it, sit in it, turn the radio on, raise the hood and trunk lid, open and shut all of the doors, sit in the back seat. I had me a nice car! I'm sure that God was smiling!

So, I was cruisin' along in my first year of recovery. I was working, I had me a car, a valid license, insurance; everything was coming around nicely now and other miracles were happening, but the greatest of them all was coming soon.

I had noticed that there was some romancing going on among these ex-drunks that I was associating with and I too began to think along those lines. Then it occurred to me that this newfound power, God, has been doing a magnificent job for me! Why don't I leave this romance matter in His hands? So I said to God, "If there is to be romance in my new life, if I am to have a loving partner, I'll wait for You to put her there." Then I put that matter out of my mind and concentrated on staying sober.

I don't remember just how long it was, but I again returned to that noon meeting place and was greeted urgently by a sweet little ol' lady named Mattie (who has since gone on to that "big meeting in the sky"). Mattie ran up to me and very excitedly announced that she had just answered the clubhouse phone and that a woman, whom she had met sometime back, needed help; that she was drunk and about to kill herself! Mattie asked me if I would go with her to see what we could do to save this poor wretch.

"What a challenge," I thought. "Here I am, less than a year sober and God has already seen fit to send me into His war against sin and evil! Me, one of his newest warriors, going on this, my very first life saving mission!"

In my mind, the world became an arena where I was about to become a combatant in a struggle with the grim reaper himself and I, "Dead Eye James", would deny him the right to take this woman's life! I bravely said to Mattie, "**LEAD ME TO HER!**" I said it in a joking way, but in my little ol' self-righteous mind, I meant it just that way!

Mattie drove her car and I went in my recently purchased Buick LeSabre, all spiffy and clean. The newness for me still hadn't worn off yet. I followed Mattie to our patient's house, which was actually pretty close to where I lived.

Mattie and I, the SWAT team, approached the front door. I knocked, but there was no answer. I knocked again——, no answer. I heard music playing inside the house so I asked Mattie if this was the right place. She assured me that it was, that she had been there before. I was doing all of the knocking because Mattie had already said that she couldn't take seeing no dead body.

The rock music was pretty loud so I figgered that the woman just hadn't heard the knocking. I pushed the door open a little and called out to whoever might be inside——, no answer. So I stuck my head inside to call out once more to whoever might be in there and *WHOOOOOHHH NELLIE!*

The first thing I saw was a large kitchen knife lying on the floor. "Shit far!", I thought, as I very nervously by now stepped into the foyer and looked further into the living room.

Just beyond the knife I saw an empty wine bottle but no blood, thank You Jesus, thank You Jesus! Then I saw where the music was coming from, an entertainment center; and at the other end of it partly blocked from my view was a human body——- dead or just passed out, I couldn't tell yet.

As badly as I wanted to, I couldn't just turn and "git the hell" out from there now, so I crept stealthily, closer to her. I had heard about folks gittin' shot in situations like this and I most certainly didn't want to startle her if she was alive and have her blow me away. "**BY DAMN,**"

I told myself, *"I'll sho' 'nuff study fer a LOOOONG SPELL before I get myself into another fix like this!"*

She was on her side, her back toward me. My mind was racing! She could just possibly be lying on a gun and here I am someone that she don't know and sho' 'nuff ain't expecting! She could look around here, see me, assume that I'm a burglar and shoot my lovely ass off and have every legal right to do it! Every nerve in my body was standing at attention. *Oh momma, momma, momma!*

"Damn", I thought, "This war on sin and evil ain't all it's cracked up to be!" I knelt down, as quietly as I could, with my pulse pounding in my ears by now. "Is she alive or dead?", I wondered. "This'll be the first time I ever found a dead person!"

Tense wadn't no name as my hands touched her shoulder and---------, *"AaaaahhhhhhEEEEEEEEEEEEEEEEEEEEEEEEEEEEEEEEEEEEEEEEEEE!"*

She had suddenly come out of it, and with great alacrity, simultaneously rolled over, saw a stranger looming over her and screamed to high heaven!!

Every one of my nerves had been stretched to its breaking point by now and they all snapped at the same time. God's brave warrior must have jumped at least three feet up and three feet back, all in one humongous *"YYAAAANNGG!"*

Now I had completely forgotten about good ol' Mattie while she, unbeknownst to me, had been creeping along right on my heels from the very start and was twice as tense as me, so when I jumped back I almost knocked her down, causing her to come unglued and scream to high heaven!

Now the screamin' was comin' from both sides of me. Her scream caused me to holler and my hollerin' scared our patient even more, causing her to scream even more in wide-eyed terror.

It was a lot like nuclear fission! *"GOD-A-MIGHTY,"* I thought, while we were all screaming our asses off, "What a revoltin' development this has turned into! This dramatic life saving mission has turned into something more like a scene from a Three Stooges movie!"

Little did I know at that moment, as we all settled back down, that God had just introduced me to Nancy; that I was, at that moment, looking through my own wide frightened eyes into the wide, frightened, alcohol-glazed eyes of my future bride. Yep, God does sometimes do His miracles in "*mighty peculiar*" ways!

There was no way for me to begin to suspect that she was for me as we lifted her into a chair and began to try to calm her down enough to talk her into going to a nearby detox center. There was absolutely no reason for me to even remotely suspect that romance could or would ever develop between me and her anymore than I should think that some day I'd live in them Biltmore Estates in North Carolina.

Sure, I couldn't help but notice that she was elegantly lovely, even in this setting, but even if I had fallen in love with her at first sight, there were too many things about us that would have made the prospect of our union look ridiculous; she was married, she had kids, she smoked, she had kids, she had cats, she had kids, she was too young for me, *SHE HAD KIDS*; she was too lovely for me to even dream of loving, living with, being with, sleeping next to, eating with, traveling with—-, and she was a drunk.

If God had written on the wall in front of my very eyes: "Dead Eye, behold thy woman!", I would have said, "God, You're very good at what You do and I appreciate what You've done for me, but You've obviously got me mixed up with some other dude!"

We finally talked her into going to the detox center. She was terrified of hospitals and such, so I lied to her by saying that they would only give her a shot of something and then I would bring her back home. I knew, however, that once I got her there, it was over. She would be there to stay for awhile—-. There wadn't no other way around that lie.

So we began our journey to the hospital in my beautiful, still new to me Buick LeSabre that I was so proud of, especially since I was using it in God's service for the first time. It was freshly washed and vacuumed, with armor-all slathered all over the vinyl top and interior. I had even put a K-Mart stereo radio and my two new speakers in her.

While I was feeling like a real hero, saving my first drunk using my beautiful new car, she was suddenly "throwing up", on my lovely maroon carpet! I mentally groped for something appropriate to say about this whole revoltin' situation because "shit far" definitely didn't adequately cover it!

I left her raisin' hell in detox that night, after she found out that she was going to be staying for awhile. I called the next day to see how she had made out and I was informed that she had "hauled ass" from there, and rather indignantly at that, so I sort of wrote her off as far as her being a star in my crown when I got to heaven.

I did see her from time to time in an AA meeting, but later discovered that she was doing the AA meeting scene because her husband and psychologist had threatened to put her into the treatment center if she didn't attend them.

Then one day, about a year later, she called to tell me that she was going to have another baby and that she wouldn't be needing us Alcoholics Anonymous misfits any longer. She thanked me very much for whatever we might have done or said to help her; in other words, "Don't y'all call me, I'll call y'all!"

I only saw her once or twice from then until her baby, Rebecca, was about two years old; maybe it was in the grocery store or gas station or some other place like that. Then she began to show up again in meetings because, I found out later, that having a baby hadn't stopped her drinking and that her husband and psychologist had made her set a "quit drinking date," or it was off to the funny farm for her and she was trying to prevent that at any cost. She came around for about a month, but couldn't seem to stay sober for any appreciable time at all.

Then one day, as I was puttering around the house looking after Dad, a car drove into the driveway. I stepped out onto the porch to greet whoever it was. To my amazement, Nancy was coming across the yard. She came onto the porch and very nervously asked me straight out if I would please come to her house and pour out all of her liquor. She said later that I had my hands behind the bib of my overalls that I always wear and that I smiled at her and even chuckled a little and said "Sure! Take it easy! Let's go!"

She picked the kids up from school and I met her at her house. She started bringing booze from all directions to the kitchen; from the bedroom, basement, bathroom and garage. It was in bottles, baby food jars and even medicine bottles. I was pouring it all down the drain as she was emphatically describing to me just what a boil on society's ass she was and how she never had felt special to anyone. She continually asked me how anybody could live without a drink now and then, as I poured; but it did seem that she was finally ready to give up alcohol. This time it was her decision. No one was pushing her or threatening her. She was finally doing this because she wanted to do it for herself and not for anybody else.

After we had finished the pouring ceremony, she asked if she could go with me to the AA meeting that night. Of course I was delighted. I picked her up later and we drove to the hospital where I had gone to my first serious meeting on that January thirty-first night, around four years before.

We found two seats and I went to get coffee for the two of us. I came back to our seats with the coffee and stopped to hand her cup to her. As she looked up and reached for her cup, my mouth fell open and I heard myself saying, "You know what, you're special to me!"

Shit far, I thought, she must think I'm crazy! I hadn't figgered on saying that! My mouth just fell open and my mind's mind just pushed them words right outta me!

She told me later that what I had said to her struck her in a powerful way; that she hadn't felt special to anyone in such a long time, and it was as if something was speaking to her through me.

The next year and some would be very stormy for her; trying to stay sober, going to meetings and trying to salvage her marriage, which by now had deteriorated beyond repair. She was divorced during her first year in recovery. It was a situation where one spouse couldn't cope with the recovery of the other.

In my street mind I was thinking: "I hope that she falls in love with the right guy this time around. I hope that she finds happiness and I'll help her all that I can." But in my mind's mind, I must have been falling in love with her since that instant when she threw up in my Buick LaSabre and she with me.

A couple of years further on down our road of recovery, she brought up the fact that our acquaintance had evolved into something significantly less formal than it had started out. I assured her that I was very much aware of that fact too, but that I hadn't spoken of my growing affection for her for fear that the combination of her enchanting loveliness and our noticeable, yet not drastic, age difference might thrust us into a "Hunchback of Notre Dame/ Esmerelda" scenario and place her in an awkward situation. "But," I quickly added, "now that it has surfaced, I hope that you don't want to stop whatever it is that seems to be drawing us closer to each other, because I surely don't!"

Six years after we met on her living room floor, we were married. I had been sober for about seven years and she for close to three years by that time.

Although alcoholism and other forms of insanity had ripped both of our families apart and we both knew that some of those old bonds still existed; and that memories of the destruction of our other lives might prevent our children from ever becoming totally committed to this new union, she and I have started into this new life and our melding has progressed into total commitment to each other and hopefully will engulf us all.

We are not now substitutes for what we lost in our other lives. We haven't tried to patch up the old using each other. We are into a new and different life together, untainted by alcohol. We have all of each other. Our lives are filled with real, all-inclusive love for each other; love that we had begun to enter into long before we even knew it. The good things from our other lives are precious memories now and on occasion we enjoy sharing those good memories with each other.

Whenever I think of having found Nancy, I think of the time that my dad volunteered to serve as lay minister for Spring Creek Baptist, a little country church in Cumming, Georgia, while the congregation searched for a preacher. I enjoyed going with Dad on Sundays to that church. I was six or seven at the time. It was also about the same time in life when I had my first drink in Granddaddy's barn. I was a hypocrite early in life! Anyhow, we rode the bus to that town each Sunday, so we had to stay for the whole day so Dad could preach that night, too.

One Sunday, a family that owned a country store invited us for dinner. After we had eaten, the father took me, the preacher's son, and his kids to his store and allowed us to pick out a treat for ourselves. I wanted chewing gum and I happened to pick out my first pack ever of Juicy Fruit chewing gum. I didn't know how to cuss good then, so I simply said, "GEE WHIZ! This has got to be the most heavenly tasting stuff that I have ever put into my mouth! I'll never again chew any other kind."

To this day, even after having tried other newer kinds, Juicy Fruit is still my favorite chewing gum! Nothing else will do! It's even still sweet the next morning, after being stuck on the bedpost overnight!

When God sent Nancy and I fell in love with her, it was like that discovery of Juicy Fruit chewing gum! There just ain't no other that can come close to her! She is my Juicy Fruit! I'm glad that I turned the choosing of my mate over to Him, because he gave me so much more than what I would have picked out for myself. I even miss her when she leaves the room for a few minutes. We hope that our bond will in time, engulf all of the children; hers and mine.

Her children were fourteen, thirteen and four when we joined our lives. The oldest one, Wendi, is nineteen now and is as fine a daughter as any one could ask for. She has graduated from high school and is already managing a music store in our town. She made me feel mighty good once when, on some special occasion, she gave me a card on which she had written, "Thanks for teaching me some of life's little lessons."

Jon is eighteen now and will graduate from high school this year. He has already, after serious consideration, signed up to go into the Marine Corps. He is developing into a fine specimen of young manhood. He was the one most profoundly affected by his family's split and has had to learn some of life's little lessons the hard way; especially that rebellion and resentments, that he was so full of at first, only bring misery to oneself in the long run. He has overcome those things and we are proud of him and his response to our interest in him. My heart "soared as the hawk" recently when I overheard him say to someone in a telephone conversation that they were having, "You get what you give, dude!" Just knowing that he has learned that much makes whatever effort that I have put into helping him along worth it all.

Rebecca is nine now and in the third grade. It is obvious that she, having been so little and not so impressionable when her family bond was shattered, will be able to develop an almost total bond with her mother and me and accumulate happy memories of our family. Recently, she needed to be corrected about something so I said to her, "It's time for one of life's little lessons." She replied "Well, lets get it over with and I hope it ain't as bad as the one about 'don't never eat no yeller' snow!'"

My children were all grown up when Nancy and I married. Tanya lives in a neighboring town with her husband Mike and their two children, Suzanne and Allie. We see them often and I am proud of them and I know that they love Nancy and me. They invite us often to be part of their family activities.

Alan also lives in a neighboring town. He is pursuing a law career and I am very proud of him. Of course, being single and handsome, he doesn't come around much, but he stays in touch and tells me from time to time that he loves me. I can't understand why he doesn't need my guidance any more than he does?

James Jr. (Jim) has adopted Trenton, Florida as his home. He chose construction as his profession; tall building, steel girder type construction. I've often thought, "Damn, I wish he'd get a safer job!" He has finally come down to ground level and is working for a company in their maintenance department—-, thank God! He has two little girls, Rebecca and Amber. I don't get to see them often, but maybe some day they will all live close to us, too. Jim stays in touch as well and he also tells me often that he loves me.

My children have come to know Nancy and to love her as my wife and their friend. We now have a new, strong family unit. A new bond has formed with all of us in it and she and I are comfortable in knowing that all of their commitments to us are in good hands now. Our families have melded together as a new family and for me, this new family has taken it's place among the vast array of phenomena called God; just as surely as the moon is part of that phenomenon called space.

As I write now at this moment, in my office in the lower level of our home, I can hear Nancy's footsteps overhead and feel my love for her welling up within me, but even more important is that I know that her commitment to me is in good hands, as long as them guns hang there. I know that I will never handle it carelessly. I also feel totally comfortable in knowing that my commitment to her is also in good, loving hands. I know that the person taking those steps up there loves me! We know that we were placed together by that power greater than ourselves that we both are very comfortable calling God.

These things have actually happened—-, they are not "fig-newtons" of my imagination. Iron **WILL** float! I can't just pass these happenings off as purely coincidental. The odds would be impossible that all of them could have just happened. So, I choose to believe that my lifestyle, my happiness today, is a product of my acceptance of God into my existence and my beliefs that He is indeed doing for me what I can't do for myself. What a deal! I do all that I can do and God will do the rest!

So how is it that I can now proclaim to the world that I am such a believer? Is it because I have spoken to God, or that God has spoken to me? NO! Nor have I had revealing visions; nor have I died and gone to heaven and come back; nor has there been a burning bush, other than the times when the whole damned yard was on fire! It's simply that I got sick enough and was hurting enough to be driven to look for recovery in the spiritual and in doing that, I have been convinced (made to feel sure) through my own experiences.

I, like those folk's centuries ago, was mentally unable to comprehend an awesome, Godlike power that was available for me if I would just flip on the spiritual switch. Now I have been given proof that there is no reason to waste time debating the existence of a Supreme Being.

Doubting that now is as dumb for me as my trying to tell everyone that it is not cold when the temperature is down to twenty degrees; that there is only an absence of heat; that in reality it is very warm at twenty degrees compared to what absolute cold really is, something like three to four hundred degrees below zero.

I do accept that there is a presence of heat until the temperature gets that low. It is a scientific fact. I have no reason to doubt that. Even though I've never seen the temperature that low, I accept it as truth; but all of my life I have been told and my own experience has been that it is cold at twenty degrees. I believe it! I don't waste time analyzing it! I **CAN FEEL IT!**

So I have wasted much of my time on this earth doubting the existence of a Supreme Being in the face of overwhelming proof in things that I can see, and in knowing that there are millions upon millions of people who believe in a Supreme Being by some name, in some form. Yet I stood against the multitudes in thinking it couldn't be true. I figgered that surely that being wouldn't have allowed his plan to become so diversified, if it was really true. He would only allow there to be one one faith and one denomination. Every one of us would be calling him God!

*"**WHoooohh** Nellie! Hold them horses!"* Somewhere deep in the recesses of my mind a little light came on and I thought, "We could all just very well be calling that Power Buddha, or Mohammed, or Allah, or the Great Spirit, or whatever else we might have first heard that Power called. I realized that I had been one who just happened to have heard that Power called God, and that name had been programmed into my little ol' computer.

"Well," I thought, "it ain't important what label I've put on it. If I'm standing with a Muslim, a Buddhist, a Native American and a Hindu and we are all admiring a beautiful snow capped mountain, we will be simultaneously thinking; God put it there, Mohammed put it there, Allah put it there, The Great Spirit put it there, Buddha put it there. Then we could each claim the credit for our own personal Deity. Then we could argue and fight all day, all night, all week or until we were all bloody and exhausted or maybe even dead and not one of us could or would change his or her conviction, but guess what? The mountain would still be there just as beautiful and as real for them as it would be for me. Wouldn't it be nice if we could just accept each other and each other's spiritual convictions and enjoy the mountain together?

Now I felt like I was beginning to learn a lot, especially for an "ignert" fellow and I was liking my new discoveries, but while I was in this mental mode, I couldn't help but know, deep down inside, that there was one more gray area in my mind, one piece of the puzzle that I hadn't found and put in it's place yet; one that I hadn't looked at straight on: Where does Jesus Christ fit into it all? He is unquestionably part of the spiritual package that was presented to me and that I am now comfortable with. I wanted, very badly, to fill in this gap too. I wanted to feel Him as well.

I again remembered those words: "If we look for Him, He will reveal Himself to us." So, I wondered, "Why is it that most of us pray directly to God, when we are told that we can only get to God through Jesus Christ?" It felt good that I could now wonder about these things without fear of "gittin' struck dead."

I recalled a time, many years before, when I had gone to our church pastor in Thomasville, Georgia, seeking some relief from some guilty feelings from having spurned not only God's, but also man's acceptable rules of life. I said to him that I felt as if I should be punished in some way for what I had done. What he said to me then became very clear for me all of these years later—-, "You were forgiven for those deeds when Jesus Christ was crucified for all of us."

I remember how I had felt when he said that to me then. I know now, that even though I had heard those exact same words hundreds of times before, I was affected in a *"mighty peculiar way"* when he spoke them then. But now, finally, after all these years and after having heard those same basic words hundreds of times since, they were about to take their place in my understanding of God.

When Milton said those words to me back then, they went deep, but I continued to have a little problem with the Jesus Christ part of this God thing. Not that I didn't believe; NO WAY!!—- I certainly wasn't going to get struck dead! It's just that I wasn't totally comfortable with that part of it. I often compare my feelings about that to my feelings about flying. I ain't afraid to do it, but I don't ever put all of my weight down when I'm in one of those airplanes!

So, for whatever reasons, there was still a mental block in my mind about Jesus Christ. I have caught myself skimming over written matter about Him because I realized that I was uncomfortable reading it; it seemed too far out. I didn't want to feel that way. I wanted to be comfortable with it. I wanted to feel it, *"As the hart panteth after the waterbrooks, so panteth my soul after thee, O God."*

So at this point in time another light came on. I began to think again about the phenomena that I now know as God and the vastness of it; of the infinite wonder, power and glory of it; and then a simple thought came into my mind: maybe God made another mistake, maybe He came on too strong for us at first, too strong in fact for simple minded people like me to believe in Him, and in our inability to believe in Him we tried to avoid Him. I think that God finally concluded that He would have to do something to prove his existence to His creation, to prove to us that "iron will float"; in other words, that He is real.

I then realized that if God could and had indeed taken away my addiction to alcohol (the greatest miracle ever!), He could certainly come to earth as a human being and suffer that pain, agony, humiliation, mental anguish and death, all so that we, His people, would never be required to suffer like that for our wrong doings simply because we weren't capable of knowing Him. And then the greatest part of it all—-, He could rise up from the grave to let His people see and therefore be compelled to know (like them iron boats a-floatin'!) that He does indeed exist, and is indeed alive!

All of these things were easy for God to arrange. I believe that now and I believe that the significance of it all was and is that humans like me saw those events "a-happenin'", and even though I might not understand, God gave me a connection; something that enables me to know that space and love and all of the wonders of the world and the miracles of the Bible are in His infinite galaxy, and that "Dead Eye James Gilmer," a once seemingly hopeless alcoholic, isn't just a forsaken little speck exiled from Him, but that I am indeed one of those shimmering little stars that is now very contentedly and happily orbiting in there, too!

I now believe that by doing all of those things, God put Himself within our reach. I'm comfortable with it now. It is a personal thing now. The story of Jesus has taken its place in the vast phenomenon that today I understand as God. Now it all ties together.

It is true for me now. I can feel it. It happened for me! Those Easter Sunday morning thoughts came back to me. There is no reason to try and analyze it. **I CAN NOW FEEL IT!!** I am comfortable believing it; just as comfortable as I am when crossing the George Washington Bridge in New York City, or going to the top of the Empire State Building. I know that they will not fail me. I have been there and done that. I have sufficient proof that they are safe. Just as surely I have sufficient proof that God is real. I am free from the bondage of alcoholic addiction!

So it is not important what package God was presented to me in. My package is good enough. I can't prove that it is all true, but it makes good sense to me and that is all that matters. If someone else finds this approach meaningful, that will just be extra. The important thing for me is that I have found proof that God is really there. The historical data is interesting, even intriguing, but I have not found my proof in it. The proof for me is in the fact that I can feel it!

When I hear the word space, I know that it is there with all of its planets; those that I can see and those that I can't see. The word love is meaningful for me now because, even though I can't define it, I can feel it. When the temperature drops to twenty degrees I am cold, I can feel it; therefore I believe that it is cold.

When I see the changes that have taken place in me and the miracles that have taken place in my life, I don't need to analyze. I know that they have happened. So I believe now that God is there; the word "God" is rich and alive for me now simply because I can feel it!

For most of my life I had been convinced that I had to prove myself to God in order to be accepted by Him. When in reality, all that I had to do was to be open-minded and willing to accept Him and then—- He would prove Himself to me! Lordy! Lordy! Lordy! It feels comfortable; even exhilarating, to know that God is really there! His name might not even be God, but I don't think that He minds if I call Him that.

Now just to be sure that I fully understood all of this, my teachers took the God thing to an even deeper philosophical level. They said, "If we believe in God, or Buddha, or Allah, or Mohammed, or The Great Spirit, or whatever, and die and discover that He DOES really exist, then we certainly will have won big!

"On the other hand, if we don't believe in God by some name, and then discover that He DOES exist, we will have really *tore our asses*!!!!"

"But," I asked, (I reckon that I'll always have a little touch of heathen in me), "What if we believe and He does NOT exist?" My teachers simply replied, "Won't matter none; we'll never know it!" Shit far!! My teachers are wise!!!

I believe that God knows that He made a mistake in His creation by making it possible for some of us to become alcoholics. I have racked my brain and have yet to come up with a good reason for God to have allowed it to happen to us. I also believe that since He did allow us alcoholics and addicts to go through more hell, torture, and agony in addiction than most other groups of people in His world, that He, if we want it, gives those of us who have recovered, an extra close companionship with Him. I believe that I would go through it all again to come back to the way that I exist today; to be one of God's pets.

I also have a theory: I believe that God created all things; therefore He created alcohol, or at least gave man the necessary ingredients for it and the ability to make it. I think that when he had completed this part of His creation, He looked it over and said, "This will bring the stubborn ones to me!"

So, there had been that time in my alcoholic life when I had resigned myself to the fact that I was just too plain sorry to be anything other than what I had become. Then as I progressed into my addiction, especially toward the end of my active alcoholic years, I had accepted the fact that I was just plain crazy. I figgered that I would surely have to be crazy to continue to remain what I had become and to continue to endure it; and I was certain, back then, that being either too sorry or just plain crazy was hopelessly incurable for me.

My teachers had correctly assured me, even back then, that I was neither sorry nor was I crazy; that like them, I was just a "garden variety" alcoholic that had learned the hard way, as they had learned, that us "real alcoholics" are a small percentage of God's people who lose our grip on reality and do insane things when we drink alcohol. But in spite of that, once we take that first drink, our alcoholic minds drive us to another, and another, and another. It again becomes: "Damn the torpedoes, full speed ahead!" Once **"WE REAL ALCOHOLICS"** start, we relinquish our power to stop ourselves from doing the very thing that is destroying us.

My teachers also assured me that if I wanted them to do it, they could help me as they had been helped by those who had gone before them, to find the power that they had found that will remove the deadly luster of that next first drink that is waiting somewhere out there for me.

My teachers had known all along what they had been talkin' about. The transition that I had convinced myself would be utterly impossible for me to attain had happened. I was free from alcohol and to my surprise, it really hadn't been all that big of a job! I can now identify with the story about the young "rassler" and the "pretzel hold. All that I had to do was inflict enough pain upon myself and the rest of it came easy"

Wise ain't no name for my teachers.

EPILOGUE

A NEW PAIR OF DRAWERS

Well now, I've done it! I've done that thing that most of us tell ourselves that we're gonna do someday: **I'VE WRITTEN A BOOK!** I must say that in all of my soul searching and through all of the countless thoughts that I've had to look at straight on while doing it, I've cried a lot and I've laughed a lot and so has Nancy, she says, in typing, retyping and cleaning up my mistakes in general. I couldn't have done it without her help.

I must admit that I feel relaxed, comfortable and clean now that I can feel it's end drawing near. Nancy says that she feels pretty good about it too, now that it's almost over. She said it in a *"mighty peculiar way"*, however. I wonder how she meant that?

Usually when I share my story with others; whether it's one on one, or in an Alcoholics Anonymous meeting room, or as a speaker, or in any other way, I end with this statement: "I hope that you enjoyed my story, because I sure did." That is a true statement because while looking back into my past, I feel assurance in my present and in my future. So I'll say now that I do hope that you enjoyed reading my story, because I surely enjoyed telling it to you.

Another spring and winter and summer have all come and gone and autumn has come around again. The beauty of the season is abundant where we live and it is especially beautiful in the mountains to the north of us. We have again made our annual fall trip to Ellijay (located in Gilmer County, Ga.) for apples and of course, soft cider and our Halloween "punkin" which will in turn become "punkin" pies for Thanksgiving and Christmas. We could get a "punkin" at Kroger or Publix or Quality food much cheaper, but it just wouldn't be the same.

Nowhere in the world is there a more splendid fall scene to be witnessed than the river valley from the top of that dam where I did my thinking that day that Stan took those little sips of whiskey and probably triggered my getting started on the writing of this book. So I go back there from time to time and sit on the grassy side of the dam and again allow my thoughts to drift with that ol' river's current.

Today I'm here thinking that of the thirty-five in my high school graduating class, there were four of us, all boys, who drank alcohol seriously. By that, I mean we were known for it. We drank often and to excess. I am the only one of us four that is alive today.

Not many of us alcoholics live to a ripe old age. One of my classmates died from an alcohol-related car wreck; one by alcohol-related suicide and one, within the last five years, of a head injury that was supposed to have been the result of an accidental fall. There are those, however, who strongly suspect that his death was not accidental. He had been seen very drunk the same night that it happened. He was the town drunk—, a bum.

Two of my drinking pals from industry, whom I drank heavily and often with, are dead because of alcoholism. I'm told that they both died very bitter men. I can understand why when I look back on the day of my last drink and remember my bitterness in realizing that, up to that point in time, I too had given all but my life in the quagmire of a meaningless, trance-like pursuit of the provocatively compelling illusion created, yet ironically made unattainable by alcohol; and that there was nothing of value, save my children and a few true friends, that I could show for it.

Those drinking pals of mine all won the grand prize. They acted out the final role of the alcoholic. They are dead. "Yet," I thought, "I survived. Here I am enjoying yet another fall season. I have lived to tell about it."

When I think of those things, I also think of when Sue and I and the kids were living in Connecticut. I was embroiled in a major project with my company at the time and the deadline for its completion was near. I had ordered some plastic label holders that we needed before we could proceed and they had arrived on Eastern Airlines air freight at LaGuardia Airport. It would take three to four days for them to be delivered through regular channels, so I decided to drive down to pick them up myself. I called Sue and asked her if she would like to go with me and have dinner in New York. Of course she was delighted. We both loved New York. She met me at my office and we tore off to New York City.

We got to the airport, parked in the usual terminal area and walked into the Eastern Airlines area to get directions to the freight terminal. We were told to step just outside; that a shuttle bus would pick us up and take us over, then bring us back. So far, so good.

We caught the next shuttle, rode over to the freight terminal, got the package, got back on the next shuttle bus and were on our way back to the main terminal when the bus suddenly stopped. The driver informed us that there had been an explosion back at the main terminal and that the bus would be going no further.

Sue and I got off amidst a lot of confusion and made our way to the parking area and to our car. The confusion and noise were getting to a level of "something bad has happened", but we were able to squeeze out of the parking area and were heading out of the airport as masses of fire trucks, police cars and all sorts of emergency vehicles were pouring into the terminal area. It was when we stopped and had dinner on the way home that we overheard some comments in the restaurant about an explosion at LaGuardia. It wasn't until we got home and turned on the news that we learned that a terrorist bomb blast had destroyed a large area of the Eastern Airlines part of the main terminal and had killed or injured several people. It had happened in the area where Sue and I had been standing only minutes before the blast.

The next day I saw the pictures and read the newspaper reports. I later saw the actual bombed-out place and I shuddered at how close we had come to probably perishing in it. I was in a state of disbelief as I looked at the pictures of the devastation of the place where we had stood. I was in awe of the fact that we had missed being destroyed by that blast by only a matter of moments. We survived it, yet it is still vivid in my memory!

The hell of the alcoholic life is over for me now. I survived it. There is peace in my valley now, yet my mind wanders back to how close I came to total destruction by my addiction. I can't help but think about the things that were destroyed by it and people who were hurt by it.

There is much that I regret—-, remember and wish that I could do again and do differently, or wish that I could erase from my mind altogether. I sometimes recall, without even trying, things that I did or said that I am embarrassed over, even now, when they pop into my mind. I sometimes hope that those who heard or witnessed them have forgotten, or at least have no reason to recall them.

It's hard for me to believe now that I made such wrong choices and committed such foolish acts. I often ask myself, "How could it have happened, how did I survive it?" Most of all, I remember the people that I hurt, especially my own children. I know that they have forgiven me, but I also know that they remember!

I also know that they know that they missed a large chunk of the family bond experience as a result of my sickness. I can't fix that. I can only try to do today those things that none of us will look back on tomorrow with regret.

It's strange also to remember how right and logical those choices seemed at the time. Such as on the day of my last drink, my plan to run to California and lose myself amongst the migrant fruit pickers and become a fugitive until all of the statutes of limitations had run out and then to come home a new man; successful, healthy, free from alcohol!

"BRILLIANT!", I thought, and was on my way out the door when God, as I understand Him, caught me in mid-air, turned me around and headed me back; away from the peril that I was hurtling toward! I believe that telephone had been placed where it was, that day, forty years earlier, so that I would see it on my way out of that door—, THAT DAY!

I also recall how funny some of the things that I did and said seemed at the time and some even now as I recall them, but it is frustrating to try and recall even one of them that I would want to relive.

Nancy and I recently took a trip so that I could visit some friends and co-workers from my past. I was appalled at how little we had to talk about outside of our alcohol- related experiences and at how unpleasant and actually awkward talking about those experiences was for me now. So those times must not have been in keeping with what I know now as normal living.

When I look back on that segment of my life, I see myself as another person, as a character in a movie or a play (I think it's called abstract thinking), trying to be part of the overall picture and whatever way that I was accepted, I would act out. The part that I acted most of the time was that of the clown. It seemed to take me further than the other roles. Unfortunately, the clown character required more alcohol than most of the others.

Most of my regrets fall under the clown scene, because I can see now that not very many of my audience were laughing. The absence of laughter would only cause me to try harder and to drink myself to greater depths of humiliation, while the alcoholic wedge was being driven deeper and deeper and deeper.

Even while the show was going on, I often thought of the portrait of the clown, all made up and looking funny in his clown outfit and make-up; but when one looks closely at the white make-up on his cheeks, it camouflages a tear. I know that feeling.

So I am sometimes compelled to mentally return to the scenes of that alcoholic time in my life, and like that airport experience, to feel the presence and fear of that almost total destruction. I must feel the real-ness of it to insure against ever forgetting that it happened. My memo-ries must serve as a deterrent to it's ever happening again, so I must keep the memories fresh in my mind.

Yes, I am also guilty of trying to excuse all of my alcoholic years as predestination and of believing that every one of those alcohol-related experiences was necessary to bring me to where I am today. Maybe that's true. I'll ask God when I see Him. In the meantime, I'll have to assume that it all happened because of my choices, which were the best that my computer could print out based on the data that it had been provided.

Remember that lots of the wrong kind of data went into my com-puter, therefore I made many, many wrong choices; most of them dev-astating for me and for those who loved me.

That pre-destiny theory is sort of shot to pieces when I think of the time that Nancy and I had our checking account at a bank where Tanya worked. The nearest branch of that bank was about forty miles from us. I usually mailed our deposits in, but on this day I had written several checks that were making their way to the bank for payment. I had to make a deposit **THAT DAY!**

So, I got all of the money and checks together and put everything in an envelope and put the envelope on the counter top in the kitchen by the door so that I couldn't leave the house without seeing it. I planned to drive down to the branch office in plenty of time to make the deposit **BY FOUR P.M.** so that it would be included in the day's business. I asked Nancy to ride down with me so that we could make a fun trip out of it.

Traffic was a little heavier than usual and getting there by cut-off time was becoming questionable. Of course, I was a little later getting started than I had planned. We were at our last red light at three fifty-five, sweating it out. The light changed and we sped the last hundred yards and finally swung into the drive-up window lane. There was nobody in front of us and the window was still open! We had made it!

"THANK YOU, O CREATOR and MASTER OVER ALL THINGS! Thou hast again delivered thy unworthy servant from his own short-comings!" I greeted the bank teller with a mighty big, confident, happy, "toothy", grinning hello, while reaching under the center armrest for the envelope containing the money and checks.

Then she watched as my countenance changed slowly to a pitiful, whimpering, pleading, Jack Benny-type stare, as my hand groped for something that wasn't there. I had begun to realize that I had left the envelope on the kitchen counter top back at home!

That little mental lapse cost us not only the wasted trip and the tension of it, but one hundred and sixty dollars in bounced check charges at the bank and an additional eighty dollars in charges by some of the people to whom I had written the checks. The total cost was two hundred and forty dollars for that little simple oversight. That was not a good experience for me! I lost two hundred and forty dollars! I'll never get it back! I might earn a million dollars after that event, but even if I do accumulate a million dollars, I'll know that I should have a million, two hundred and forty dollars! The two hundred and forty dollars will be forever lost.

Some comfort comes from knowing that the two hundred and forty dollars is not something that I just threw away, but was the result of an involuntary act or series of acts; and that my mistake triggered other actions that I couldn't stop. I didn't know that it was going to happen. I surely didn't WANT it to happen, but it happened and it can't be undone. As the old saying goes: "You can't un-ring a bell."

Just as surely, I couldn't know that my alcoholic choices back then would cause me to remember with regret a huge chunk of my life that cannot be changed. It is lost! I cannot regain it and I wonder—-, "What happened? How could it have happened?"

I wonder because when I look back and see the pattern of my life, it is obvious that before alcohol was in total control, I made good choices; right decisions. I, on my own, decided that I needed to continue my education after high school. I went to an aunt of mine and asked her if she would help me to go to college and she did. I finished college. Sue and I chose to let love begin to grow between us and we chose to marry at the right time. Then we logically chose to have children when we had them. We chose our jobs and moves logically. I climbed the ladder of success. I was respected for my abilities in my work. I was moved up to the home office in Connecticut; the New York scene. I traveled to far away places frequently. We did such things as Sunday brunch in New York and Broadway plays afterward. We flew high!

Then the same person, me, with the same basic mentality, but having held onto that alcoholic rope for too long, eventually begged for work, slept in an old Volkswagen bus from time to time, got de-loused in jails, slept on concrete floors in jails when there was no bunk available, went through trash cans to find empty whiskey bottles to accumulate the last few drops that might have been left in them and maybe get enough for a noticeable sip. I was talked to by employers, judges, probation officers, policemen and the others like I was trash and could only take their abuse and nod my already-bowed head in agreement with them. And sometimes in my aloneness, I would be unable to hold back tears while wondering what was happening, why was I this way; wondering what was mentally or morally wrong with me?

Alcohol closed on me like a vise and I can't make myself believe that God wanted it that way. The choices were mine and as long as I poured alcohol into my brain, activating that phenomenon of craving that compelled me to pour more and more of it in, I couldn't possibly make right choices.

Finally, on January the thirty-first, nineteen hundred and eighty-six, alcohol was miraculously removed from my life and once again I am making right choices and right decisions. I am living a normal life.

I can be comfortable that I am not going to lose two hundred and forty dollars because of a bad mental error on my part. We have moved our account to a bank about five miles away and I make sure that my checks are covered before I write them. I learned from my mistake.

Likewise, I don't have to be concerned about losing any more of my life to alcohol, because the craving for it has been placed in the care of a Power infinitely greater than myself and it will stay there as long as I want to leave it there. That Power is more than sufficient to cover it.

So I can put the loss of that part of my life in it's proper perspective, knowing that I didn't just throw it away; that in fact I was sick and couldn't have done any better and that I can bask in the good life now and for as long as I live——; as long as them guns hang there.

I suppose that I also mentally return because the old life is sort of like an old love affair. I fell in love a few times after my divorce, before God gave me Nancy.

I know now that these were love affairs that stemmed from a deep longing to find a loving bond with someone, somewhere, that would be a reasonable facsimile of the one that I had once had with my own family; the one that my alcoholic mind had shattered.

Those love affairs however, were real enough in my mind to bring excruciating pain in the realization that each, in turn, was in reality only a mirage that I was groping for, yet I can remember affectionately the special times from every one of them.

Long before those other loves, I had fallen head over heels in love with alcohol and her tantalizing lifestyle. I had reached the point where I was doing anything and giving up everything to please her, until she made it clear to me, "If you keep on loving me, I will kill you!" Then came the agony in the realization that it too, had all been a cruel mirage.

I believe I must also go back to those places and things of the past to remember and to know that in spite of my alcoholic sickness, there are also some wonderful memories from those years. In fact, we had a family gathering recently to celebrate Father's Day. The occasion gave me an opportunity to explore those pleasant archives again. My children and Nancy's children were all here and two of my grandchildren. They call Nancy "Grandma."

During the chatting, Tanya told of how, when she and Jim were little, I would sometimes emerge from the basement of the house where we lived then, wearing a pair of coveralls with a nylon stocking over my head; me chasing them through the house and them screaming and hiding and then finally running to mommy.

The "booger man" would then disappear and I would reappear as myself asking if the "booger" had run away. I would then tell them of how the "booger" had jumped me and tied me up in the basement so that he could eat them up, and that he must have run when he heard me gettin' loose!

Tanya also recalled the time when her mother was going to teach her to drive our straight shift car. They left the house and were back in about fifteen minutes, Sue mad as hell and Tanya frustrated as hell! Of course, Deadeye took over. Tanya and I left and she ended up driving all over town before we came back.

Jim told of how I always liked to show him off at the swimming pool at the Riviera motel when we were in Clearwater Beach, Florida. He was only about four then but had already taken to water like a duck. He would jump off of the diving board and swim underwater to the ladder on the other side of the pool and climb out. I would always go out to the pool before he was quite ready and would be reading a book or newspaper when he appeared. Of course, he would head straight for the deep end, which would alarm anybody who might be sitting around the pool.

Then he would climb onto the diving board (which really scared anyone who might be watching!), and just as someone was about to stop him, he would plunge into the water! Then as he climbed the ladder and stepped onto the pool side, I would look over the top of my book or paper and very calmly say, "Good swimmin' ain't no name, Jimmy!", letting them all know that he was MY son!

Jim also recalled our times with our dune buggy in El Paso; how every time we would take it out for a ride, the frame would get broken and we would have to take it to Bill, a welder way out in the desert, to have it repaired. Jim said in recent years that Ol' Bill was probably the one that influenced him to become a welder!

We also remembered the time that he took his mom for her first ride on that "thang", as she called it. He said that he got up to about thirty miles per hour (which on a dune buggy seems like a hundred and thirty!), flyin' across that sand with her hollerin' and draggin' her foot tryin' and slow it down!

Alan told of his memories of our Indian guide times, making a tom-tom from a coffee can and of other little father/son projects. He remembered how I would teach him one of life's little lessons each day. He would sometimes ask, "What's the lesson for today, Dad?" Another of his favorite memories was sitting in my lap and guiding the car the last half-mile on our way home from wherever we had been.

Alan also talked of when he was playing little league baseball, after his mother and I had gone our separate ways. I would go to his games and I noticed that he couldn't hit the ball. In fact, as the old saying goes, "He couldn't hit a bull in the ass with a bass fiddle." I made arrangements to meet him at home one day and, with Jim chasing the balls, I taught Alan to keep his eye ON THE BALL and NOT on the bat; that his brain would guide his hands and the bat to the ball. From then on he started hittin' "homers". I was mighty proud of that boy and I also let everyone know whose son he was when he would smack one out of the park! I really felt warm and good knowing that I had brought some joyful memories to them; not just those other memories that weren't so joyful.

So when I am in the various towns that I lived in during that life, I always ride by the houses where we lived and the places that we went: the churches, schools, parks and so on; and I think on the good things. Maybe I want to squeeze all of the good that I can from those memories to prove to myself that I wasn't all bad; that I was indeed just sick.

Looking back on the good things I can't help but be mystified by the fact that my life was so drastically diverted from them simply because an accumulation of my experiences developed an alcoholic mentality in me. I can't help but wonder how things might have been but for those quirks of fate that came together in such a way to cause me to steer away from the good life and to travel in the wrong direction for so many years.

If God would grant me answers to a few questions (now that I don't have to worry about "gittin' struck dead" for asking!), I think that I would ask Him why my life was so viciously side-tracked. Why did I, a person that seems normal in every other respect and who had all of the dreams and aspirations that others have, get switched onto such a treacherous course when I took that first drink of alcohol? In simple terms, why did He let this disease, the ol' wrecking ball of alcoholism, "whang me?"

I doubt that I will ever be able to come up with satisfactory answers to those questions or that I will ever be totally at peace with that disruption, knowing now that I really didn't choose to be that way. Surely nobody would have chosen to do it; yet I can't help but sometimes think on what might have been. So as best I can, I must believe that there were reasons for it and then try to put it all behind me.

I must also remember how miserably I failed when I alone tried to go back and pick up where I left off the life that alcohol had broken and shattered with my own feeble attempts to create love and happiness again. It was only when I fully realized that I couldn't go back (because that life was no longer there), that I was able to put my affairs in God's hands and He started to put together this brand new life for me.

Of course when I put the romance matter in God's hands, He gave me Nancy; albeit in a *"mighty peculiar way!"* She has become the hub around which my new life revolves. She has brought a joy into my existence that I had never before dreamed of knowing. I often wonder, "How could I have lived so long without her?"

I have discovered over time, that of all the assurances we have in recovery, the one that gives me the most comfort is that we will not regret the past. I have found that when the ugliness of my past forces itself into my mind, I can call upon God as I understand God to remove those thoughts; then I can fill that space that was occupied by them with the fact that it doesn't matter any more. I have this day and I can live this day doing, thinking, and saying those things that won't bring me, or those who care for me, regrets tomorrow.

There have been, and probably always will be times in my recovery when I have been awakened during the night by those thoughts of my past. I especially remember those awakenings on frosty nights when it had been snowing or sleeting outside and I could hear the wind blowing the little ice particles against the bedroom windows.

When these awakenings come, I think back on those times when I was being taken into a jail cell or especially once when I was trying to sleep in my old Volkswagen bus with no heat, out in the cold and snow. I was trying to cover up with the floor mat that I had ripped up, trying just to stop some of my shivering. Or I might think of some cold, lonely, run-down mobile homes that I rented, and then other thoughts of the alcoholic life would come to mind as I lie there. I allow myself to keep those thoughts for a little while for even more assurance for myself that it was all indeed real and that it was all brought about by my alcoholic addiction.

But then when I ask God to remove those thoughts, I can lie there and cherish the realization that I am in a warm house, in a warm bed, next to my beautiful companion who loves me. That we, and those who love and depend on us, are protected and safe and warm and comfortable, too. And that we all can be comfortable again in being part of a powerful, loving family structure with all of her children and mine knowing that their commitments to us are in good hands. I feel the bond that has developed with all of us in it.

Then I snuggle down a little further into the covers and feeling her warmth next to me, I can return to a peaceful, untroubled sleep with assurance that a power greater than ourselves (that we both very comfortably call God!) brought us together and that we don't have to worry about steering our vessel, even though our journey may be treacherous at times. For now we both know that He is at the helm.

I am very much aware that, being the addicted one, I alone am accountable for the pain and suffering that was thrust upon others whose lives touched mine. And for sometime, I was painfully programmed to believe that being accountable for it, I should have to pay suitable penalties for it: perhaps misery for the rest of my life and then eternity in a burning hell. There was therefore a nagging question in my mind: "Why am I being allowed to enjoy the goodness of a life that I am now comfortable and happy with?"

It seemed that I had gotten away with something; as if I came to this undeservingly and at their expense. The last barrier between me and total comfort in my recovery was the feeling of having cheated those near and dear to me; that I had just lucked out for awhile and that in time, I would loose it all again. I went to my new teachers with this fear as if to say to them, "Now I've got something that you can't explain!" As usual, they gave me a very simple explanation.

"Dead-Eye," they said, "you tell us and others of the miracles that have happened in your life, of things that have happened for you that you could not have possibly had any control over, and you say that the odds against them having happened by chance are so overwhelming that you must rule out pure circumstance." I had to agree.

They continued, "You yourself have said that those things could have only been brought about by some Power not of this world, a spiritual thing; a Power that you call God." Once again, I had to agree.

Then they said, "If you believe what you say and that it has been proven to you beyond any doubt by your own experiences, then you must believe that God gave you this new life because He wants you to have it." That's right, I thought! Then they said, "If He wants you to have it, then He must have forgiven you for any part that you played in your past, RIGHT?" I had to agree!

Then they finished by saying, "With all of this knowledge and proof of what God is capable of doing and HAS done for you, aren't you sort of slapping Him in the face by saying 'God, I think that you are wrong in forgiving me, so I'm not going along with your decision! I'm not going to forgive myself!'? Don't you think that in choosing not to forgive yourself or accept God's miracles in your life, that you are questioning His wisdom and saying to Him, in effect, "I am still a little smarter than You, God!" I very sheepishly, and probably very humbly said, "Yep!", and to my own pleasant surprise, I knew that I meant it.

The last loose end had finally been tied up. I know now that my life is God's business and that He can take care of His business without my help. All that I have to do is let Him do it. All that I need to do is all that I can humanly do in any situation, and God will then do the rest! No matter how hard a person tries, you can't beat a deal like that!

I was recently driving to town. I do that often now simply because I can exercise that freedom. It was early morning, not much traffic yet. I saw a dog that had obviously broken loose during the night because he still had a chain, eight to ten feet long and nice and shiny, that was dragging from his collar. He was a Doberman and to a dog lover, I'm sure would qualify as a fine, beautiful dog.

He was obviously well cared for; sleek, shining, alert, eyes bright and searching, ears and tail straight up, responding to every sound. In fact, he appeared to be quite arrogant in his newly found freedom and independence.

I didn't give that dog any more thought, until late that afternoon when I saw him again. He was dirty and bloody by then from all of the punishment that he had taken throughout the day. His chain wasn't shining anymore, but was caked with blood and dirt. I slowed down as he crossed the road in front of my car.

When my wheels rolled across his chain, I saw the vicious jerk that occurred. His ears weren't up now and his tail wasn't wagging. He was in much pain and fear. He was frustrated and desperate to find safety.

I stopped and called out to him to check for his identification, but he wouldn't come to me. His confidence in anything or anybody had turned to fear. I could see it in his now terror-filled eyes.

I recalled how I had felt after many years of dragging that alcoholic chain around and being jerked unmercifully by it; I had been beaten down to a point where I was pleading for something to please just not let me be hurt by it anymore, but backing away from anyone who might be trying to help me and fearing that all was hopeless.

If that dog made it back to his home, I'm sure that he must have felt the same as I felt when I made it back home by asking God, as best as I knew how to ask, to please just not let me be driven by alcohol any more; to take away my craving for it and to salvage what he would of the rest of my life.

When that dog and I each knew that our master was near, we each must have sensed, "It's over, it's finished; I'm safe now. My wounds will heal, I'll be cleaned up and I'll have food and drink and warmth and comfort and love again." I sensed that the misery of a drunken, alcoholic life and the loneliness of that kind of existence were finished for me; that it was over and done. I'm sure that my Master, like that dog's master, wasn't concerned at all that I had run away, but was just very happy that I had survived my journey back home.

So here I am back in my little basement isolation booth, as Nancy calls it; eleven years since my last drink of alcohol and coming to the end of a pretty good size book that started out as just a few notes that I wanted to jot down so that my children might have a little better understanding of their dad after I'm gone. I never dreamed that it would come to this. Maybe it was supposed to be.

Anyway, I can't end my story here because it's not over yet. I'm still alive and life is getting better and better; but I've got to stop writing somewhere, so it might as well be here since I hear Nancy calling me anyhow.

The family is gathering in and she's already said that she wants me to make some biscuits for supper. I've always wanted to be able to make biscuits and I've learned to make them recently. It's just another little part of my new life and the family is constantly askin' for 'em. They're goood biscuits and Nancy lets me think that I am the only one that can make 'em that good.

So I'll leave you for now and I'll climb those stairs up to the kitchen and step into a warm, happy atmosphere. Nancy will greet me with a hug, even though I've only been down here for a little while. I'll hug her back and then I'll make them biscuits. Jim, my oldest son, is visiting us again so our whole new family will be here.

When the biscuits are done, we will all gather around what we call our "happy table" to eat supper. We call our table that because no one can sit at our happy table if they are crabby. There will be laughter mixed in with the conversation and comments about the scrumptious pork chops that Nancy has fixed in the special sauce that only she can make. We'll all comment on how hungry we are as the tea and coffee are at last being poured.

To an outsider, all would appear that we are a family that has always been happy and have never suffered any major upheavals, and there probably won't be any talk during this time together about alcoholic addiction or anything about those times; but as we all join hands and the quietness settles over us for a moment as we bow our heads for Rebecca to ask the blessing, mine and Nancy's eyes will meet for an instant, and in that glance we will say to each other, "We are aware of the way that things might have been. WE ARE AWARE that in this very moment we are smack-dab in the middle of the miracle of healing from the seemingly hopeless malady of alcoholic addiction!"

These are all just simple things that normal folks take for granted, but that recovered alcoholics like us, having been pulled back from the brink of insanity and destruction, hold as being absolutely fantastic—- *GOOD AIN'T NO NAME!*

I sometimes feel that anyone out there can look at me and know that I once was a miserable, helpless, hopeless drunk and can see recovery written all over me, but I know very well that they can't possibly know that. As good as it feels to me being sober and free from addiction, I know that they can't feel it, unless they've been there.

It's sort of like "a new pair of drawers" feels, after you've gotten used to wearing them old ones that are so worn and stretched that no part of them is touching the body except the waistband. No one can see or feel the newness and snugness of a new pair of drawers on someone else. The only one who can enjoy the newness and snugness of them is the one who is wearing them. It's sort of like that old underwear commercial used to say: "I feel good all under!"

So thanks, Red Ryder; I knew that I had been affected in a *"mighty peculiar way"* when you said them words many years ago. I sho' 'nuff understand the meaning of them now! I know now that as long as them guns hang there where I left 'em, there will be peace in my Red Rock Valley.

THE BEGINNING

ABOUT THE AUTHOR

James Gilmer grew up in the small town of Buford, Georgia. He gradu-ated from North Georgia College in Dahlonega, Georgia with a Bachelor of Science Degree in Business Administration. He had a very successful career as an Industrial Engineer and enjoyed the "American Dream" lifestyle with his family until his addiction to alcohol destroyed it all.

James began his recovery on January thirty-first, nineteen hundred and eighty-six. He met Nancy along the way and they were married six years after their meeting. They now live in Buford.

Nancy has three children, and James' relationship with his own three children has been richly restored. Today he and Nancy enjoy a brand new lifestyle that embraces them all.

Watch for "That Took A Lotta Guts" coming next from the pen of "Deadeye" Gilmer.